- Go to **awmi.net/sg431** to download PDFs of the following resources for each lesson in this study guide:
    - Outlines
    - Discipleship Questions
    - Scriptures
- Share as many copies as you'd like.
- These documents are not for resale.

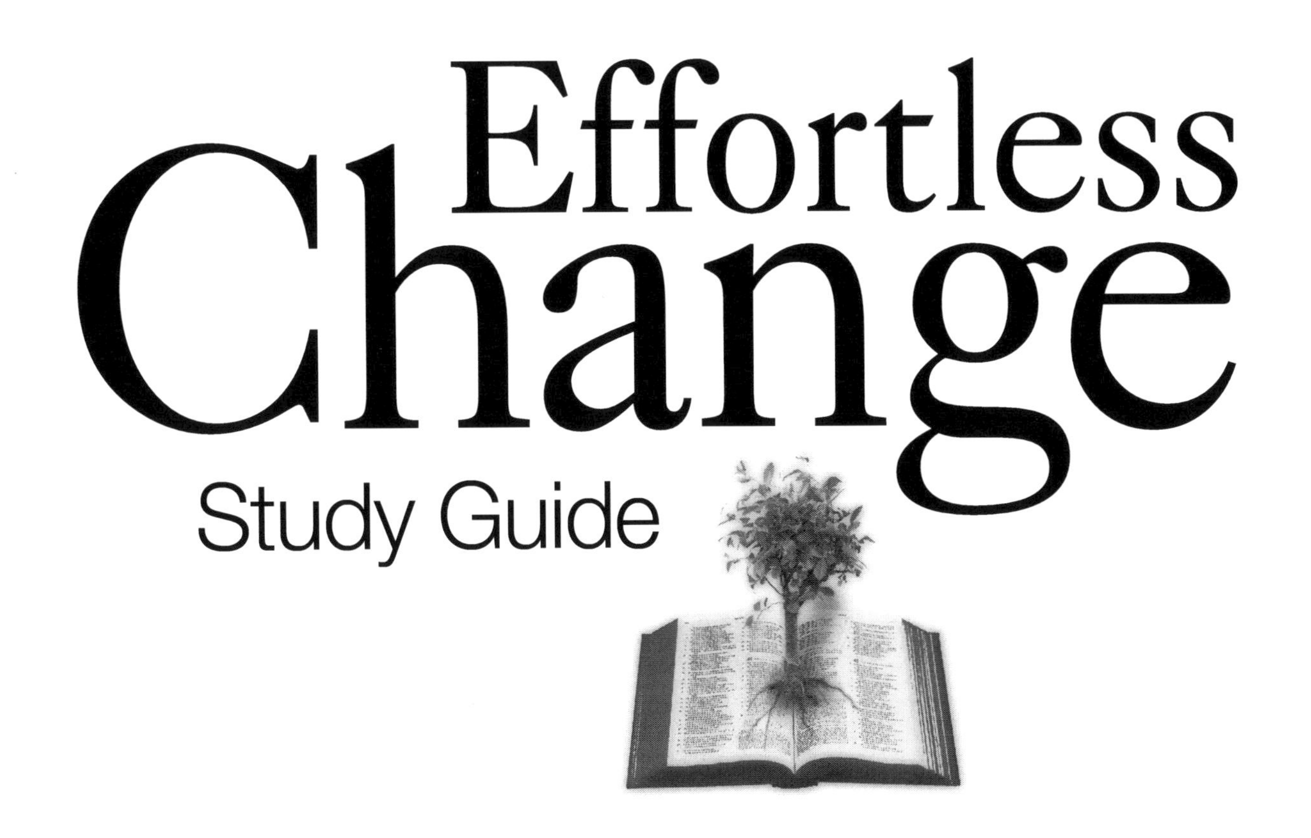

Effortless Change

Study Guide

The Word is the seed
that can change your life.

ANDREW WOMMACK

Unless otherwise indicated, all Scripture quotations are taken from the *King James Version* of the Bible.

The author has emphasized some words in Scripture quotations in italicized type.

Effortless Change Study Guide
ISBN: 978-1-59548-238-9

PO Box 3333
Colorado Springs CO 80934-3333

Contents

Introduction

Effortless change—it sounds impossible. Yet that's what the Word reveals about how the kingdom of God works.

Most people view change as a difficult, painful, and labor-intensive process. To their way of thinking, it takes a huge amount of effort to change their thoughts, actions, and circumstances. Due to this, change is something they resist. It's hard to change routines, traditions, and long-standing problems. People get stuck in ruts—ways of thinking and doing. Therefore, there's just a natural resistance toward change.

In this book, I want to share with you some truths from the Word of God that can totally transform the way you understand and approach change. If you receive these truths into your heart and apply them to your life, you'll be able to see change take place in your life effortlessly.

Many people don't even recognize their need to change. Others are very aware and have a strong desire to change. If you're sick, you probably desire to walk in health. If you're in poverty, it's likely you want to experience more of God's financial provision. You may realize that you would like certain changes in your life externally. However, all true change begins internally. It starts with what's on the inside of you.

Taking the Limits off God

On January 31, 2002, the Lord spoke to me in a personal and powerful way. He told me I had been limiting what He wanted to do in and through my life because of my small thinking. This word literally shook my world. So, I spent about a week or so really meditating on this until it became a revelation in my life. Then I called my staff together and told them what God had convicted me of, saying, "I don't know how long it will take to change the image that's inside me. It may take a week, a month, a year, five years—I don't know. But I am going to change, and we will start seeing increase!" I remember that within one week, things started happening so quickly that it just amazed me.

Before I even had time to write a letter, send it to our mailing list, and receive a response (which normally takes at least three months), we saw a huge financial increase. All that changed was the inside of me—my attitude, thoughts, and expectations. Other than that, we weren't doing anything different. Yet we immediately set records three months in a row in donation receipts. This was before my letter on this subject went out—before the people had a chance to even hear what God had said to me and respond! When I changed on the inside, immediately everything in my life began to change on the outside. This example is just one of many. External change began to happen when I started to change the way I thought on the inside.

If you want to see change outwardly, it has to begin on the inside. That's what this book is all about—how to start changing on the inside. If you can change the way you think—the way you are on the inside—then you'll see a change on the outside...effortlessly.

How to Use Your Study Guide

Whether you are teaching a class, leading a small group, discipling an individual, or studying *Effortless Change* on your own, this **Study Guide** is designed for you! Here's how it works:

Each study consists of a **Lesson Outline**, **Teacher's Guide**, **Discipleship Questions**, **Answer Key**, and **Scriptures**. Some **Lessons** also have **Additional Information**.

The teacher reads the **Lesson** aloud. While the **Lesson** is being read, each student follows along with their own copy of the **Lesson Outline**.

Once the **Lesson** is read, the teacher then facilitates a group Bible study using the **Teacher's Guide**. Simply read aloud one numbered section at a time, ask the corresponding questions that follow, and have the group answer them. Then, repeat the process for the next numbered section. For your convenience, answers are provided in parentheses.

Except for the corresponding questions and answers, the information on the **Teacher's Guide** is the same as the **Lesson Outline**. Therefore, the group should use their **Lesson Outlines** to assist them in answering the questions.

Whenever a question mentions a specific scripture, be sure to have the group look it up in their Bibles and read it together before answering the question. Feel free to interact with the group over the scriptures and points from the **Lesson** as time allows. Don't let any individual dominate the discussion, but try to draw out the quieter ones for the group conversation. As much as possible, keep the discussion centered on the scriptures and the **Lesson** points at hand. Remember, the goal is understanding (Matt. 13:19).

Discipleship Questions are provided for further study and meditation. They are designed for use as "homework," but—according to the teacher's discretion—may be helpful during the group study sometimes as well. Each **Lesson** comes with an **Answer Key**. As a brief review before launching into the current **Lesson**, the teacher may wish to go over the **Answer Key** for the previous study's **Discipleship Questions** with the group.

Some **Lessons** also have **Additional Information.** This section, geared toward the teacher, contains resource recommendations for further study.

Scriptures from the *King James Version* of the Bible are included as another tool for reference and meditation.

For personal study, read the **Lesson** and review the **Teacher's Guide**. Then, answer the **Discipleship Questions** and check your work with the **Answer Key**. For maximum impact, be sure to utilize the **Additional Information** and **Scriptures** sections.

OUTLINE FOR GROUP STUDY:

I. Briefly review previous study by going over the **Answer Key** for the **Discipleship Questions** (homework).

II. Read the current **Lesson** aloud.
   A. Be sure that each student has a copy of the **Lesson Outline**.
   B. While the **Lesson** is being read, students should use their **Lesson Outlines** to follow along.

III. Once the **Lesson** is read, facilitate a group Bible study using the **Teacher's Guide**.
   A. Read one entire numbered section (top of page).
   B. Ask the corresponding questions (bottom of page).
   C. Have the group look up and read aloud each specifically mentioned scripture before answering the question.
   D. Discuss the scripture and the answer/point from the **Lesson** as desired.
   E. Repeat the process by reading the next numbered section (top of page).

IV. Distribute copies of the **Discipleship Questions** to be worked on as homework.

Materials Needed:

Study guide, Bible, and enough copies of the **Outline**, **Discipleship Questions**, and **Scriptures** for each student. (PDFs of the **Outlines**, **Discipleship Questions**, and Scriptures can be downloaded via the URL located on the first page of this study guide.)

OUTLINE FOR PERSONAL STUDY:

I. Read **Lesson**.
   A. Read **Additional Information**, if any.
   B. Meditate on the given scriptures, as desired.

II. Review **Teacher's Guide**.

III. Answer **Discipleship Questions**.

IV. Check your work with the **Answer Key**.

Materials Needed:

Study guide, Bible, and a writing utensil.

It Begins on the Inside
LESSON 1

The Word of God clearly reveals that as you think in your heart, so are you:

> **For as he thinketh in his heart, so is he.**
>
> **Proverbs 23:7**

If you can't—or should I say won't—change on the inside, then you aren't going to change on the outside. You can pray, beg God, and get other people to intercede for you all you want. They could even lay hands on you until they rub all the hair off the top of your head. But you aren't going to see change in your life externally until you change internally.

Many people say, "But I do desire to change. I've done everything I know, yet it seems like things are just continually the same." God's Word is true. As you think in your heart, so are you. This is a law of God. Romans 8:6 confirms this truth, revealing that...

> **...to be carnally minded is death; but to be spiritually minded is life and peace.**

Before you take offense, resenting and disagreeing with what I'm sharing, consider this truth. Of course, everyone has a bump in the road now and again, whether they are walking with the Lord or not. You live in a fallen world, and you have an Enemy who comes against you. Not every single problem in your life is a direct result of something on the inside of you. However, if your life overall is spiraling downward, nothing ever works, and problems are all you seem to experience, then you should stop to consider what I'm saying.

What Have You Planted?

People typically respond by blaming someone or something else: "It's the color of my skin. It's my family background. I was disadvantaged. This person mistreated me." They'll blame anybody: "It's my employer who's the jerk, not me." It's always somebody else's fault.

However, the Word makes it clear that your experience—your situation—is basically because of the way you think. As you think in your heart, that's the way it is. When you are spiritually minded, all you get is life and peace. When you aren't, you get death. You may not like that. You might be saying "No, that's not true," but it is.

If I came to your house to see what you planted in your garden, I wouldn't have to be with you when you sowed the seeds. All I'd have to do is be there when the plants start growing up.

If you have corn growing, you planted corn. If there are peas, you sowed peas. Perhaps someone else could have come in and planted something in your garden. However, it's your responsibility to guard and protect your garden. Whatever is growing there is what you've planted or what you've allowed to be planted.

Just as this is true in the natural realm, it's true in the spiritual realm. Whatever is growing in the garden of your life is what you've planted or allowed to be planted in your heart. Before you can really see change, you must quit using excuses and blaming anybody and everybody else for what is wrong in your life. You have to stop saying, "It's just fate or luck, and nothing ever works for me." Scripture reveals that as you think in your heart, that's the way you're going to be (Prov. 23:7). If you think spiritually minded, all it produces is life and peace (Rom. 8:6).

The Knowledge of God

Second Peter 1:2 agrees, saying,

> **Grace and peace be multiplied unto you through the knowledge of God, and of Jesus our Lord.**

Many people want grace and peace to be multiplied to them. They desire peace in their lives, but they're praying for it. They're asking other people to help them get it. Actually, they're looking for peace to come externally—from outside of them—into their circumstances. This scripture reveals that peace comes through the knowledge of God.

Peace in your life isn't going to be the absence of problems or challenging circumstances around you. God's kind of peace is there even in the midst of a storm. It resides on the inside. Then, eventually, that peace on the inside of you will begin to change the circumstances on the outside.

> **According as his divine power hath given unto us all things that pertain unto life and godliness, through the knowledge of him that hath called us to glory and virtue.**
>
> **2 Peter 1:3**

This says that His divine power has (past tense) already given all things to us. Most people want God to just come with His power from the outside in. They pray, "O Lord, stretch forth Your mighty hand and touch me!" They're looking for God to send a spiritual bolt of lightning to hit them and—BOOM—they're healed, prospered, delivered, or whatever they need. However, this scripture says that all things that pertain to life and godliness come through the knowledge of God. This includes healing, prosperity, deliverance, joy, peace, success in business, good relationships, and anything else that is of God. Everything that pertains to life and godliness comes through the knowledge of God. The born-again Christian already has the peace of God in their spirit, and as they renew their mind to who they are and what they have in Christ, they draw that peace out into their experience.

The dominant experience of your life is the way you think on the inside (Prov. 23:7). Instead of looking for a change to take place externally in everybody and everything else around you, the first thing you need to do is recognize that change begins on the inside of you. It's according to the knowledge of God you have (2 Pet. 1:2-3).

Reality

This is a simple truth, but it's profound. In fact, most people miss it because it's so simple, thinking, *No, it must be more complex than that. It can't just be the fact that I'm not thinking properly about things.* God's Word is true. You can turn any circumstance around in your life by getting His perspective and starting to think His thoughts. Some people call this by different names, but I believe this is what the Bible calls *faith.*

Faith is simply seeing things from God's perspective. When someone wrongs you, instead of just reacting in the natural, physical realm—based on your emotions—faith considers, *What does God's Word say?* So, you take a scripture like Ephesians 6:12, which says that you aren't wrestling...

> **...against flesh and blood, but against principalities, against powers, against the rulers of the darkness of this world, against spiritual wickedness in high places.**
>
> **Ephesians 6:12**

So, instead of just going by the fact that this person has pushed your hot button, because of God's knowledge that you have through His Word, you recognize that the devil can speak through people and use them to come against you. Instead of just seeing things in the natural, you have a different perspective because of the knowledge of God. You think differently on the inside. You realize that it's not really that person who is angry at you and resisting God inside you. Because of this, you just constantly respond differently than other people do. You love that person instead of getting into strife, and it produces different results. All of this begins with you thinking differently.

I could give you hundreds of testimonies from my life and the lives of others who have personally experienced this truth. This is reality. However, most people want change in their circumstances, but they don't recognize that the change begins on the inside of them.

Insanity

At each of our *Gospel Truth Seminars,* I tell people about our Bible colleges. I often ask, "How many of you realize that there's more; you desire more and you want change in your life?"

It's not unusual to see 80 to 90 percent of the crowd respond. Most of these are Christians—Spirit-filled believers—who recognize that there needs to be change in their lives. They aren't satisfied with where they are, and they want something more.

After all these people admit "Yes, I want change," I ask, "What are you going to do to effect change? What's going to be different? One of the definitions of insanity is to do the same thing over and over again expecting different results. If you want something to change on the outside, then you're going to have to start changing something on the inside. First of all, you must change in your heart. Then you'll have to take some steps to cooperate with that change. Change isn't going to come from the outside; it begins on the inside. If you want change in your life, then you're going to have to do something different."

The moment I bring this up, I instantly meet resistance because people are afraid to change. I've actually met people who were in terrible, miserable situations, yet they had adjusted to them. They knew they could survive. It may not be what they wanted—their dreams or goals—but they had been there a long time. They knew they could survive, and they were afraid of failure.

If that's you, one of the things that must happen in order to effect change in your life is you have to get to a place where you are sick and tired of being sick and tired. You have to really reach a place where you say, "I'm going to do whatever it takes to see these external changes in my life. I'm going to start changing the way I think. I'm going to start taking some risks." Unless you're willing to do these things, you'll never see external change.

"How Long?"

The Bible relates the story of when the city of Samaria was surrounded and besieged by the Assyrian army (2 Kin. 6:24—7:20). The Samaritans were starving so much that they were eating their own children. Animal dung, being sold as food, was commanding a high price. This city was suffering terribly from the siege, drought, and famine. The people were just about to be completely destroyed, yet they couldn't do anything about it because the Syrians had Samaria completely surrounded.

Four lepers sat at the gate of Samaria. As they talked to each other, they said, "How long are we going to sit here—until we die? If we stay here, we'll die. If we go into the city, the famine will destroy us. Let's go out to the Syrians. If they kill us, we're just going to die here anyway. We don't have anything to lose. Perhaps they'll show us mercy."

So, these four lepers got up and went into the Syrian camp. It turned out that the Lord had already been there. He had caused the Syrians to hear a noise. They thought the Israelites had hired another nation against them, so they had fled in terror leaving behind all their food, animals, tents, provisions, gold, and silver. The Syrians had fled for their lives and left everything behind!

These four lepers, who were facing starvation just a few minutes before, experienced a tremendous personal deliverance. They went out to the camp and discovered food that was still warm. They began to eat their fill. They found clothes, gold, and silver. After doing all these things, eventually they were the ones who brought the good news back to the city of Samaria. They became the heroes that actually proclaimed deliverance to the entire area. All of this happened because four lepers, shunned by their city, sitting out at the gates, starving to death, finally made a decision. Even though their outlook seemed terrible, they declared, "We've got to do something. We're going to die if we stay where we are. We must head in some direction." So, they considered their options. Even though this one didn't look real good, it was better than sitting still and dying. And because they did something different, they experienced tremendous deliverance.

Change Is Needed

Right now you may be dying like these lepers, if not physically, then perhaps emotionally—you know you're dying, your marriage is falling apart, things aren't going right. You're keenly aware that something is wrong. You know there's more, yet you are fearful to take any steps because you're afraid you might fail. If you would just look at things properly, you'd realize that you're failing now. Even if you have a guaranteed income, live in a relatively nice house, and your circumstances are going well, if you aren't satisfied and fulfilled in your heart, then you are dying and change is necessary. If you don't wake up in the morning and feel like saying "Praise God, another opportunity to do what the Lord has called me to do and make a difference in this world," then whether you realize it or not, change is needed.

If you want different results, then you're going to have to do something different. To keep doing the same thing over and over again, and praying for different results, is insane. If you want different results, do something different.

True change begins on the inside. Now, you can sit there and pray for God to do something externally. Many people are praying to win the lottery, or some other roll of the dice. If that's what you are believing for, you aren't following God. That's not the way He's going to meet your need. The odds of that happening are millions to one. Nobody is going to walk into your office and, out of the blue, ask you to become the CEO of a Fortune 500 company. That's not how life works. Change doesn't happen that way. If you want change on the outside, it begins on the inside.

It Begins on the Inside
LESSON 1 – OUTLINE

I. If you can't—or should I say won't—change on the inside, then you aren't going to change on the outside.

   A. Many people say, "But I do desire to change. I've done everything I know, yet it seems like things are just continually the same."

   B. As you think in your heart, so are you (Prov. 23:7).

   C. This is a law of God.

   D. Romans 8:6 confirms this truth, revealing that…

   ...to be carnally minded is death; but to be spiritually minded is life and peace.

   E. When you are spiritually minded, all you get is life and peace.

   F. When you aren't, you get death.

   G. You might be saying "No, that's not true," but it is.

II. If I came to your house to see what you planted in your garden, I wouldn't have to be with you when you sowed the seeds.

   A. Whatever is growing there is what you've planted or what you've allowed to be planted.

   B. Just as this is true in the natural realm, it's true in the spiritual realm.

   C. Whatever is growing in the garden of your life is what you've planted or allowed to be planted in your heart.

III. Many people want grace and peace to be multiplied to them.

   A. They desire peace in their lives, but they're praying for it.

   Grace and peace be multiplied unto you through the knowledge of God, and of Jesus our Lord.

   2 Peter 1:2

B. This scripture reveals that peace comes through the knowledge of God.

> **According as his divine power hath given unto us all things that pertain unto life and godliness, through the knowledge of him that hath called us to glory and virtue.**
>
> **2 Peter 1:3**

C. This scripture says that all things that pertain to life and godliness come through the knowledge of God.

D. This includes healing, prosperity, deliverance, joy, peace, success in business, good relationships, and anything else that is of God.

E. The dominant experience of your life is the way you think on the inside.

F. Instead of looking for a change to take place externally in everybody and everything else around you, the first thing you need to do is recognize that change begins on the inside of you.

G. It's according to the knowledge of God you have.

IV. You can turn any circumstance around in your life by getting God's perspective and starting to think His thoughts.

A. Some people call this by different names, but I believe this is what the Bible calls *faith.*

B. When someone wrongs you, instead of just reacting in the natural, physical realm—based on your emotions—faith considers, *What does God's Word say?*

C. Because of God's knowledge that you have through His Word, you recognize that the devil can speak through people and use them to come against you (Eph. 6:12).

D. You realize that it's not really that person who is angry at you and resisting God inside you.

E. Because of this, you just constantly respond differently than other people do.

F. You love that person instead of getting into strife, and it produces different results.

G. All of this begins with you thinking differently.

V. One of the things that must happen in order to effect change in your life is you have to get to a place where you are sick and tired of being sick and tired.

   A. You have to really reach a place where you say, “I’m going to do whatever it takes to see external changes in my life. I’m going to start changing the way I think. I’m going to start taking some risks.”

   B. Unless you’re willing to do these things, you’ll never see external change.

VI. If you want different results, then you’re going to have to do something different.

   A. To keep doing the same thing over and over again, and praying for different results, is insane.

   B. True change begins on the inside.

   C. If you want change on the outside, it begins on the inside.

It Begins on the Inside
LESSON 1 – TEACHER'S GUIDE

1. If we can't—or should I say won't—change on the inside, then we aren't going to change on the outside. Many people say, "But I do desire to change. I've done everything I know, yet it seems like things are just continually the same." As we think in our hearts, so are we (Prov. 23:7). This is a law of God. Romans 8:6 confirms this truth. When we are spiritually minded, all we get is life and peace. When we aren't, we get death. We might be saying "No, that's not true," but it is.

2. If I came to your house to see what you planted in your garden, I wouldn't have to be with you when you sowed the seeds. Whatever is growing there is what you've planted or what you've allowed to be planted. Just as this is true in the natural realm, it's true in the spiritual realm. Whatever is growing in the garden of our lives is what we've planted or allowed to be planted in our hearts.

3. Many of us want grace and peace to be multiplied to us. We desire peace in our lives, but we're praying for it. Second Peter 1:2 reveals that peace comes through the knowledge of God. The next verse says that all things that pertain to life and godliness come through the knowledge of God. This includes healing, prosperity, deliverance, joy, peace, success in business, good relationships, and anything else that is of God. The dominant experience of our lives is the way we think on the inside. Instead of looking for a change to take place externally in everybody and everything else around us, the first thing we need to do is recognize that change begins on the inside of us. It's according to the knowledge of God we have.

1. A. We have to change on the inside before we change where? (On the outside)
   B. Read Romans 8:6. What do we get if we are spiritually minded? (Life and peace)
2. Whatever is growing in the garden of our lives is what we've planted or allowed to be planted in our _____. (Hearts)
3. A. Does 2 Peter 1:2 tell us to pray for grace and peace? (No)
   B. How do they come, then? (Through the knowledge of God and of our Lord Jesus Christ)
   C. Read 2 Peter 1:3. What kinds of things pertain to life and godliness? (Healing, prosperity, deliverance, joy, peace, success in business, good relationships, and anything else that's of God)

4. We can turn any circumstance around in our lives by getting God's perspective and starting to think His thoughts. Some people call this by different names, but I believe this is what the Bible calls *faith*. When someone wrongs us, instead of just reacting in the natural, physical realm—based on our emotions—faith considers, *What does God's Word say?* Because of God's knowledge that we have through His Word, we recognize that the devil can speak through people and use them to come against us (Eph. 6:12). We realize that it's not really that person who is angry at us and resisting God inside us. Because of this, we just constantly respond differently than other people do. We love that person instead of getting into strife, and it produces different results. All of this begins with us thinking differently.

5. One of the things that must happen in order to effect change in our lives is we have to get to a place where we are sick and tired of being sick and tired. We have to really reach a place where we say, "I'm going to do whatever it takes to see external changes in my life. I'm going to start changing the way I think. I'm going to start taking some risks." Unless we're willing to do these things, we'll never see external change.

6. If we want different results, then we're going to have to do something different. To keep doing the same thing over and over again, and praying for different results, is insane. True change begins on the inside. If we want change on the outside, it begins on the inside.

4. A. What can turn around in our lives when we get God's perspective and start thinking His thoughts? (Any circumstance)
   B. When someone wrongs us, instead of just reacting in the natural, physical realm—based on our emotions—what does faith consider? (*What does God's Word say?*)
   C. What do we do instead of getting into strife? (We love that person)
5. What is one thing that must happen in order to effect change in our lives? (We have to get to a place where we're sick and tired of being sick and tired)
6. A. If we want different results, what do we have to do? (Something different)
   B. Where does true change begin? (On the inside)

It Begins on the Inside
LESSON 1 – DISCIPLESHIP QUESTIONS

1. Read Proverbs 23:7. What's more important, what a person says or what they think in their heart?

2. According to Romans 8:6, what is death?

3. What is life and peace?

4. Read 2 Peter 1:2-3. Peter wants God's grace and peace to be _____ unto you.
   A. Divided
   B. Added
   C. Multiplied
   D. All of the above
   E. None of the above

5. What has God called you to?

6. Read Ephesians 6:12. If your conflict is not with flesh and blood, what is it with?
   A. Circumstances
   B. Stinkin' thinkin'
   C. Government
   D. Principalities, powers, rulers of the darkness of this world, spiritual wickedness in high places
   E. Traditions of man

7. Read 2 Kings 6:24—7:20. Who did the king of Israel blame for Samaria's troubles?

8. What did the lepers sound like to the Syrians?

9. How did the Syrians flee their camp?

10. Everything Elisha prophesied came to pass according to what?

It Begins on the Inside

LESSON 1 – ANSWER KEY

1. What they think in their heart
2. Being carnally minded
3. Being spiritually minded
4. C. Multiplied
5. Glory and virtue
6. D. Principalities, powers, rulers of the darkness of this world, spiritual wickedness in high places
7. Elisha
8. A great host (army)
9. In haste
10. The word of the Lord

It Begins on the Inside

LESSON 1 – SCRIPTURES

PROVERBS 23:7

For as he thinketh in his heart, so is he: Eat and drink, saith he to thee; but his heart is not with thee.

ROMANS 8:6

For to be carnally minded is death; but to be spiritually minded is life and peace.

2 PETER 1:2-3

Grace and peace be multiplied unto you through the knowledge of God, and of Jesus our Lord, [3] **According as his divine power hath given unto us all things that pertain unto life and godliness, through the knowledge of him that hath called us to glory and virtue.**

EPHESIANS 6:12

For we wrestle not against flesh and blood, but against principalities, against powers, against the rulers of the darkness of this world, against spiritual wickedness in high places.

2 KINGS 6:24—7:20

And it came to pass after this, that Benhadad king of Syria gathered all his host, and went up, and besieged Samaria. [25] **And there was a great famine in Samaria: and, behold, they besieged it, until an ass's head was sold for fourscore pieces of silver, and the fourth part of a cab of dove's dung for five pieces of silver.** [26] **And as the king of Israel was passing by upon the wall, there cried a woman unto him, saying, Help, my lord, O king.** [27] **And he said, If the LORD do not help thee, whence shall I help thee? out of the barnfloor, or out of the winepress?** [28] **And the king said unto her, What aileth thee? And she answered, This woman said unto me, Give thy son, that we may eat him to day, and we will eat my son to morrow.** [29] **So we boiled my son, and did eat him: and I said unto her on the next day, Give thy son, that we may eat him: and she hath hid her son.** [30] **And it came to pass, when the king heard the words of the woman, that he rent his clothes; and he passed by upon the wall, and the people looked, and, behold, he had sackcloth within upon his flesh.** [31] **Then he said, God do so and more also to me, if the head of Elisha the son of Shaphat shall stand on him this day.** [32] **But Elisha sat in his house, and the elders sat with him; and the king sent a man from before him: but ere the messenger came to him, he said to the elders, See ye how this son of a murderer hath sent to take away mine head? look, when the messenger cometh, shut the door, and hold him fast at the door: is not the sound of his master's feet behind him?** [33] **And**

while he yet talked with them, behold, the messenger came down unto him: and he said, Behold, this evil is of the LORD; what should I wait for the LORD any longer? [1] Then Elisha said, Hear ye the word of the LORD; Thus saith the LORD, To morrow about this time shall a measure of fine flour be sold for a shekel, and two measures of barley for a shekel, in the gate of Samaria. [2] Then a lord on whose hand the king leaned answered the man of God, and said, Behold, if the LORD would make windows in heaven, might this thing be? And he said, Behold, thou shalt see it with thine eyes, but shalt not eat thereof. [3] And there were four leprous men at the entering in of the gate: and they said one to another, Why sit we here until we die? [4] If we say, We will enter into the city, then the famine is in the city, and we shall die there: and if we sit still here, we die also. Now therefore come, and let us fall unto the host of the Syrians: if they save us alive, we shall live; and if they kill us, we shall but die. [5] And they rose up in the twilight, to go unto the camp of the Syrians: and when they were come to the uttermost part of the camp of Syria, behold, there was no man there. [6] For the LORD had made the host of the Syrians to hear a noise of chariots, and a noise of horses, even the noise of a great host: and they said one to another, Lo, the king of Israel hath hired against us the kings of the Hittites, and the kings of the Egyptians, to come upon us. [7] Wherefore they arose and fled in the twilight, and left their tents, and their horses, and their asses, even the camp as it was, and fled for their life. [8] And when these lepers came to the uttermost part of the camp, they went into one tent, and did eat and drink, and carried thence silver, and gold, and raiment, and went and hid it; and came again, and entered into another tent, and carried thence also, and went and hid it. [9] Then they said one to another, We do not well: this day is a day of good tidings, and we hold our peace: if we tarry till the morning light, some mischief will come upon us: now therefore come, that we may go and tell the king's household. [10] So they came and called unto the porter of the city: and they told them, saying, We came to the camp of the Syrians, and, behold, there was no man there, neither voice of man, but horses tied, and asses tied, and the tents as they were. [11] And he called the porters; and they told it to the king's house within. [12] And the king arose in the night, and said unto his servants, I will now shew you what the Syrians have done to us. They know that we be hungry; therefore are they gone out of the camp to hide themselves in the field, saying, When they come out of the city, we shall catch them alive, and get into the city. [13] And one of his servants answered and said, Let some take, I pray thee, five of the horses that remain, which are left in the city, (behold, they are as all the multitude of Israel that are left in it: behold, I say, they are even as all the multitude of the Israelites that are consumed:) and let us send and see. [14] They took therefore two chariot horses; and the king sent after the host of the Syrians, saying, Go and see. [15] And they went after them unto Jordan: and, lo, all the way was full of garments and vessels, which the Syrians had cast away in their haste. And the messengers returned, and told the king. [16] And the people went out, and spoiled the tents of the Syrians. So a measure of fine flour was sold for a shekel,

and two measures of barley for a shekel, according to the word of the LORD. [17] **And the king appointed the lord on whose hand he leaned to have the charge of the gate: and the people trode upon him in the gate, and he died, as the man of God had said, who spake when the king came down to him.** [18] **And it came to pass as the man of God had spoken to the king, saying, Two measures of barley for a shekel, and a measure of fine flour for a shekel, shall be to morrow about this time in the gate of Samaria:** [19] **And that lord answered the man of God, and said, Now, behold, if the LORD should make windows in heaven, might such a thing be? And he said, Behold, thou shalt see it with thine eyes, but shalt not eat thereof.** [20] **And so it fell out unto him: for the people trode upon him in the gate, and he died.**

Meditate the Word
LESSON 2

I remember when the Word of God first came alive to me. It was immediately after my life-changing encounter with the Lord on March 23, 1968. The Bible was no longer just a book about what God said. As I read it, I knew the Lord was speaking directly to me. I just fell in love with the Word. When I studied it, He imparted truths to me. I could tell that change was happening in my life.

I remember how the Lord spoke to me one time and gave me a vision of what He wanted to do through me. He had already impacted my life, and I felt called to the ministry. I was in my bedroom at home and still single at the time. I saw in my heart some of the things God wanted to do in my life. While kneeling down at my bed and praying with my Bible open in front of me, I was just overwhelmed when I thought about seeing blind eyes open, deaf ears hear, people raised from the dead—all kinds of miracles. I knew that God had called me to teach His Word and that people's lives would be changed. As an eighteen-year-old, I was praying over all these things.

Then I remember having a vision of many different things happening, including me ministering to people on television (like what I'm doing now). I saw these things and knew they were going to happen. Yet I was an introvert. I couldn't even look at a person in the face and talk to them. How was an introverted hick from Texas ever going to be on radio or television? I sure wouldn't have chosen me.

"How Do I Do This?"

So, there I was, seeing in my heart a vision of all these things that God was calling me to do—seeing the absolute impossibility of it all in the natural realm. I was kneeling by my bed, praying and asking, "Lord, how do I get from where I am to where I know You're telling me I'm supposed to go? It seems like such a huge distance, and I don't have a track to run on. I don't know how to get there. How do I do this?"

As I was praying, I just opened my eyes and looked. There was my Bible lying open on the bed in front of me. When I saw it, I heard the Lord say, "If you will take My Word and meditate in it day and night, then My Word will teach you everything you need to know. My Word will change everything."

I know that sounds really simple, but if it hadn't have been simple, I wouldn't have been able to get it! I took that as God's direction to me. From that time forward, I just poured myself into the Word of God. I didn't think about all of the things that needed to happen for that vision to come to pass. I didn't keep asking, "Lord, how do I overcome my shyness? How do

I get the money? How do I overcome this and do that?" I just forgot all of those issues, and I immersed myself for long periods of time in God's Word. Up until the time I got married, I was spending anywhere from ten to sixteen hours a day studying the Word and learning the truths of God. As I took God's Word and meditated in it day and night, it began to change me.

God is no respecter of persons (Rom. 2:11). If you put His Word first place in your life and meditate in it on a consistent basis, it will change you.

Joshua

That's what God told Joshua to do. He was about to take over the leadership role from Moses. Now, if you stop and think about it, Moses would be a hard act to follow. Joshua was struggling with this, praying, "God, what do I do? How do I lead these people?"

The Lord answered and said, "The same way I was with Moses, I will be with you. Wherever your feet trod, I'll give that land to you." He gave Joshua several promises (Josh. 1:1-7). Then He continued, saying,

> **This book of the law shall not depart out of thy mouth.**
>
> **Joshua 1:8**

Now, at this time, all they had was the first five books of the Bible, the ones that Moses had written out. For us today, I believe that instead of saying **"this book of the law,"** we can say, the Bible, the Word of God...

> **...shall not depart out of thy mouth; but thou shalt meditate therein day and night, that thou mayest observe to do according to all that is written therein: for then thou shalt make thy way prosperous, and then thou shalt have good success.**
>
> **Joshua 1:8**

If you start at the end of this verse and work backward, most people want to be prosperous and have good success. Yet I find it amazing that the vast majority of people bypass the first part of this verse. They'll spend their prayer time asking God "Please prosper my business, please cause my marriage to succeed, please heal my body," but they won't do what the Word says. Joshua 1:8 reveals that the way you get prosperity and good success in every area of your life is to take the Word of God and meditate in it to the degree that it saturates what you think about, what you talk about, and how you act. When God's Word literally begins to control your life, you will prosper and have good success physically, emotionally, relationally, financially—in every area.

I'm living proof of this truth. This is exactly what my life is based upon.

Focusing Your Attention

You may be thinking, *But, Andrew, I work a job. I can't meditate in the Word day and night.* Or you may be saying, "I have two or three kids at home. I'm constantly running around here and there, doing this and that. I can't just sit there reading my Bible and not pay any attention to what's going on with my children." Most people don't believe they can literally meditate in the Word of God day and night. They think that this is a totally impractical demand. But meditation is simply focusing your attention on something to the point that it never leaves your consciousness.

Worry is meditation. It's just meditation on something negative or evil. Whatever your daily demands—watching children, running errands, cleaning the house, taking your kids places, preparing food—you've gone through days accomplishing all of your activities, yet your mind was fixed on, *How am I going to pay for this? What are we going to do? Is my spouse running around on me? Are they with someone? Are we heading for a divorce?* You were able to do all the things you needed to do, yet your mind still worried about those other things.

Maybe you have a career. You could be doing whatever kind of job, yet your mind could still be focused on, *How is this situation going to work out?* You could be sitting there working, yet have something else occupying your mind. You're worrying about it day and night. If you're honest, there have probably been times when certain problems have bothered you to the point where you dream about them. You have a fitful night of sleep because your mind was stayed on, *What am I going to do? How am I going to get out of this situation?* That's worry, which is a form of meditation.

The part of you that worries is the exact same part of you that meditates. Meditation is just the positive side of it.

If you have children at home or you're working a job, it's wrong for you to study the Word sixteen hours a day. It's not being faithful to your family, boss, or employer—to the responsibilities you have. But you can take a passage of Scripture, read it, and then meditate on it the rest of the day and night. You can be thinking on the Word of God and considering *How does this apply to me?* while you're going about your daily activities.

"Believe!"

Recently I was studying King Jehoshaphat in 2 Chronicles 20. He had been faithful to the Lord and serving Him, yet three nations came out against him. The armies of these three nations joined together into what seemed to be an overwhelming force to King Jehoshaphat. There seemed to be no way for him and his people to win. So, Jehoshaphat built a platform, assembled all of the people together, and addressed them. He stood on the platform, lifted his hands to heaven in front of all the people, and began to pray: "God, we don't have any help, any power against this great multitude that has come against us. Our only help is in You. We're standing here. We're waiting on You. God, we need You to do something!"

In the midst of his prayer, a prophet stood up and prophesied, "You won't even have to fight in this battle. In the morning, assemble yourself. You will go out and find that it has already been won." Then, very early the next morning...

> **...Jehoshaphat stood and said, Hear me, O Judah, and ye inhabitants of Jerusalem; Believe in the LORD your God, so shall ye be established; believe his prophets, so shall ye prosper.**
>
> **2 Chronicles 20:20**

He spoke powerful words of faith, saying, "Believe the word of God!" Then they went out to meet these three armies that were coming against them. They didn't just say that they believed God; they proved it by acting on their faith and putting the singers up front (2 Chr. 20:21).

As I've been meditating on this passage of Scripture, I've thought, *What a miracle!* Some people read Bible stories like they didn't really happen, or they think they happened so long ago to somebody else, somewhere else that they just don't connect with the stories. Don't just read the information; begin to think about it. Ask, "God, what if I was Jehoshaphat? What would it have been like to tell the soldiers to get in the back and to put the choir in the front? How must it have sounded as they sang **'Praise the LORD; for His mercy endureth for ever'** on their way out to meet the three armies (2 Chr. 20:21)—over a million people armed to the hilt?"

It's one thing to read that, but another to meditate on it. I read those passages of Scripture again and again for two or three days. I'd go back to the same passages and spend thirty minutes to an hour reading, looking up cross references, and gathering information. Then I'd spend time meditating on it during the day. I was on an airplane traveling to a *Gospel Truth Seminar*. My eyes were closed, but I was thinking about what a huge step of faith this was for Jehoshaphat and how God rewarded him.

All You Need

Sure enough, when the Israelites came over the hill and looked, these three armies had turned on each other. Two of them had agreed to kill the third. Then, after they wiped out that army, they began killing each other. The very last two people standing killed each other. So, when the armies of Israel came over the hill, they looked and there was nothing but corpses. They found so much gold, silver, and clothes that it took the entire nation of Israel three days to gather the spoils.

Most people read through a Bible story like that and glibly say, "Oh, there was a victory for trusting God." But you can milk this passage for tremendous truths. Here was Jehoshaphat, his life and kingdom looked like they were just about to be snuffed out. In the midst of that, he cried out to God. The Lord gave him a prophecy. He believed it, and in less than twenty-four hours after he began trusting God, the very thing that looked like it would be the destruction of the nation turned out to be one of the best things that ever happened. They didn't even have to lift a sword. They went out and gathered so much spoil, and Jehoshaphat dedicated all of it to the temple. Prior to that time, some other people had come in and stolen all of the gold and silver from the temple. Through faith in God's Word, Jehoshaphat saw this situation, which looked like it was going to be his destruction, turn out to be the very thing God used to supply the needed resources to refurbish the temple. It turned out great!

For days after I read that, I just meditated on those scriptures, thinking about how those truths applied to my life and some of the problems that faced me, problems that appeared like they could be the end of Andrew Wommack Ministries. I started thinking that in the same way God did this for Jehoshaphat, He can do it for me. This situation that looks like it could destroy me could very well turn out to be one of the best things that ever happens to me.

As you meditate in the Word, faith rises in you. Many people miss this because they read the Word but don't meditate in it. So, everyone may not be able to spend large quantities of time in the Word, but *everyone* can meditate in it day and night.

Regardless of what your circumstances or problems are, you're never more than one word from God away from absolute victory. The Lord knows exactly where you are and how to get you to where you're supposed to be. All you need is just the slightest instruction, an impartation of God's wisdom. All you need is a word from God!

Meditate the Word
LESSON 2 – OUTLINE

I. As I took God's Word and meditated in it day and night, it began to change me.

   A. God is no respecter of persons (Rom. 2:11).

   B. If you put His Word first place in your life and meditate in it on a consistent basis, it will change you.

> **This book of the law shall not depart out of thy mouth; but thou shalt meditate therein day and night, that thou mayest observe to do according to all that is written therein: for then thou shalt make thy way prosperous, and then thou shalt have good success.**
>
> **Joshua 1:8**

   C. This verse reveals that the way you get prosperity and good success in every area of your life is to take the Word of God and meditate in it to the degree that it saturates what you think about, what you talk about, and how you act.

   D. When God's Word literally begins to control your life, you will prosper and have good success physically, emotionally, relationally, financially—in every area.

   E. This is exactly what my life is based upon.

II. Most people don't believe they can literally meditate in the Word of God day and night.

   A. They think that this is a totally impractical demand.

   B. But meditation is simply focusing your attention on something to the point that it never leaves your consciousness.

   C. You can take a passage of Scripture, read it, and then meditate on it the rest of the day and night.

   D. You can be thinking on the Word of God and considering *How does this apply to me?* while you're going about your daily activities.

III. Recently I was studying King Jehoshaphat in 2 Chronicles 20.

   A. He had been faithful to the Lord and serving Him, yet three nations came out against him.

B. Some people read Bible stories like they didn't really happen, or they think they hap pened so long ago to somebody else, somewhere else that they just don't connect with the stories.

C. Don't just read the information; begin to think about it.

D. I was thinking about what a huge step of faith this was for Jehoshaphat and how God rewarded him.

E. It turned out great!

F. For days after I read that, I just meditated on those scriptures, thinking about how those truths applied to my life and some of the problems that faced me, problems that appeared like they could be the end of Andrew Wommack Ministries.

G. I started thinking that in the same way God did this for Jehoshaphat, He can do it for me.

H. This situation that looks like it could destroy me could very well turn out to be one of the best things that ever happens to me.

IV. As you meditate in the Word, faith rises in you.

A. Many people miss this because they read the Word, but don't meditate in it.

B. So, everyone may not be able to spend large quantities of time in the Word, but *everyone* can meditate in it day and night.

Meditate the Word
LESSON 2 – TEACHER'S GUIDE

1. As I took God's Word and meditated in it day and night, it began to change me. God is no respecter of persons (Rom. 2:11). If you put His Word first place in your life and meditate in it on a consistent basis, it will change you. Joshua 1:8 reveals that the way we get prosperity and good success in every area of our lives is to take the Word of God and meditate in it to the degree that it saturates what we think about, what we talk about, and how we act. When God's Word literally begins to control our lives, we will prosper and have good success physically, emotionally, relationally, financially—in every area. This is exactly what my life is based upon.

2. Most of us don't believe we can literally meditate in the Word of God day and night. We think that this is a totally impractical demand. But meditation is simply focusing our attention on something to the point that it never leaves our consciousness. We can take a passage of Scripture, read it, and then meditate on it the rest of the day and night. We can be thinking on the Word of God and considering *How does this apply to me?* while we're going about our daily activities.

3. Recently I was studying King Jehoshaphat in 2 Chronicles 20. He had been faithful to the Lord and serving Him, yet three nations came out against him. Some of us read Bible stories like they didn't really happen, or we think they happened so long ago to somebody else, somewhere else that we just don't connect with the stories. We shouldn't just read the information; we need to begin to think about it. I was thinking about what a huge step of faith this was for Jehoshaphat and how God rewarded him. It turned out great! For days after I read that, I just meditated on those scriptures, thinking about how those truths applied to my life and some of the problems that faced me, problems that appeared like they could be the end of Andrew Wommack Ministries. I started thinking that in the same way God did this for Jehoshaphat, He can do it for me. This situation that looks like it could destroy me could very well turn out to be one of the best things that ever happens to me.

1. A. What would happen if we put God's Word first place in our lives and meditated in it on a consistent basis? (It will change us)
   B. How do we get prosperity and good success in every area of our lives? (By taking the Word of God and meditating in it to the degree that it saturates what we think about, what we talk about, and how we act)
2. A. What is meditation? (It's simply focusing our attention on something to the point that it never leaves our consciousness)
   B. When we're thinking on the Word of God, what can we consider? (How does this apply to me?)
3. A. When we read Bible stories, what do we need to do with the information? (Think about it)
   B. What did Andrew think about God as he meditated on Jehoshaphat's story? (He thought that in the same way God rewarded Jehoshaphat, He can do it for him)

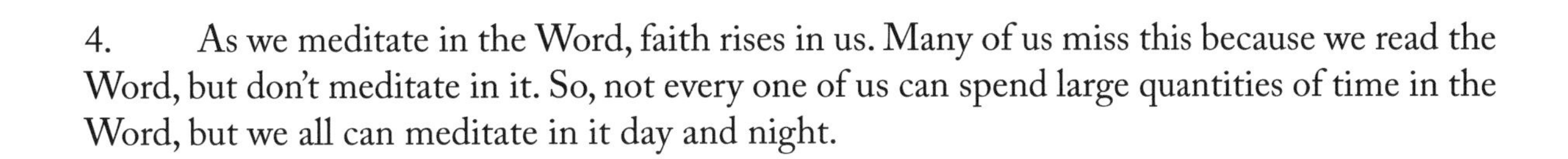

4. As we meditate in the Word, faith rises in us. Many of us miss this because we read the Word, but don't meditate in it. So, not every one of us can spend large quantities of time in the Word, but we all can meditate in it day and night.

4. A. What happens as we meditate in the Word? (Faith rises in us)
   B. What can we all do? (We can all meditate in the Word day and night)

Meditate the Word
LESSON 2 – DISCIPLESHIP QUESTIONS

1. Read Romans 2:11. What does this verse mean?
   A. Some people are God's favorites
   B. God thinks people are not to be respected
   C. God can't tell the difference between His people and those who are not His people
   D. God shows favoritism to no one
   E. God doesn't care about anyone

2. Read Joshua 1:1-8. Was God concerned that He could no longer work through Moses?

3. How would God be with Joshua?

4. What was the only thing God wanted Joshua to be?

5. What did He want Joshua to do?

6. Read 2 Chronicles 20:20-21. What was the first thing Jehoshaphat told the people to do?

7. What did Jehoshaphat do before he appointed singers?
   A. He consulted with the people
   B. He proclaimed a feast
   C. He took up an offering
   D. All of the above
   E. None of the above

8. What did the people praise God for?

Meditate the Word
LESSON 2 – ANSWER KEY

1. D. God shows favoritism to no one
2. No
3. In the same way He was with Moses
4. Strong and very courageous
5. To not let the book of the Law depart from his mouth but to meditate in it day and night that he might observe to do all that is written in it
6. To believe in the Lord and to believe His prophets
7. A. He consulted with the people
8. His mercy, which endures for forever

Meditate the Word
LESSON 2 – SCRIPTURES

ROMANS 2:11
For there is no respect of persons with God.

JOSHUA 1:1-8
Now after the death of Moses the servant of the LORD it came to pass, that the LORD spake unto Joshua the son of Nun, Moses' minister, saying, [2] Moses my servant is dead; now therefore arise, go over this Jordan, thou, and all this people, unto the land which I do give to them, even to the children of Israel. [3] Every place that the sole of your foot shall tread upon, that have I given unto you, as I said unto Moses. [4] From the wilderness and this Lebanon even unto the great river, the river Euphrates, all the land of the Hittites, and unto the great sea toward the going down of the sun, shall be your coast. [5] There shall not any man be able to stand before thee all the days of thy life: as I was with Moses, so I will be with thee: I will not fail thee, nor forsake thee. [6] Be strong and of a good courage: for unto this people shalt thou divide for an inheritance the land, which I sware unto their fathers to give them. [7] Only be thou strong and very courageous, that thou mayest observe to do according to all the law, which Moses my servant commanded thee: turn not from it to the right hand or to the left, that thou mayest prosper whithersoever thou goest. [8] This book of the law shall not depart out of thy mouth; but thou shalt meditate therein day and night, that thou mayest observe to do according to all that is written therein: for then thou shalt make thy way prosperous, and then thou shalt have good success.

2 CHRONICLES 20:20-21
And they rose early in the morning, and went forth into the wilderness of Tekoa: and as they went forth, Jehoshaphat stood and said, Hear me, O Judah, and ye inhabitants of Jerusalem; Believe in the LORD your God, so shall ye be established; believe his prophets, so shall ye prosper. [21] And when he had consulted with the people, he appointed singers unto the LORD, and that should praise the beauty of holiness, as they went out before the army, and to say, Praise the LORD; for his mercy endureth for ever.

God Speaking
LESSON 3

God isn't wringing His hands and wondering how He can pull it out for us. There is a simple solution for every person. Our biggest problem is our inability to hear His voice. The way we know what God is saying is by His Word. If we would get into the Word of God and meditate in it, the Lord would speak to us. He would give us wisdom and direction.

I deal with all kinds of people all around the world. They vary greatly in maturity. Many of them nod their heads and tell me, "We know that this is God's Word, and it has our answers." They say that because they know it's what they're supposed to say. But in a practical sense, most people don't really believe they can solve their problems at work, at home—anywhere—by the Word of God.

Wisdom and Instruction

In chapter 1, Solomon described why he wrote the book of Proverbs.

> **To know wisdom and instruction; to perceive the words of understanding; To receive the instruction of wisdom, justice, and judgment, and equity; To give subtilty to the simple, to the young man knowledge and discretion.**
>
> **Proverbs 1:2-4**

He said it's to give wisdom to the simple and understanding to those who don't have any. Then he spoke about the good it will bring you and the bad it will help you avoid. The truths contained in the book of Proverbs alone will instruct you concerning all kinds of things.

> **A man's gift maketh room for him, and bringeth him before great men.**
>
> **Proverbs 18:16**

This isn't talking about just your talents and abilities. Literally, it's speaking of a gift—a present given to a person. The negative side of this truth is a bribe. It's easy to understand how a bribe can affect people and change things. Gifts have tremendous potential for positive influence as well.

Another proverb says,

> **Cast out the scorner, and contention shall go out; yea, strife and reproach shall cease.**
>
> **Proverbs 22:10**

I've applied this in my own ministry. When there are problems among people, go to the person who is the root of it. Cast out the scorner—the critical person who's stirring everything up—and contention, strife, and reproach will cease.

Perfect Representation

Through God's Word, you can learn how to deal with people. You can gain wisdom if you're a boss, an employee, or a salesperson. If you are a parent and you're struggling with your children, there's a wealth of information in the Bible. I have yet to run across a problem in life that the Word of God doesn't provide an answer for. And if you will take His Word, meditate in it, and put His knowledge on the inside of you, then the Holy Spirit will, at the appropriate time, quicken things to you and show you what to do.

God speaks to me this way. This is what makes my life tick. What has changed my life is my love for the Word of God.

Sometimes I get criticized by people, who say, "You love the Word of God more than you love God." I don't separate the two! Jesus is the Word made flesh who dwelt among us (John 1:14). When I refer to the Word, I'm not talking about just a physical book. You could tear a page out of the Bible, even a whole book, but you haven't changed the Word of God. The words contained in the Bible perfectly represent the heart of God.

When I read the Word, it's not me reading a book about God; this is the Lord writing to me! Even some of the things that were said thousands of years ago to other people, He speaks to me today.

"I'll Give You Anything"

The Lord told Jeremiah,

> **Before I formed thee in the belly I knew thee; and before thou camest forth out of the womb I sanctified thee, and I ordained thee a prophet unto the nations.**
>
> **Jeremiah 1:5**

Some people read that and say, "Well, this was something written specifically to Jeremiah over 3,000 years ago. Yet here you are, getting excited over it as if it was written to you!"

I can tell you the exact time and place where God spoke that to me. I was in an apartment in Kingsley Place Apartments in Dallas, Texas, in 1973. I read those scriptures and went to bed, but couldn't fall asleep (which was very unusual for me). I wondered, *What is going on?* Then all of a sudden, the presence of God manifested in that room. This was soon after Jamie and I were married. I got up and went into our living room. The Lord came to me and said (just as He had to Solomon), "I'll give you anything you ask for." So, I answered, saying, "I want the ability to speak Your Word effectively so that it changes people's lives." Then He ministered to me and led me to Jeremiah 1:5.

Then the Lord continued speaking to me, saying,

> **Behold, I will make my words in thy mouth fire, and this people wood, and it shall devour them.**
>
> **Jeremiah 5:14**

Yes, God did speak these words to Jeremiah thousands of years ago, but He's also spoken them to me. They're mine. Say what you will, but it's working for me. I'm seeing the power of God manifest. This is an important way God has spoken to me in my life—through His Word.

Alive, Not Dead

Some folks say, "Well, I want God to speak to me outside of His Word." I don't need that. I really believe that God inspired people to write down His Word. Many others have given their lives to preserve it. Many people take God's Word for granted. They don't respect and honor it for what it is—God speaking to us. That's why they don't get the benefit out of it that I do. Believe me, God's Word has everything in it that you need to succeed. If you would simply do what the Word says and meditate in it day and night, you would prosper and have good success (Josh. 1:8).

Average Christians don't believe this truth. That's why they don't meditate in the Word of God day and night, which is the reason they're not prospering and succeeding more than they are.

Many Christians don't honor the Word of God and look at it as God literally speaking to them. When they read it, they do it more as a religious obligation and duty. They don't read it expecting God to speak to them.

When I open up the Word of God, I literally view it as God talking to me—and He does. These are living words. The Bible is alive; it's not dead (Heb. 4:12). There's a difference between this Book and any other book. That's why I choose not to read very much else. I might read one or two other books in a year, and that's mainly because I have so many people pressing me to read their books. Usually these are people I like and know that they have some good things to say. However, my desire is for the Word. Everything I need is right there in the Word of God.

A man came to me recently at one of my meetings in California. He told me he really enjoyed the ministry, that the message blessed him, and that he had never heard the truths I shared that day. Since he was a scientist, he told me, "You ought to read this and that book about science and the Bible. Then you could get to where you could come at the Bible from a scientific perspective and answer all of these questions and so forth." He gave me several books and really wanted me to read them.

The Real Thing

Finally, because he kept pushing me so hard, I had to push back. I didn't do it out of anger or anything like that. I just told him, "The way people learn how to recognize counterfeit money isn't by studying all of the counterfeits. There are so many different ways to counterfeit money that you just can't learn every counterfeit. Instead, the people who are going to be on the frontlines of deciding which bills are counterfeit are given the real thing. They study the grain, the weight, the texture, the look—everything about genuine bills. In the process, they become so familiar with the real that they're able to instantly recognize a counterfeit.

"That's how I feel about it. I'm going to be so familiar with God through His Word that I don't have to go to this person over here or learn this, that, and these other things. I'm going to be so single minded, so focused on the Word of God that I don't have to have all these supplemental things."

I realize that this is a departure from how most people live. Most people advocate reading a book a week, a book a month, or something like that. I'm not saying that's wrong or of the devil; I'm just saying that there is a definite difference between anybody else's book and the Word of God!

I've written books. In fact, you're reading one right now. So, I'm not against books. But there is a difference between my books and the Word of God. The only reason I like my books as much as I do is because they're crammed full of the Word of God. Actually, my purpose in writing books is simply to explain truths and share personal examples in order to help people understand the Word of God. However, it wouldn't bother me one bit if you bypassed all of my books and just meditated in the Word of God day and night. You'd be better off.

Take God's Word. Meditate in it day and night. Get to where the Word of God is more real to you than a person sitting next to you. When you're at work, even though you interact with people and do your job well, the truth is, you're constantly thinking about scriptures and what

God is speaking to you. You're meditating on God's Word and trying to relate it to different circumstances and situations. If you would do that, you would prosper more accidentally than you ever have on purpose.

Give Attention

Proverbs says,

> **My son, attend to my words; incline thine ear unto my sayings.**
>
> **Proverbs 4:20**

"Attend to my words" simply means give attention.

You've been in school when the teacher was in front talking. Perhaps even though you were looking straight at him or her, you weren't attending to those words. They were going in one ear and out the other. You were daydreaming. Your focus was somewhere else.

Likewise, many people go through the motions of reading passages of Scripture. You could probably read an entire chapter of the Word and close your Bible as soon as you're done. Then I could immediately ask you "What chapter were you reading? What book of the Bible was it in?" and you wouldn't even have a clue. You certainly couldn't tell me what you read. I'm not trying to condemn you. I just want you to realize that's not attending to God's words.

Life and Health

Whenever I emphasize how important and powerful God's Word is, people always say to me, "I've studied the Bible. I've read the Word. In fact, I've read the Bible all the way through, and it hasn't done this for me." You must do what Proverbs 4 says, which is to attend to His words and incline your ear.

The phrase **"incline thine ear"** isn't telling you to change the position of your head; it's talking about listening with your heart. It's speaking of focus and commitment. You must listen to God's Word with your heart, not just your head.

Place a high priority and value on the Word of God. Start taking each one of these words as being a direct word from God to you. Attend to it. Incline your ear to it. Then you'll start getting the results I'm describing.

> **My son, attend to my words; incline thine ear unto my sayings.**
> **Let them not depart from thine eyes; keep them in the midst of**

thine heart. For they [God's words] **are life unto those that find them, and health to all their flesh.**

Proverbs 4:20-22, brackets mine

God's Word is life. No matter how grave the situation you're in, God's Word is life and health to all your flesh!

God Speaking
LESSON 3 – OUTLINE

I. Our biggest problem is our inability to hear God's voice.

   A. The way we know what God is saying is by His Word.

   B. If we would get into the Word of God and meditate in it, the Lord would speak to us.

   C. He would give us wisdom and direction.

   D. God speaks to me this way.

   E. This is what makes my life tick.

II. Sometimes I get criticized by people, who say, "You love the Word of God more than you love God."

   A. I don't separate the two!

   B. Jesus is the Word made flesh who dwelt among us (John 1:14).

   C. When I refer to the Word, I'm not talking about just a physical book.

   D. When I read the Word, it's not me reading a book about God; this is the Lord writing to me!

   E. Even some of the things that were said thousands of years ago to other people, He speaks to me today.

III. Some folks say, "Well, I want God to speak to me outside of His Word."

   A. That's why they don't meditate in the Word of God day and night, which is the reason they're not prospering and succeeding more than they are.

   B. They don't read it expecting God to speak to them.

   C. When I open up the Word of God, I literally view it as God talking to me—and He does.

IV. There's a difference between this Book and any other book.

   A. That's why I choose not to read very much else.

   B. My desire is for the Word.

   C. Everything I need is right there in the Word of God.

   D. Most people advocate reading a book a week, a book a month, or something like that.

   E. I'm not saying that's wrong or of the devil.

   F. I've written books. In fact, you're reading one right now.

   G. However, it wouldn't bother me one bit if you bypassed all of my books and just meditated in the Word of God day and night.

V. Take God's Word.

   A. Meditate in it day and night.

   B. Get to where the Word of God is more real to you than a person sitting next to you.

   C. If you would do that, you would prosper more accidentally than you ever have on purpose.

VI. Whenever I emphasize how important and powerful God's Word is, people always say to me, "I've studied the Bible. I've read the Word. In fact, I've read the Bible all the way through, and it hasn't done this for me."

   A. You must do what Proverbs 4:20 says, which is to attend to God's words and incline your ear.

   B. The phrase **"incline thine ear"** is speaking of focus and commitment.

   C. You must listen to God's Word with your heart, not just your head.

   D. Place a high priority and value on the Word of God.

   E. Then you'll start getting the results I'm describing.

> **My son, attend to my words; incline thine ear unto my sayings. Let them not depart from thine eyes; keep them in the midst of thine heart. For they** [God's words] **are life unto those that find them, and health to all their flesh.**
>
> **Proverbs 4:20-22, brackets mine**

F. No matter how grave the situation you're in, God's Word is life and health to all your flesh!

God Speaking
LESSON 3 – TEACHER'S GUIDE

1. Our biggest problem is our inability to hear God's voice. The way we know what God is saying by His Word. If we would get into the Word of God and meditate in it, the Lord would speak to us. He would give us wisdom and direction. God speaks to me this way. This is what makes my life tick.

2. Sometimes I get criticized by people, who say, "You love the Word of God more than you love God." I don't separate the two! Jesus is the Word made flesh who dwelt among us (John 1:14). When I refer to the Word, I'm not talking about just a physical book. When I read the Word, it's not me reading a book about God; this is the Lord writing to me! Even some of the things that were said thousands of years ago to other people, He speaks to me today.

3. Some folks say, "Well, I want God to speak to me outside of His Word." That's why they don't meditate in the Word of God day and night, which is the reason they're not prospering and succeeding more than they are. They don't read it expecting God to speak to them. When I open up the Word of God, I literally view it as God talking to me—and He does.

1. A. What is our biggest problem? (Our inability to hear God's voice)
   B. How do we know what God is saying? (By His Word)
   C. What would the Lord do if we got into the Word of God and meditated in it? (He would give us wisdom and direction)
2. Read John 1:14. Why doesn't Andrew separate his love for the Word of God from his love for God? (Because Jesus [God] is the Word made flesh)
3. A. Why don't some folks meditate in the Word of God day and night? (Because they want God to speak to them outside of His Word)
   B. That's also the reason they're not what? (Prospering and succeeding more than they are)

4. There's a difference between this Book and any other book. That's why I choose not to read very much else. My desire is for the Word. Everything I need is right there in the Word of God. Most people advocate reading a book a week, a book a month, or something like that. I'm not saying that's wrong or of the devil. I've written books. In fact, you're reading one right now. However, it wouldn't bother me one bit if you bypassed all of my books and just meditated in the Word of God day and night.

5. We need to take God's Word. We need to meditate in it day and night. We need to get to where the Word of God is more real to us than a person sitting next to us. If we would do that, we would prosper more accidentally than we ever have on purpose.

6. Whenever I emphasize how important and powerful God's Word is, people say to me, "I've studied the Bible. I've read the Word. In fact, I've read the Bible all the way through, and it hasn't done this for me." We must do what Proverbs 4:20 says, which is to attend to God's words and incline our ears. The phrase **"incline thine ear"** is speaking of focus and commitment. We must listen to God's Word with our hearts, not just our heads. We need to place a high priority and value on the Word of God. Then we'll start getting the results I'm describing. No matter how grave the situation we're in, God's Word is life and health to all our flesh (Prov. 4:20-22)!

4. A. What does Andrew have a desire for? (The Word)
   B. Is Andrew saying it's wrong, or of the devil, to read a book other than the Word of God? (No)
   C. What wouldn't bother Andrew? (If we bypassed all of his books and just meditated in the Word of God day and night)
5. A. What do we need to take? (The Word of God)
   B. Where do we need to get? (Where the Word of God is more real to us than a person sitting next to us)
   C. How would we prosper? (More accidentally than we ever have on purpose)
6. A. We must listen to God's Word with our _____, not just our heads. (Hearts)
   B. Read Proverbs 4:20-22. Is God's Word life and health to all our flesh in only favorable situations? (No, no matter how grave the situation we're in)

God Speaking
LESSON 3 – DISCIPLESHIP QUESTIONS

1. Read Proverbs 1:2-4. You are to _____ wisdom and instruction.

2. You are to _____ the words of understanding.

3. You are to _____ the instruction of wisdom, justice, judgment, and equity.

4. Read Proverbs 18:16. What makes room for a person and brings them before great people?

5. According to Proverbs 22:10, casting out the scorner will cause what to go out as well?
   A. The scorner's brother
   B. Contention
   C. The lights
   D. All of the above
   E. None of the above

6. What shall cease?

7. Read John 1:14. The only begotten of the Father was full of what two things?

8. According to Jeremiah 1:5, when was Jeremiah's ordination as a prophet?

9. Read Jeremiah 5:14. Why was God going to make Jeremiah's words fire and the people wood?

10. Read Joshua 1:8. Whose responsibility is it to make your way prosperous and have good success?

11. According to Hebrews 4:12, what can divide soul and spirit?

12. The Word of God is a _____ of the thoughts and intents of the heart.
    A. Condemner
    B. Follower
    C. Endorser
    D. Finisher
    E. Discerner

13. Read Proverbs 4:20-22. Who is instructed to incline their ear?

14. Where are you to keep God's sayings?

15. Why?

God Speaking
LESSON 3 – ANSWER KEY

1. Know
2. Perceive
3. Receive
4. Their gift
5. B. Contention
6. Strife and reproach
7. Grace and truth
8. Before he came forth out of the womb
9. Because he spoke what God said
10. Mine
11. The Word of God
12. E. Discerner
13. A son
14. In the midst of my heart
15. Because they are life to those who find them and health to all their flesh

God Speaking
LESSON 3 – SCRIPTURES

PROVERBS 1:2-4
To know wisdom and instruction; to perceive the words of understanding; [3] To receive the instruction of wisdom, justice, and judgment, and equity; [4] To give subtilty to the simple, to the young man knowledge and discretion.

PROVERBS 18:16
A man's gift maketh room for him, and bringeth him before great men.

PROVERBS 22:10
Cast out the scorner, and contention shall go out; yea, strife and reproach shall cease.

JOHN 1:14
And the Word was made flesh, and dwelt among us, (and we beheld his glory, the glory as of the only begotten of the Father,) full of grace and truth.

JEREMIAH 1:5
Before I formed thee in the belly I knew thee; and before thou camest forth out of the womb I sanctified thee, and I ordained thee a prophet unto the nations.

JEREMIAH 5:14
Wherefore thus saith the LORD God of hosts, Because ye speak this word, behold, I will make my words in thy mouth fire, and this people wood, and it shall devour them.

JOSHUA 1:8
This book of the law shall not depart out of thy mouth; but thou shalt meditate therein day and night, that thou mayest observe to do according to all that is written therein: for then thou shalt make thy way prosperous, and then thou shalt have good success.

HEBREWS 4:12
For the word of God is quick, and powerful, and sharper than any twoedged sword, piercing even to the dividing asunder of soul and spirit, and of the joints and marrow, and is a discerner of the thoughts and intents of the heart.

PROVERBS 4:20-22

My son, attend to my words; incline thine ear unto my sayings. [21] **Let them not depart from thine eyes; keep them in the midst of thine heart.** [22] **For they are life unto those that find them, and health to all their flesh.**

Transformed
LESSON 4

If you're struggling with depression, you're not meditating in the Word of God day and night. Romans 8:6 reveals,

> **For to be carnally minded is death; but to be spiritually minded is life and peace.**

If you have death in any form working in you—including depression, discouragement, anger, un-forgiveness, bitterness, and so forth—it's because you've planted death. I don't mean that to condemn you, but rather to enlighten you and show you where the problem is.

Remember, I don't have to be with you when you plant a garden to see what you've sown. All I have to do is be there when the garden grows up (See **Lesson 1**). If you have death in your life—if you're depressed, discouraged, angry, or bitter—you haven't been meditating in the Word of God. Spiritual-mindedness only produces life and peace.

Take a Gos-pill

Jesus said,

> **The words that I speak unto you, they are spirit, and they are life.**
>
> **John 6:63**

Since God's Word is spirit, to be spiritually minded is to be Word-of-God minded. If you were Word-of-God minded, all it would produce is life and peace.

> **Thou wilt keep him in perfect peace, whose mind is stayed on thee: because he trusteth in thee.**
>
> **Isaiah 26:3**

Some might say, "But I've done all of these things, and I still have terrible problems in my life." You may have read the Word of God or heard somebody else quote it, but you haven't attended to it. You haven't inclined your ear and kept His sayings in the midst of your heart (Prov. 4:20-22). You've let your eyes depart and focus on other things. If you do what God's Word says, all it will produce is the results that the Word said it will produce. Proverbs 4:20-22 reveals that God's Word will be life to those who find His sayings, and health to all their flesh.

Literally thousands of people have come to me with sickness in their bodies and asked, "Would you pray for me?" "Yes," I tell them, "I'll pray for you." But what do I do, after I've prayed for everybody else, when I get sick? Do I run to somebody every time an illness is fighting against me? No, I go to the Word of God. Just like if you have a pain, you may take a pill, if I have a pain, I take a Gos-pill (Gospel). I take the Word of God.

Health Flows Through

Whenever I have any physical symptoms hitting me, I'll stand against them, rebuke them, and speak my faith. Normally, that will take care of everything. For over forty years, I've lived in divine health. I took a couple of asprins after having a tooth removed, and I got so weak after ministering eighty-two times in two weeks that I had a sinus infection for a couple of days, but that's it. I don't get sick. I don't believe in being sick. But I've had the symptoms of sickness hit me. They'll last for an hour or two. If I don't see instantaneous results when I immediately rebuke it, then I take the Word of God. I start going over scriptures that I already know, like 1 Peter 2:24, which says that by His stripes, I was healed. It's not good enough just to quote them from memory. I go back and look them up again because of this principle. God's words are life to those that find them and health to all their flesh (Prov. 4:22). The Word of God is health to your flesh!

He sent his word, and healed them, and delivered them from their destructions.

Psalm 107:20

If I need healing in my body, I take the Word of God and meditate on it. I eat these words because they're life and health to my flesh. I could even quote them, but I'll still go back and study them. As I do, the Bible reveals that…

...faith cometh by hearing, and hearing by the word of God.

Romans 10:17

Notice that verse doesn't say, "Faith comes by having heard." No, it's in the present. We have to continually hear God's Word. When I meditate on those scriptures, I stir up the faith that I already have on the inside of me (Rom. 12:3). As I start meditating on them, health flows through me.

I've only gone a maximum of a few hours over the past forty years with any symptom of sickness in my body. I've overcome broken bones, swelling, sprains, fevers, and nausea. I actually have a doctor's report saying I had an incurable disease. Yet within hours of that doctor's visit, I was totally healed. I've operated this way for decades and it works.

This is what the Word of God teaches about itself. Yet most people, even those who say "God's Word is important," don't really live this way. They don't meditate in the Word day and night. That's the reason they don't have good success and aren't prosperous.

Made Manifest

God used the first two verses of Romans 12 to totally transform my life. It was the first passage of Scripture that ever came alive to me, back in 1967. These verses impacted me so deeply that they literally changed the course of my life.

> **I beseech you therefore, brethren, by the mercies of God, that ye present your bodies a living sacrifice, holy, acceptable unto God, which is your reasonable service. And be not conformed to this world: but be ye transformed by the renewing of your mind, that ye may prove what is that good, and acceptable, and perfect, will of God.**
>
> **Romans 12:1-2**

That's what I was seeking in my life. I wanted to know God's will. So, I looked up the word **"prove,"** and it means to make manifest to the physical senses. That was exactly what I desired. God already had a plan for my life. I believed that. I just didn't know what it was. It wasn't manifest to my physical senses. I believed it was there—somewhere. I just wanted it to be manifest. So, for months I focused on this passage of Scripture. I wanted the result promised at the end of verse 2 where I would make manifest to my physical senses the good, acceptable, and perfect will of God. So, I went back to verse 1 and to the beginning of verse 2 to see what I had to do to get there.

Verse 1 radically transformed my life and gave me a totally brand-new direction. After meditating on it for three and a half months, I had this experience where God poured out His love in my life. That was March 23, 1968. It literally changed the course of my life. I've never been the same since.

As important as that experience was, I would have lost the benefit of just an encounter with God if I had not continued to grow in the knowledge of His Word. You may be struggling to understand that, thinking, *Oh, if only I could really encounter God. If I had a vision or if the Lord were to appear to me, then my life would never be the same.* I've had some very miraculous encounters with God, but I'm telling you that you can't just live off of an experience or emotions. It's been over forty years since I encountered God this way. If all I was living from was an experience that happened to me over forty years ago, I would be dry, dead, and lifeless today. That encounter got me jump-started. It opened up my eyes and gave me a vision. It provided me with motivation. That was good, and I praise God for it, but what really changed my life was Romans 12:2:

Be not conformed to this world: but be ye transformed by the renewing of your mind.

That's what happened to me: I've been transformed by the renewing of my mind. I had this supernatural experience that got my attention, changed my desires, and started me moving in a different direction. However, it was the renewing of my mind through the Word of God that has completely, thoroughly, and totally transformed me. I attribute every bit of the power and victory that I've experienced to the Word of God becoming alive and speaking to me.

Melted

Verse 2 says,

Be not conformed to this world.

The Greek word translated **"conformed"** here literally means to pour into the mold.

You aren't going to exit this life the same way you came in. You came as a baby—innocent, naïve, without a firm direction or plan for your life. By the time you live twenty, forty, sixty, or however many years, the pressures of this life are going to melt you. Everyone will be melted. You'll change shape, form, and direction. However, the good news is that you get to choose what mold you fit into.

The pressures of this life tend to fit everybody into the world's mold of being a pessimist (i.e, you lose your dreams and goals, harbor un-forgiveness, and become bitter). That's the mold the problems in this life are trying to force you into. But you don't have to go into that mold; you can choose to be transformed.

I first truly understood this concept on the day we received our orders to be shipped to Vietnam. Like most of my fellow soldiers, I was still a teenager. At nineteen years old, I had already been through infantry training. Every one of us, except one, received orders to go to Vietnam. Immediately, most of these young men broke down in fear and started crying.

As I write this today, we're at war in Iraq. Many brave men and women have given their lives for the cause of freedom. Each one has a story, beloved family and friends who miss them, and unfulfilled hopes and dreams. However, as of today, the sheer volume of American blood that flowed in Vietnam makes the over 4,000 deaths over seven years in Iraq pale in comparison. Although the car bombs and other dangers in Iraq are bad enough, it's nothing compared to what was happening at that time in Vietnam. There were mortars, bombs, booby traps, and people with guns coming at you. When you got shipped to Vietnam, you knew you were going to come into contact with the enemy. It wasn't just some of the people over there getting shot at; it was everyone. Due to this, people were just falling apart left and right like two-dollar suitcases.

After we received our orders and all these young men were weeping all over the room, the chaplain came in and made this statement: "Going to Vietnam is a fire, and it will melt you. But you get to pick what mold you fit into. This doesn't have to be a negative experience that destroys you; it can be a positive experience." God used that chaplain's words to speak directly to me.

Renew Your Mind

You may not be a soldier in the midst of a war zone, but you will have pressures come against you in this life that will melt you. However, you get to pick whether you'll be like the other people who become negative, bitter, and unforgiving. You can choose whether you'll murmur and complain or if you'll let these things drive you to the Lord and make you stronger and more stable in your commitment to God. How do you make that choice?

> **Be not conformed to this world: but be ye transformed by the renewing of your mind, that ye may prove what is that good, and acceptable, and perfect, will of God.**
>
> **Romans 12:2**

The Greek word rendered **"transformed"** here is *metamorphoo*. It's the word we derive our English word *metamorphosis* from. A little worm spins a cocoon and then, after time, comes out a beautiful butterfly. If you want to be transformed from something creepy, crawly, and earthbound into something beautiful that flies, you need to go through metamorphosis. Do you want to change from being weak, inferior, and bound by all kinds of problems into someone who releases and experiences the abundant life of God from within? The Word of God reveals that the way to do this is by the renewing of your mind. You must renew your mind to the Word of God.

You can't just turn your mind off and think of nothing. Sometimes when you ask someone what they are thinking, they'll answer, "Nothing." The truth is, they were thinking of something. You can't not think. Your mind is constantly going. Even when you're asleep, your subconscious mind will inspire dreams. Whether you're awake or not, you can't turn your mind off and not think. All you can do is choose what you think on—the things of the Lord or the things of the world.

The things of the world could simply be physical, natural things. They don't even have to be demonic—X-rated, R-rated, terrible, ungodly—things. They can even be decent things. They don't have to be bad. But just be occupied with them, and you'll never experience this transformation.

The Greatest Thing in the World

If you want to be transformed like a caterpillar into a butterfly, you must put your mind on God through His Word. If you desire to be poured into His mold, you do it through the Word of God. There is no other system God has in place.

Now, you can experience a touch from God. He loves you, and especially in times of crisis, you can cry out to Him and He'll touch you. Some people call this an epiphany. You could have an encounter with the Lord. God could speak to you, and it would touch your life. But I guarantee you that these emotional types of experiences only last a very short period of time. You will never be able to sustain a relationship with God on an emotional level only.

You have to renew your mind. If you want to be transformed long-term and see your life change, you must be transformed by the Word. You must renew your mind. Some folks say, "To me, that seems restrictive." To me, it's awesome. I love it because it's so simple. You just meditate in the Word day and night (Josh. 1:8). You just keep the Lord and His truths in your thoughts. You go over and over them, keeping your mind stayed on the Word of God and not on "As the Stomach Turns" on television. If you'll keep your mind stayed on the Lord by meditating in His Word, then without effort—automatically—your life will begin to change.

Some people really struggle to believe that this is true. If that's you, don't knock it until you've tried it. I've tried it. I have spent thousands, tens of thousands, perhaps even hundreds of thousands of hours meditating in the Word of God.

There's nothing that challenges and inspires me more than being in the Word of God and hearing Him speak to me. All of a sudden, I recognize an application between the principles I see in the Scriptures, or a certain Bible character's life and my own. God makes a direct connection between His Word and my life. The greatest thing in the world to me is to see or experience God speaking to me through His Word.

A Byproduct, Not the Cause

Many Christians don't feel this way. They've read the Bible. They may not have found it boring, but it wasn't as stimulating to them as a novel. Personally, I think the subject matter in God's Word beats any novel, any plot you could ever come up with. The Bible is full of so many wonderful things. Yet many Christians just read it as a book and don't meet with Him and receive from Him like He wants them to. They couldn't honestly say that spending time with God through His Word is the most exciting thing they've ever done.

I can truthfully say that the greatest joy and excitement I think I have ever had in my life has been being alone with God studying His Word. All of a sudden, I connect with God's heart. I know what He is saying to me through the Scriptures. God gives me a direct revelation. I can truthfully say that's the greatest thing that's ever happened in my life. I've seen several people raised from the dead, including my own son. I've seen great miracles and healings manifest. I'm not saying they aren't wonderful and exciting. They are. But it's the Word of God and my relationship with Him through His Word that have caused all those things to happen. They're a byproduct, not the cause. Renewing my mind to God's Word is what has turned my life around.

If you want to be transformed like this, the way you do it is to take God's Word and meditate in it day and night. Dwell on it and it just changes you. Now, that's exciting!

Transformed
LESSON 4 – OUTLINE

I. Literally thousands of people have come to me with sickness in their bodies and asked, "Would you pray for me?"

   A. But what do I do, after I've prayed for everybody else, when I get sick?

   B. Do I run to somebody every time an illness is fighting against me?

   C. No, I go to the Word of God.

   D. If I have a pain, I take a Gos-pill (Gospel).

   E. I'll stand against symptoms, rebuke them, and speak my faith.

   F. Normally, that will take care of everything.

II. I don't believe in being sick.

   A. But I've had the symptoms of sickness hit me.

   B. I take the Word of God and meditate on it.

   C. I eat these words because they're life and health to my flesh.

   D. I could even quote them, but I'll still go back and study them.

Faith cometh by hearing, and hearing by the word of God.

Romans 10:17

   E. As I start meditating on them, health flows through me.

   F. I've only gone for a maximum of a few hours over the past forty years with any symptom of sickness in my body.

   G. I actually have a doctor's report saying I had an incurable disease.

   H. Yet within hours of that doctor's visit, I was totally healed.

III. God used the first two verses of Romans 12 to totally transform my life:

> **I beseech you therefore, brethren, by the mercies of God, that ye present your bodies a living sacrifice, holy, acceptable unto God, which is your reasonable service. And be not conformed to this world: but be ye transformed by the renewing of your mind, that ye may prove what is that good, and acceptable, and perfect, will of God.**

A. I looked up the word **"prove,"** and it means to make manifest to the physical senses.

B. I wanted the result promised at the end of verse 2 where I would make manifest to my physical senses the good, acceptable, and perfect will of God.

C. So, I went back to verse 1 and to the beginning of verse 2 to see what I had to do to get there.

D. After meditating on it for three and a half months, I had an experience where God poured out His love in my life.

E. As important as that experience was, I would have lost the benefit of just an encounter with God if I had not continued to grow in the knowledge of His Word.

IV. What really changed my life was Romans 12:2.

A. The Greek word translated **"conformed"** here literally means to pour into the mold.

B. By the time you live twenty, forty, sixty, or however many years, the pressures of this life are going to melt you.

C. However, the good news is that you get to choose what mold you fit into.

D. You get to pick whether you'll be like the other people who become negative, bitter, and unforgiving.

E. You can choose whether you'll murmur and complain or if you'll let these things drive you to the Lord and make you stronger and more stable in your commitment to God.

F. The Greek word rendered **"transformed"** here is the word we derive our English word *metamorphosis* from.

G. Do you want to change from being weak, inferior, and bound by all kinds of problems into someone who releases and experiences the abundant life of God from within?

H. The Word of God reveals that the way to do this is by the renewing of your mind.

V. You can't just turn your mind off and think of nothing.

  A. All you can do is choose what you think on—the things of the Lord or the things of the world.

  B. The things of the world don't have to be bad. But just be occupied with them, and you'll never experience this transformation.

  C. If you desire to be poured into God's mold, you do it through the Word of God.

  D. There is no other system He has in place.

  E. Some folks say, "To me, that seems restrictive." To me, it's awesome.

VI. If you'll keep your mind stayed on the Lord by meditating in His Word, then without effort—automatically—your life will begin to change.

  A. Don't knock it until you've tried it.

  B. There's nothing that challenges and inspires me more than being in the Word of God and hearing Him speak to me.

  C. All of a sudden, I connect with God's heart.

  D. I know what He is saying to me through the Scriptures.

  E. I can truthfully say that's the greatest thing that's ever happened in my life.

  F. I've seen several people raised from the dead, including my own son. I've seen great miracles and healings manifest.

  G. But it's the Word of God and my relationship with Him through His Word that have caused all those things to happen.

  H. Renewing my mind to God's Word is what has turned my life around.

  I. If you want to be transformed like this, the way you do it is to take God's Word and meditate in it day and night.

  J. Now, that's exciting!

Transformed

LESSON 4 – TEACHER'S GUIDE

1. Literally thousands of people have come to me with sickness in their bodies and asked, "Would you pray for me?" But what do I do, after I've prayed for everybody else, when I get sick? Do I run to somebody every time an illness is fighting against me? No, I go to the Word of God. If I have a pain, I take a Gos-pill (Gospel). I'll stand against symptoms, rebuke them, and speak my faith. Normally, that will take care of everything.

2. I don't believe in being sick. But I've had the symptoms of sickness hit me. I take the Word of God and meditate on it. I eat these words because they're life and health to my flesh. I could even quote them, but I'll still go back and study them (Rom. 10:17). As I start meditating on them, health flows through me. I've only gone for a maximum of a few hours over the past forty years with any symptom of sickness in my body. I actually have a doctor's report saying I had an incurable disease. Yet within hours of that doctor's visit, I was totally healed.

3. God used the first two verses of Romans 12 to totally transform my life. I looked up the word **"prove,"** and it means to make manifest to the physical senses. I wanted the result promised at the end of verse 2 where I would make manifest to my physical senses the good, acceptable, and perfect will of God. So, I went back to verse 1 and to the beginning of verse 2 to see what I had to do to get there. After meditating on it for three and a half months, I had an experience where God poured out His love in my life. As important as that experience was, I would have lost the benefit of just an encounter with God if I had not continued to grow in the knowledge of His Word.

1. What does Andrew do every time an illness is fighting against him or if he has a pain? (He goes to the Word of God, he stands against symptoms, rebukes them, and speaks his faith)
2. A. Read Romans 10:17. Why does Andrew go back and study God's words? (Because faith comes by hearing)
   B. What happens as he starts meditating on them? (Health flows through him)
3. A. What did Andrew want to make manifest? (The good, acceptable, and perfect will of God)
   B. What would have happened if Andrew had not continued to grow in the knowledge of God's Word? (He would have lost the benefit of just an encounter with Him)

4. What really changed my life was Romans 12:2. The Greek word translated **"conformed"** here literally means to pour into the mold. By the time we live twenty, forty, sixty, or however many years, the pressures of this life are going to melt us. However, the good news is that we get to choose what mold we fit into. We get to pick whether we'll be like the other people who become negative, bitter, and unforgiving. We can choose whether we'll murmur and complain or if we'll let these things drive us to the Lord and make us stronger and more stable in our commitment to God. The Greek word rendered **"transformed"** here is the word we derive our English word *metamorphosis* from. Do we want to change from being weak, inferior, and bound by all kinds of problems into people who release and experience the abundant life of God from within? The Word of God reveals that the way to do this is by the renewing of our minds.

5. We can't just turn our minds off and think of nothing. All we can do is choose what we think on—the things of the Lord or the things of the world. The things of the world don't have to be bad. But if we're occupied with them, we'll never experience this transformation. If we desire to be poured into God's mold, we do it through the Word of God. There is no other system He has in place. Some folks say, "To me, that seems restrictive." To me, it's awesome.

6. If we'll keep our minds stayed on the Lord by meditating in His Word, then without effort—automatically—our lives will begin to change. We shouldn't knock it until we've tried it. There's nothing that challenges and inspires me more than being in the Word of God and hearing Him speak to me. All of a sudden, I connect with God's heart. I know what He is saying to me through the Scriptures. I can truthfully say that's the greatest thing that's ever happened in my life. I've seen several people raised from the dead, including my own son. I've seen great miracles and healings manifest. But it's the Word of God and my relationship with Him through His Word that have caused all those things to happen. Renewing my mind to God's Word is what has turned my life around. If we want to be transformed like this, the way we do it is to take God's Word and meditate in it day and night. Now, that's exciting!

4. A. What really changed Andrew's life? (Romans 12:2)
   B. What do we get to choose? (What mold we fit into)
   C. What does the Word of God reveal is by the renewing of our minds? (Changing from being weak, inferior, and bound by all kinds of problems into people who release and experience the abundant life of God from within)
5. A. We can choose _____. (What we think on—the things of the Lord or the things of the world)
   B. How are we poured into God's mold? (By the Word of God)
   C. Does God have another system in place? (No)
6. A. How would our lives begin to change without effort—automatically? (If we would keep our minds stayed on the Lord by meditating in His Word)
   B. Even though Andrew has seen great miracles and healings manifest, what caused all those things to happen? (The Word of God and his relationship with Him through His Word)

Transformed
LESSON 4 – DISCIPLESHIP QUESTIONS

1. Read Romans 8:6. Does carnal-mindedness tend toward death? Does spiritual-mindedness tend toward life and peace?

2. According to John 6:63, what does the flesh profit?

3. What are Jesus' words?
   A. Easy and light
   B. Fire and brimstone
   C. Spirit and life
   D. All of the above
   E. None of the above

4. Read Isaiah 26:3. What is needed to be kept in perfect peace?

5. According to Proverbs 4:20-22, what are God's words?

6. Read 1 Peter 2:24. We are _____ to sins and should _____ unto righteousness.

7. Read Psalm 107:20. To heal us and deliver us from our destructions, what did God do with His word?

8. Read Romans 10:17. Faith comes before or after hearing the Word of God?

9. Read Romans 12:1-3. What is holy and acceptable to God?

10. If you're conformed to this world, what won't you be?

11. How are you not to think?

12. According to Joshua 1:8, the book of the Law (Word of God) is not to depart from your _____.

13. Therefore, other than the mind, what does meditation include?
    A. Speaking what the Law (Word of God) says
    B. A certain posture
    C. Soft music
    D. Having a sinless day
    E. Fasting

Transformed
LESSON 4 – ANSWER KEY

1. No, carnal-mindedness *is* death. Spiritual-mindedness *is* life and peace
2. Nothing
3. C. Spirit and life
4. Having a mind stayed on God and trusting in Him
5. Life to those who find them and health to all their flesh
6. Dead, live
7. He sent it
8. After
9. My body being presented to Him as a living sacrifice
10. Transformed by the renewing of your mind
11. More highly than I ought to think
12. Mouth
13. A. Speaking what the Law (Word of God) says

Transformed
LESSON 4 – SCRIPTURES

ROMANS 8:6
For to be carnally minded is death; but to be spiritually minded is life and peace.

JOHN 6:63
It is the spirit that quickeneth; the flesh profiteth nothing: the words that I speak unto you, they are spirit, and they are life.

ISAIAH 26:3
Thou wilt keep him in perfect peace, whose mind is stayed on thee: because he trusteth in thee.

PROVERBS 4:20-22
My son, attend to my words; incline thine ear unto my sayings. [21] **Let them not depart from thine eyes; keep them in the midst of thine heart.** [22] **For they are life unto those that find them, and health to all their flesh.**

1 PETER 2:24
Who his own self bare our sins in his own body on the tree, that we, being dead to sins, should live unto righteousness: by whose stripes ye were healed.

PSALM 107:20
He sent his word, and healed them, and delivered them from their destructions.

ROMANS 10:17
So then faith cometh by hearing, and hearing by the word of God.

ROMANS 12:1-3
I beseech you therefore, brethren, by the mercies of God, that ye present your bodies a living sacrifice, holy, acceptable unto God, which is your reasonable service. [2] **And be not conformed to this world: but be ye transformed by the renewing of your mind, that ye may prove what is that good, and acceptable, and perfect, will of God.** [3] **For I say, through the grace given unto me, to every man that is among you, not to think of himself more highly than he ought to think; but to think soberly, according as God hath dealt to every man the measure of faith.**

JOSHUA 1:8

This book of the law shall not depart out of thy mouth; but thou shalt meditate therein day and night, that thou mayest observe to do according to all that is written therein: for then thou shalt make thy way prosperous, and then thou shalt have good success.

Converting the Soul
LESSON 5

I vividly remember what was going on in my life when the Lord showed me the importance of His Word. I had just made a commitment to Him. As I sought Him, I felt like He told me to drop out of college. This was during the Vietnam War, so for me to follow Him meant to be immediately drafted and sent to Vietnam. Also, I would lose the social security income that I had been receiving since my father's death. I could keep it as long as I was still in school. So, following the Lord cost me financially. It sent me to a war zone where I quite possibly could have been killed.

Beyond that, every person in my life that I had ever looked up to until then told me in one way or another that "this isn't God." They told me this was of the devil and that if I was going to be a preacher, then I needed to get a seminary education. Everyone was telling me what a dunce I was and how my ministry wouldn't happen unless I followed the prescribed way of doing things. I wasn't trying to rebel. I just wanted to be obedient to what I knew God was speaking to my heart.

When I came across those scriptures in Romans 12, God showed me that if I would take His Word and meditate in it, it would accomplish everything I needed in my life. I can't tell you how much comfort and direction that gave me at that crucial crossroads of my life. So, I poured myself into the Word of God, and here I am, over forty years, later fulfilling God's will for my life. It's the revelation of God's Word that has transformed my life and ministry, and the same will work for you.

All 176 verses of Psalm 119—the longest chapter in the Bible—are about the importance of God's Word.

> **Wherewithal shall a young man cleanse his way? by taking heed thereto according to thy word.**
>
> **Psalm 119:9**

> **Thy word have I hid in mine heart, that I might not sin against thee.**
>
> **Psalm 119:11**

> **Great peace have they which love thy law: and nothing shall offend them.**
>
> **Psalm 119:165**

Restored

Psalm 19 also affirms the importance of God's Word and how it will change your life. These different phrases—**"the law of the Lord"** (verse 7), **"statutes of the Lord"** (verse 8), **"commandments of the Lord"** (verse 8), and **"testimony of the Lord"** (verse 7)—are all just referring to the Word of God.

The law of the Lord is perfect, converting the soul.

Psalm 19:7

In Hebrew, this word rendered **"converting"** here means "to turn back" (Strong's Concordance).

Many people have experienced tragedy in their lives. Their souls have been bruised, battered, and damaged. The average person continues to carry this pain. They don't seem able to break free. Therefore, most people have just embraced it as, "This is the way that it is." One of the reasons they accept this is because that's the way the world—apart from access to God's supernatural power—looks at it.

In the natural realm, without God, that's true. You are a product of your environment. If you were verbally, physically, or sexually abused, that's going to scar you. If you were beat down, condemned, and told you could do nothing and would amount to nothing, that could very well influence you for the rest of your life.

However, God won't just give you the ability to cope; He can totally change you so that it's like those things never happened. Through His Word, He wants to convert your soul—restore you to an original condition (Ps. 19:7).

If you were damaged by something or someone, you don't have to bear that for five, ten, twenty, or thirty years. You can get over it. The Word of God will convert your soul and turn it back to what God meant it to be.

Wisdom

This isn't only true on an individual basis; it's true of mankind as a whole. Since Adam and Eve's Fall, our existence and surroundings have been so negative and different than what God originally intended man to be. By the time an average child graduates from high school, they've seen tens of thousands of brutal murders on television. They've been exposed to sexual immorality and ungodliness that the Lord never intended for mankind to be burdened with. How do you overcome all that? The law of the Lord is perfect—it's not just good. It's not just better than anything else that's out there. It's perfect, and it will convert—restore—your soul to an original condition.

So many people carry around baggage—hurts and pains from previous years—from all kinds of things: previous marriages, losses, disappointments, and broken relationships. They never seem to recover. That's because they aren't taking the Word of God and properly using it in their lives. This is a promise that God's Word is perfect. It will convert your soul. It will restore you to an original condition.

Psalm 19:7 continues, saying,

The testimony of the Lord is sure, making wise the simple.

God's Word makes wise those who are stupid—people who don't think properly and who make mistakes.

I've heard all kinds of stories from people who made stupid decisions and suffered from them. They commit adultery and then wind up with shame and disgrace. They lose their jobs, their churches, and their friends. They end up with physical problems, like AIDS. On and on the repercussions go from the stupid things that people do. Every once in a while, I just want to tell folks, "How dumb can you get and still breathe?" It's amazing what some people do.

You may be thinking, *I've done some of those same things. I just don't seem to be able to help it.* Right here in Psalm 19:7, God's Word promises to give wisdom to the simple. It will make you wise even if you have been stupid in the past. You don't have to submit to the lie that says, "Well, my mind just isn't as bright as somebody else's." The Word of God will quicken your thinking and give you understanding.

Get Happy

So many people are depressed and defeated. They can't seem to find any reason to rejoice. They're struggling, and they give this reason and that excuse, saying, "This and that happened to me." Do you know what it all comes down to?

The statutes of the Lord are right, rejoicing the heart.

Psalm 19:8

If you aren't full of joy, peace, and rejoicing, the problem isn't your circumstances (1 Pet. 1:8). If you have ashes, mourning, and a spirit of heaviness instead of the oil of joy and the garment of praise, it's the fact that there's a vacuum on the inside of you (Is. 61:3). You don't know the truth of God's Word. The statutes of the Lord are right, and they will rejoice your heart. If you're discouraged, take the Word of God. Start speaking the promises of God to yourself. You can get happy in a hurry!

Psalm 19:8 continues, saying,

The commandment of the LORD is pure, enlightening the eyes.

Is it worth it to be able to see clearly instead of having a negative perception that always makes every cup look half empty? What a benefit it is to be able to see the positive side and to see a way through everything. That's what the Word of God does.

Great Reward

The fear of the LORD is clean, enduring for ever: the judgments of the LORD are true and righteous altogether. More to be desired are they than gold, yea, than much fine gold: sweeter also than honey and the honeycomb.

Psalm 19:9-10

God's Word is worth far more to me than gold, even much fine gold. To me, the Word of God is better than honey. How would you treat God's Word if you truly desired it more than money—even large amounts of it—and more than your favorite food? You'd be able to say along with Job...

I have esteemed the words of his mouth more than my necessary food.

Job 23:12

If you were to seek God through His Word like that, your life would be transformed.

Moreover by them is thy servant warned: and in keeping of them there is great reward.

Psalm 19:11

How much benefit would it be to your life if you could be warned before you get into a problem, pursue an ungodly relationship, take the wrong job, buy the wrong car, do something that damages your health, or take a wrong turn? How much would it be worth to you if you could see problems before they happened so you could take evasive action? That's exactly what the Word of God will do.

And in keeping God's Word, there is great reward!

Keep on Planting

Take the Word of God and center your life on it. Meditate in the Word day and night. As you do, the Word will cause change to come in your life effortlessly. It would be automatic. As you renew your mind to God's Word, you, too, will begin to prove—make manifest to your physical senses—God's good, acceptable, and perfect will.

If you aren't experiencing the abundance and victory that the Lord has promised, it's not God who has failed. Praying longer and petitioning harder won't change anything; you must take the incorruptible seed of God's Word and keep on planting it in the garden of your heart.

Converting the Soul
LESSON 5 – OUTLINE

I. I vividly remember what was going on in my life when the Lord showed me the importance of His Word.

   A. And here I am, over forty years later, fulfilling His will for my life.

   B. It's the revelation of God's Word that has transformed my life and ministry, and the same will work for you.

   C. All 176 verses of Psalm 119—the longest chapter in the Bible—are about the importance of God's Word.

II. Psalm 19 also affirms the importance of God's Word and how it will change your life.

   A. In verse 7, the Hebrew word rendered **"converting"** means "to turn back" (Strong's Concordance).

   B. Through His Word, He wants to convert your soul—restore you to an original condition.

   C. If you were damaged by something or someone, you don't have to bear that for five, ten, twenty, or thirty years.

   D. You can get over it.

   E. This is a promise that God's Word is perfect.

III. God's Word makes wise those who are stupid—people who don't think properly and who make mistakes (Ps. 19:7).

   A. I've heard all kinds of stories from people who made stupid decisions and suffered from them.

   B. You may be thinking, *I've done some of those things. I just don't seem to be able to help it.*

   C. The Word of God will quicken your thinking and give you understanding.

IV. So many people are depressed and defeated.

   A. They can't seem to find any reason to rejoice.

B. Do you know what it all comes down to?

C. You don't know the truth of God's Word (Ps. 19:8).

D. If you're discouraged, take the Word of God.

E. Start speaking the promises of God to yourself.

F. You can get happy in a hurry!

V. Is it worth it to be able to see clearly instead of having a negative perception that always makes every cup look half empty?

A. What a benefit it is to be able to see the positive side and to see a way through everything.

B. That's what the Word of God does (Ps. 19:8).

VI. How would you treat God's Word if you truly desired it more than money—even large amounts of it—and more than your favorite food (Ps. 19:9-10)?

A. You'd be able to say along with Job...

> **I have esteemed the words of his mouth more than my necessary food.**
>
> **Job 23:12**

B. If you were to seek God through His Word like that, your life would be transformed.

VII. How much would it be worth to you if you could see problems before they happened so you could take evasive action?

A. That's exactly what the Word of God will do (Ps. 19:11).

B. And in keeping God's Word, there is great reward!

Converting the Soul
LESSON 5 – TEACHER'S GUIDE

1. I vividly remember what was going on in my life when the Lord showed me the importance of His Word. And here I am, over forty years later, fulfilling His will for my life. It's the revelation of God's Word that has transformed my life and ministry, and the same will work for you. All 176 verses of Psalm 119—the longest chapter in the Bible—are about the importance of God's Word.

2. Psalm 19 also affirms the importance of God's Word and how it will change our lives. In verse 7, the Hebrew word rendered **"converting"** means "to turn back" (Strong's Concordance). Through His Word, He wants to convert our souls—restore us to an original condition. If we were damaged by something or someone, we don't have to bear that for five, ten, twenty, or thirty years. We can get over it. This is a promise that God's Word is perfect.

3. God's Word makes wise those who are stupid—people who don't think properly and who make mistakes (Ps. 19:7). I've heard all kinds of stories from people who made stupid decisions and suffered from them. You may be thinking, *I've done some of those things. I just don't seem to be able to help it.* The Word of God will quicken your thinking and give you understanding.

1. A. What has transformed Andrew's life and ministry? (The revelation of God's Word)
   B. Will the same work for us? (Yes)
2. A. What does God want to do through His Word? (Convert our souls—restore us to an original condition)
   B. Read Psalm 19:7. What is a promise that God's Word is perfect? (That if we were damaged by something or someone, we can get over it)
3. A. What will God's Word do for people who don't think properly and who make mistakes? (It makes them wise)
   B. What will it quicken, and what will it give us? (It will quicken our thinking and give us understanding)

4. So many of us as Christians are depressed and defeated. We can't seem to find any reason to rejoice. Do you know what it all comes down to? We don't know the truth of God's Word (Ps. 19:8). If we're discouraged, we need to take the Word of God. Let's start speaking the promises of God to ourselves. We can get happy in a hurry!

5. Is it worth it to be able to see clearly instead of having a negative perception that always makes every cup look half empty? What a benefit it is to be able to see the positive side and to see a way through everything. That's what the Word of God does (Ps. 19:8).

6. How would we treat God's Word if we truly desired it more than money—even large amounts of it—and more than our favorite food (Ps. 19:9-10)? We'd be able to say along with Job, **"I have esteemed the words of his mouth more than my necessary food"** (Job 23:12). If we were to seek God through His Word like that, our lives would be transformed.

7. How much would it be worth to us if we could see problems before they happened so we could take evasive action? That's exactly what the Word of God will do (Ps. 19:11). And in keeping God's Word, there is great reward!

4. A. Read Psalm 19:8. If we're depressed, defeated, and can't seem to find any reason to rejoice, what does it come down to? (We don't know the truth of God's Word)
   B. What do we need to start speaking to ourselves? (The promises of God)
5. What does the Word of God do? (It makes us able to see the positive side and to see a way through everything)
6. Read Job 23:12. What was Job able to say? (**"I have esteemed the words of his mouth more than my necessary food"**)
7. A. Read Psalm 19:11. This verse says the Word of God will _____. (Enable us to see problems before they happen so we can take evasive action)
   B. What is there in keeping God's Word? (Great reward)

Converting the Soul
LESSON 5 – DISCIPLESHIP QUESTIONS

1. Read Psalm 119:9. A young person should take heed to God's Word in order to do what?

2. Read Psalm 119:11. What do you have to hide in your heart so you don't sin against God?

3. According to Psalm 119:165, if you want great peace and nothing to offend you, what do have to love?
   A. My pastor's sermons
   B. God's Word
   C. My denomination's statement of faith
   D. All of the above
   E. None of the above

4. Read Psalm 19:7-11. Since the Word of God is perfect, that means there are no _____.
   A. Points of discussion
   B. Adequate ministers
   C. Questions
   D. False interpretations
   E. Flaws

5. What is the fear of the Lord?

6. By the judgments of the Lord, His servants are _____.
   A. Warmed
   B. Judged
   C. Warned
   D. All of the above
   E. None of the above

7. According 1 Peter 1:8, you don't need to see God in order to what?

8. Read Isaiah 61:3. When you're called the tree of righteousness, the planting of the Lord, what will that result in?

9. Read Job 23:12. Job said he had not gone back from the _____ of God's lips.

10. What did he say he did with the words of God's mouth?

Converting the Soul
LESSON 5 – ANSWER KEY

1. Cleanse his or her way (manner)
2. His Word
3. B. God's Word
4. E. Flaws
5. Clean, enduring forever
6. C. Warned
7. Love and believe Him
8. The Lord will be glorified
9. Commandment
10. He esteemed them more than his necessary food

Converting the Soul
LESSON 5 – SCRIPTURES

PSALM 119:9
BETH. Wherewithal shall a young man cleanse his way? by taking heed thereto according to thy word.

PSALM 119:11
Thy word have I hid in mine heart, that I might not sin against thee.

PSALM 119:165
Great peace have they which love thy law: and nothing shall offend them.

PSALM 19:7-11
The law of the LORD is perfect, converting the soul: the testimony of the LORD is sure, making wise the simple. [8] The statutes of the LORD are right, rejoicing the heart: the commandment of the LORD is pure, enlightening the eyes. [9] The fear of the LORD is clean, enduring for ever: the judgments of the LORD are true and righteous altogether. [10] More to be desired are they than gold, yea, than much fine gold: sweeter also than honey and the honeycomb. [11] Moreover by them is thy servant warned: and in keeping of them there is great reward.

1 PETER 1:8
Whom having not seen, ye love; in whom, though now ye see him not, yet believing, ye rejoice with joy unspeakable and full of glory.

ISAIAH 61:3
To appoint unto them that mourn in Zion, to give unto them beauty for ashes, the oil of joy for mourning, the garment of praise for the spirit of heaviness; that they might be called trees of righteousness, the planting of the LORD, that he might be glorified.

JOB 23:12
Neither have I gone back from the commandment of his lips; I have esteemed the words of his mouth more than my necessary food.

Subject to Doubt

LESSON 6

You will become as you think (Prov. 23:7). The reason most people have the problems they do is because they aren't controlling their thinking. Unless you do something specifically to keep your mind on the Lord, it will naturally go somewhere else. There aren't very many things outside of God's Word that reflect God and point us to and draw us closer to Him. However, the Word of God is pure light (Ps. 19:8). When you study and meditate in God's Word, it changes the way you think. As your thinking changes, so does your life. That's why you must get to where you're dominated by the Word of God.

When John the Baptist had doubts, Jesus pointed him to the Word of God to overcome them. This is simple, but so profound. And although this is true, not many people believe it.

Personal Responsibility

I'm not one of these ministers who sneak in and walk up to the stage after the praise and worship is nearly over. I talk to lots of people. At our meetings, I'll spend two or three hours personally ministring to people on a one-on-one basis outside of my preaching in the service. I know by dealing firsthand with hundreds of people on a regular basis that many folks are struggling. They have doubt and fear. The doctor told them they're going to die, and they want me to help them overcome. They want me to wave my hand over them to take away their fears. They're looking to me to impart healing to them. I'm not saying that I can't help people. However, it's wrong for us to look for our help in another human being.

When John the Baptist had doubts, Jesus didn't just say, "Oh, John. I know how you feel. I'm going to take care of this for you. I'll handle it from here." The Lord didn't just wave His hand, and then John was free of doubt and guilt. That's not at all what happened. Jesus referred John back to the Word of God.

If you would just take God's Word and use it yourself, you wouldn't have to follow people around from meeting to meeting begging them to pray for you.

Don't take what I'm saying out of context. I'm not against you having someone else pray for you. It takes time to get into the Word of God and start seeing the life that's in the Word released into your life. During that period of time, when you're sowing the seed and waiting for it to increase and grow to the point that it will bring liberty in your life, don't be so stubborn or proud that you won't go to others for help and ask them to pray for you.

But don't be like those people who refuse to take personal responsibility. These people don't get into the Word of God for themselves to let it transform them, and neither do they have any plans of doing so. Their lives are occupied with work, pleasures, or whatever. They aren't going to make the Word of God a central part of their lives. Like many others, they try to substitute someone like me or a church pastor for themselves seeking the Lord. That's just not going to work.

While you're in the process of seeking the Lord, growing to maturity, and getting the Word of God working in you, don't be too proud to ask for help if you come into a problem. But don't be like people who aren't even trying, who don't even have a desire to try to get into the Word for themselves. If your life is too busy to be in the Word of God and you just want to bootleg the Gospel off of me or someone else, it's not going to work.

I'm glad if you like to watch my television program or listen to my radio show. I'm not against anybody's program, or Christian programming in general. It's a real blessing from the Lord in many people's lives. However, if all you're doing is receiving your nourishment from God after it's already been digested by someone else, you aren't going to grow much. If you aren't going to take the Word firsthand, then you aren't going to mature.

Absolutely Committed

The Lord dealt with John the Baptist's doubt by referring him back to the Word of God. He didn't just take care of it for him. He didn't wave His hand and solve the problem. Jesus told John to go back to the Word of God.

> **Now when John had heard in the prison the works of Christ, he sent two of his disciples, And said unto him, Art thou he that should come, or do we look for another?**
>
> **Matthew 11:2-3**

John the Baptist was a man who was mightily used of God. He is the only person in the Bible—Old or New Testament—who was baptized in the Holy Spirit while he was still in his mother's womb (Luke 1:15). Before he was physically born, he was filled with the Holy Spirit. Jesus didn't even have that happen to Him. John was a unique character, mightily anointed and blessed by God.

John spent thirty years in the desert preparing for his ministry. He never experienced the normal things that people go through. He was totally focused on his calling.

Then he burst onto the scene and, in six months' time, turned not only the Jewish nation but also all of the nations surrounding Israel to an expectancy of the Messiah's coming. John saw the greatest revival that had ever happened in history up until that time, possibly the greatest revival that's ever taken place anywhere. This was the man who caused it.

At one time, John was absolutely certain Jesus was the Messiah. He sent his own disciples off after Christ, saying, **"He must increase, but I must decrease"** (John 3:30). The Pharisees came out to John and tried to make him envious of Jesus by saying, "Don't you realize that Jesus now has more disciples than you? He's baptized more people than you." Instead of becoming envious, John responded by saying, "I'm not even worthy to stoop over and undo His sandals." He knew his place. John knew who Jesus was, and he was absolutely committed to Him.

Fireball on Ice

But John wasn't so sure after being in prison for an unspecified amount of time. It had been a minimum of six months—possibly as long as two years—that this fireball for God had been put on ice. John had been forbidden to communicate with his followers and to influence people. After such a long period of time, this hardship began to wear on him.

So, when John the Baptist sent two of his remaining disciples to inquire if Jesus was the Messiah or if he should look for another, this wasn't some newcomer to the Lord who was asking this question. This was someone who had this question answered before. This was the man who knew beyond a shadow of a doubt at one time that Jesus was the Christ. Yet afterward, here he was, doubting that Jesus was the Messiah.

> **Art thou he that should come, or do we look for another?**
>
> **Matthew 11:3**

This is nothing but pure doubt! This was a major problem on John the Baptist's part because at one time, he had been absolutely certain of who Jesus was. He had even been given a sign from God regarding Jesus being the Messiah.

> **Jesus, when he was baptized, went up straightway out of the water: and, lo, the heavens were opened unto him, and he saw the Spirit of God descending like a dove, and lighting upon him: And lo a voice from heaven, saying, This is my beloved Son, in whom I am well pleased.**
>
> **Matthew 3:16-17**

> **And the Holy Ghost descended in a bodily shape like a dove upon him, and a voice came from heaven, which said, Thou art my beloved Son; in thee I am well pleased.**
>
> **Luke 3:22**

God told John that upon whom he saw the Spirit of God descending in the shape of a dove and remaining on would be the Messiah (John 1:33). So, John the Baptist had a visible sign when he baptized Jesus in water, and the Holy Spirit descended in the form of a dove. He also heard an audible voice from heaven, saying, "This is My beloved Son, in whom I am well pleased" (Matt. 3:17). John not only had the Scriptures and the witness in his own heart, but he also had an audible and visible sign.

Hope Deferred

What do you need to be able to believe? That's a really good question. Some people think, *If I was one of Jesus' twelve disciples, I wouldn't struggle with doubt. If I could see a vision, if I had a tangible tingling in my hands, if I could hear an audible voice from God—then I would believe.* John had every one of those things, yet he doubted.

It doesn't matter who you are or how strong in faith you've been, everyone is capable of doubt. When you're in a negative situation over a long period of time, the tendency is to doubt. Negative circumstances tend to just beat faith out of you and cause doubt to come.

That's exactly what happened with John the Baptist. He had been in prison for at least six months, possibly as long as two years by this time. John had been a stark, raving mad fanatic. He was bold, wild, and fearless. John pronounced judgment against Herod because he had married his brother's wife while his brother was still alive (Matt. 14:3-4). It was an ungodly alliance, and he risked everything by speaking the truth about it. In time, it did cost him everything. He was imprisoned because of it and then killed.

John was fearless in proclaiming what was right and wrong. He lived for speaking God's truth and seeing people change. Once he came on the scene, his preaching changed an entire nation in six months' time. John was a high-energy guy who just loved to be in the center of it all, speaking forth God's Word. He was a bony-fingered prophet. That's the way John was. Yet he had been silenced and put in prison. Sure, he probably talked to the prison guards, but he was kept physically restrained from being able to continue to fulfill his ministry.

Proverbs 13:12 reveals that...

> **Hope deferred maketh the heart sick.**

John the Baptist's hope was to be out there preaching the Gospel, preparing the way for the Lord and turning people to Him. Yet it just wasn't coming to pass. So, this began to wear on him.

The Church Age

Another important factor regarding John the Baptist's doubt was the misunderstanding of what the Messiah would do when He came. During the time of Jesus, the people didn't have a clear understanding that the coming of the Lord would take place in two advents, as we call it. The first coming of Jesus culminated in His crucifixion, resurrection, and ascension. Since then, there's been this intervening period of time of more than 2,000 years, which we call the "church age." Today believers everywhere continue to look forward to the Second Coming of the Lord (Rev. 22:20).

This was prophesied in the Old Testament, but it all ran together. Take, for instance, Isaiah 61:1-2, which Jesus quoted in Luke 4, saying,

> **The Spirit of the Lord is upon me, because he hath anointed me to preach the gospel to the poor; he hath sent me to heal the brokenhearted, to preach deliverance to the captives, and recovering of sight to the blind, to set at liberty them that are bruised, To preach the acceptable year of the Lord.**
>
> **Luke 4:18-19**

This was definitely a prophecy of the Messiah that was fulfilled when He came to this earth. Jesus did, was doing, and would later do all of these things. He Himself declared,

> **This day is this scripture fulfilled in your ears.**
>
> **Luke 4:21**

Yet in comparing Luke 4:18-19 with Isaiah 61:1-2, notice how the Lord stopped right before completing verse 2, which says,

> **To proclaim the acceptable year of the Lord, and the day of vengeance of our God.**

Why did Jesus stop before proclaiming the day of vengeance of our God? Because that portion of the prophecy about Him will come to pass at His second coming when He brings judgment to the earth. But if you just read the Old Testament scripture without the benefit of the New Testament commentary, it would be easy to run these things together.

Heartsick

In a nutshell, all of these Old Testament prophecies concerning the Messiah gave the impression that the first and second comings of Jesus would take place as one event. People didn't clearly understand that there would be two advents. Due to this, the people of Jesus' time eagerly anticipated that the Lord would not only come and reconcile us back to God but that He would also put down Roman rule, institute the kingdom of God, judge the ungodly, and physically rule on the earth. That's what they were expecting.

Personally, I believe that John the Baptist was of the same opinion, which was one of the reasons he began to doubt that Jesus was indeed the Christ. At one time, John had no doubt. He'd heard an audible voice and had seen a visible sign, but things weren't playing out the way he thought they would. He thought Jesus would've come and destroyed the Romans. He thought Jesus would've come and taken him out of prison. He thought Jesus would've ushered in the kingdom of God and begun to physically rule upon this earth. Those things weren't happening. It could have been up to two or two and a half years' time since John had baptized Him, but Jesus still hadn't yet made a political statement. He hadn't tried to reform society. Jesus was simply speaking to individuals about their personal relationship to God.

Hope deferred makes the heart sick (Prov. 13:12). If John the Baptist's hope wasn't right on, this negative experience could have made his heart sick. If he was like almost everybody else in Scripture, he, too, was wondering,

Lord, wilt thou at this time restore again the kingdom to Israel?

Acts 1:6

If John the Baptist didn't have a clear understanding that there was going to be this church age intervening between the first and second comings of the Lord, then these negative circumstances could have made his heart sick.

John wasn't seeing his hope for the kingdom of God coming to pass. He was locked up in prison and couldn't minister anymore. Prisons in those days were horrible places. Yet not being able to fulfill your God-given calling can be very frustrating and discouraging too. It's obvious that all of these negative circumstances worked together to cause John the Baptist to reconsider, *Have I heard from God correctly? Did I miss Him?*

If you're in negative circumstances, your hope has been deferred and you aren't seeing things come to pass the way you thought you should, you could also fall into this same trap. John the Baptist was the greatest man who had ever lived on the face of the earth up until this time. Jesus Himself said that (Matt. 11:11 and Luke 7:28). Yet John was subject to doubt. When he got into a high-pressure situation, he began to doubt even the things that had been so emphatically confirmed to him. This just shows that anybody is capable of doubt.

Maintain Thrust

In your Christian life, you must continue to seek the Lord. You can't just turn off the engine and coast. Like an airplane, you must maintain that thrust in order to be able to maintain your lift. A helicopter has the aerodynamics of a rock if you turn the engine off and the blades quit turning. It's going to fall. You must maintain that power and lift in order to overcome gravity and fly.

All of us are subject to doubt. John the Baptist was a man who had been filled with the Holy Spirit before he was even born. He was a man who walked with God constantly, who caused the greatest revival in the history of the world. John had an audible and visible sign from God and at one time had no doubt whatsoever. If negative pressures and circumstances over a period of time could make someone like that doubt, it can happen to you.

Are you someone who only seeks God every once in a while? Do you just seek Him when your back is against the wall so you can receive deliverance and then go back to your carnal ways? You need to be on guard and be watchful. You need to recognize that unbelief is like gravity—it's always pulling. It never turns off. You can rise above it by applying the power of God in your life, but you can't just turn your faith engine off and coast. The moment you start coasting, you're coming down. You may float and go farther than someone else, but the moment you switch off that power of faith, you're headed down.

If John the Baptist could doubt, you can doubt. You need to maintain your focus on the Lord and resist—actively fight against—doubt (James 4:7).

Subject to Doubt
LESSON 6 – OUTLINE

I. The reason most people have the problems they do is because they aren't controlling their thinking.

   A. Unless you do something specifically to keep your mind on the Lord, it will naturally go somewhere else.

   B. When you study and meditate in God's Word, it changes the way you think.

   C. As your thinking changes, so does your life.

   D. That's why you must get to where you're dominated by the Word of God.

II. I know by dealing firsthand with hundreds of people on a regular basis that many folks are struggling.

   A. They want me to wave my hand over them to take away their fears.

   B. If you would just take God's Word and use it yourself, you wouldn't have to follow people around from meeting to meeting begging them to pray for you.

   C. When you're sowing the seed (Word of God) and waiting for it to increase and grow to the point that it will bring liberty in your life, don't be so stubborn or proud that you won't go to others for help and ask them to pray for you.

   D. But don't be like those people who refuse to take personal responsibility.

   E. They try to substitute someone like me or a church pastor for themselves seeking the Lord.

   F. That's just not going to work.

   G. If you aren't going to take the Word firsthand, then you aren't going to mature.

III. The Lord dealt with John the Baptist's doubt by referring him back to the Word of God.

> **Now when John had heard in the prison the works of Christ, he sent two of his disciples, And said unto him, Art thou he that should come, or do we look for another?**
>
> **Matthew 11:2-3**

A. At one time, John was absolutely certain Jesus was the Messiah.

B. But John wasn't so sure after being in prison for an unspecified amount of time.

C. He had even been given a sign from God regarding Jesus being the Messiah.

D. Some people think, *If I was one of Jesus' twelve disciples, I wouldn't struggle with doubt. If I could see a vision, if I had a tangible tingling in my hands, if I could hear an audible voice from God—then I would believe.*

E. John had every one of those things (John 1:33 and Matt. 3:16-17), yet he doubted.

IV. It doesn't matter who you are or how strong in faith you've been, everyone is capable of doubt.

A. Negative circumstances tend to just beat faith out of you and cause doubt to come.

> **Hope deferred maketh the heart sick.**
>
> **Proverbs 13:12**

B. If you're in negative circumstances, your hope has been deferred and you aren't seeing things come to pass the way you thought you should, you could also fall into this same trap.

C. John the Baptist was the greatest man who had ever lived on the face of the earth up until this time.

D. Yet he was subject to doubt.

V. In your Christian life, you must continue to seek the Lord.

A. Are you someone who only seeks God every once in a while?

B. Do you just seek Him when your back is against the wall so you can receive deliverance and then go back to your carnal ways?

C. You need to be on guard and be watchful.

D. You need to recognize that unbelief is like gravity—it's always pulling.

E. You can rise above it by applying the power of God in your life, but you can't just turn your faith engine off and coast.

F. You may float and go farther than someone else, but the moment you switch off that power of faith, you're headed down.

G. You need to maintain your focus on the Lord and resist—actively fight against—doubt (James 4:7).

Subject to Doubt
LESSON 6 – TEACHER'S GUIDE

1. The reason most of us have the problems we do is because we aren't controlling our thinking. Unless we do something specifically to keep our minds on the Lord, they will naturally go somewhere else. When we study and meditate in God's Word, it changes the way we think. As our thinking changes, so do our lives. That's why we must get to where we're dominated by the Word of God.

2. I know by dealing firsthand with hundreds of people on a regular basis that many folks are struggling. They want me to wave my hand over them to take away their fears. If we would just take God's Word and use it ourselves, we wouldn't have to follow people around from meeting to meeting begging them to pray for us. When we're sowing the seed (Word of God) and waiting for it to increase and grow to the point that it will bring liberty in our lives, we shouldn't be so stubborn or proud that we won't go to others for help and ask them to pray for us. But we shouldn't be like those people who refuse to take personal responsibility. They try to substitute someone like me or a church pastor for themselves seeking the Lord. That's just not going to work. If we aren't going to take the Word firsthand, then we aren't going to mature.

3. The Lord dealt with John the Baptist's doubt by referring him back to the Word of God. At one time, John was absolutely certain Jesus was the Messiah. But John wasn't so sure after being in prison for an unspecified amount of time (Matt 11:2-3). He had even been given a sign from God regarding Jesus being the Messiah. Some people think, *If I was one of Jesus' twelve disciples, I wouldn't struggle with doubt. If I could see a vision, if I had a tangible tingling in my hands, if I could hear an audible voice from God—then I would believe.* John had every one of those things (John 1:33 and Matt. 3:16-17), yet he doubted.

1. A. Why do most of us have the problems we do? (Because we aren't controlling our thinking)
   B. What happens when we study and meditate in God's Word? (It changes the way we think)
2. A. When we're sowing the seed (Word of God) and waiting for it to increase and grow to the point that it will bring liberty in our lives, what shouldn't we be? (So stubborn or proud that we won't go to others for help and ask them to pray for us)
   B. We aren't going to mature if we don't what? (Take the Word firsthand)
3. How did the Lord deal with John the Baptist's doubt? (By referring him back to the Word of God)

4. It doesn't matter who we are or how strong in faith we've been, we are all capable of doubt. Negative circumstances tend to just beat faith out of us and cause doubt to come (Prov. 13:12). If we're in negative circumstances, our hope has been deferred and we aren't seeing things come to pass the way we thought we should, we could also fall into this same trap. John the Baptist was the greatest man who had ever lived on the face of the earth up until this time. Yet he was subject to doubt.

5. In our Christian lives, we must continue to seek the Lord. Do we only seek God every once in a while? Do we just seek Him when our backs are against the wall so we can receive deliverance and then go back to our carnal ways? We need to be on guard and be watchful. We need to recognize that unbelief is like gravity—it's always pulling. We can rise above it by applying the power of God in our lives, but we can't just turn our faith engines off and coast. We may float and go farther than someone else, but the moment we switch off that power of faith, we're headed down. We need to maintain our focus on the Lord and resist—actively fight against—doubt (James 4:7).

4. A. What are we all capable of? (Doubt)
   B. Read Proverbs 13:12. What do negative circumstances tend to do? (Beat faith out of us and cause doubt to come)
5. A. What do we need to continue doing? (Seeking the Lord)
   B. What is like gravity—always pulling? (Unbelief)
   C. Read James 4:7. What do we need to do with doubt? (Resist—actively fight against—it)

Subject to Doubt
LESSON 6 – DISCIPLESHIP QUESTIONS

1. Read Proverbs 23:7. Even though this person eats and drinks with you, where is his heart?

2. Read Psalm 19:8. What do the statutes of the Lord do?

3. What does the commandment of the Lord do?

4. Read Matthew 11:2-3. John sent two of his disciples to Jesus after he heard what?

5. According to Luke 1:15, in whose sight would John be great?
   A. His peers'
   B. His boss's
   C. His parents'
   D. The Lord's
   E. The Pharisees'

6. Read John 3:30. **"He must increase, but I _____ decrease."**

7. Read Matthew 3:16-17. How did the Spirit of God descend?

8. **"This is my _____ Son, in whom I am _____ pleased."**
   A. "Favorite," "always"
   B. "Last," "also"
   C. "Beloved," "well"
   D. All of the above
   E. None of the above

9. Read Luke 3:22. Who descended in bodily shape?

10. Read John 1:33. The Spirit who descended and remained on Jesus is whom Jesus would do what with?

11. According to Matthew 14:3-4, why was John put in prison?

12. Read Proverbs 13:12. What happens when what is desired comes?

13. Read Revelation 22:20. Jesus said he *might* come quickly?

14. According to Isaiah 61:1-2, what is the Spirit of the Lord about?

15. Read Luke 4:18-19. Whose ministry is this describing?

16. Read Luke 4:21. When was this scripture fulfilled?

17. According to Acts 1:6, the disciples were asking if Jesus was about to do what with the kingdom?

18. Read Matthew 11:11. Who is greater than John the Baptist?

19. Read Luke 7:28. John the Baptist was a prophet, but he was _____ than a prophet.

20. Read James 4:7. Does this scripture indicate that God will make you submit to Him and resist the devil?

Subject to Doubt
LESSON 6 – ANSWER KEY

1. Not with me
2. They rejoice the heart
3. It enlightens the eyes
4. About the works of Christ
5. D. The Lord's
6. **"Must"**
7. Like a dove
8. C. **"Beloved," "well"**
9. The Holy Ghost
10. Baptize
11. Because He told Herod it was not lawful for him to have his brother's wife
12. It is a tree of life
13. No, *surely* He will come quickly
14. Preaching good tidings unto the meek, binding up the brokenhearted, proclaiming liberty to the captives, opening of the prison to them that are bound, proclaiming the acceptable year of the Lord and the day of vengeance of our God, and comforting all that mourn
15. Jesus'
16. That day
17. Restore it to Israel
18. The least in the kingdom of heaven

19. Greater

20. No

Subject to Doubt
LESSON 6 – SCRIPTURES

PROVERBS 23:7
For as he thinketh in his heart, so is he: Eat and drink, saith he to thee; but his heart is not with thee.

PSALM 19:8
The statutes of the LORD are right, rejoicing the heart: the commandment of the LORD is pure, enlightening the eyes.

MATTHEW 11:2-3
Now when John had heard in the prison the works of Christ, he sent two of his disciples, [3] And said unto him, Art thou he that should come, or do we look for another?

LUKE 1:15
For he shall be great in the sight of the Lord, and shall drink neither wine nor strong drink; and he shall be filled with the Holy Ghost, even from his mother's womb.

JOHN 3:30
He must increase, but I must decrease.

MATTHEW 3:16-17
And Jesus, when he was baptized, went up straightway out of the water: and, lo, the heavens were opened unto him, and he saw the Spirit of God descending like a dove, and lighting upon him: [17] And lo a voice from heaven, saying, This is my beloved Son, in whom I am well pleased.

LUKE 3:22
And the Holy Ghost descended in a bodily shape like a dove upon him, and a voice came from heaven, which said, Thou art my beloved Son; in thee I am well pleased.

JOHN 1:33
And I knew him not: but he that sent me to baptize with water, the same said unto me, Upon whom thou shalt see the Spirit descending, and remaining on him, the same is he which baptizeth with the Holy Ghost.

MATTHEW 14:3-4
For Herod had laid hold on John, and bound him, and put him in prison for Herodias' sake, his brother Philip's wife. [4] For John said unto him, It is not lawful for thee to have her.

PROVERBS 13:12
Hope deferred maketh the heart sick: but when the desire cometh, it is a tree of life.

REVELATION 22:20
He which testifieth these things saith, Surely I come quickly. Amen. Even so, come, Lord Jesus.

ISAIAH 61:1-2
The Spirit of the LORD GOD is upon me; because the LORD hath anointed me to preach good tidings unto the meek; he hath sent me to bind up the brokenhearted, to proclaim liberty to the captives, and the opening of the prison to them that are bound; [2] To proclaim the acceptable year of the LORD, and the day of vengeance of our God; to comfort all that mourn.

LUKE 4:18-19
The Spirit of the Lord is upon me, because he hath anointed me to preach the gospel to the poor; he hath sent me to heal the brokenhearted, to preach deliverance to the captives, and recovering of sight to the blind, to set at liberty them that are bruised, [19] To preach the acceptable year of the Lord.

LUKE 4:21
And he began to say unto them, This day is this scripture fulfilled in your ears.

ACTS 1:6
When they therefore were come together, they asked of him, saying, Lord, wilt thou at this time restore again the kingdom to Israel?

MATTHEW 11:11
Verily I say unto you, Among them that are born of women there hath not risen a greater than John the Baptist: notwithstanding he that is least in the kingdom of heaven is greater than he.

LUKE 7:28
For I say unto you, Among those that are born of women there is not a greater prophet than John the Baptist: but he that is least in the kingdom of God is greater than he.

James 4:7
Submit yourselves therefore to God. Resist the devil, and he will flee from you.

A Crisis Situation
LESSON 7

As John the Baptist wrestled with doubt, he sent two of his disciples to Jesus to ask if He really was the Christ.

> **Jesus answered and said unto them, Go and shew John again those things which ye do hear and see: The blind receive their sight, and the lame walk, the lepers are cleansed, and the deaf hear, the dead are raised up, and the poor have the gospel preached to them. And blessed is he, whosoever shall not be offended in me.**
>
> **Matthew 11:4-6**

Luke's account of this same event adds a minor detail that makes all the difference in the world:

> **When the men were come unto him, they said, John Baptist hath sent us unto thee, saying, Art thou he that should come? or look we for another? And in that same hour he cured many of their infirmities and plagues, and of evil spirits; and unto many that were blind he gave sight. Then Jesus answering said unto them, Go your way, and tell John what things ye have seen and heard; how that the blind see, the lame walk, the lepers are cleansed, the deaf hear, the dead are raised, to the poor the gospel is preached. And blessed is he, whosoever shall not be offended in me.**
>
> **Luke 7:20-23**

Matthew's account of this instance simply recorded John's disciples asking their question and Jesus answering them (Matt. 11:2-6). However, here in Luke's account, we see that before Jesus answered John the Baptist's disciples, He performed many miracles:

> **In that same hour he cured many of their infirmities and plagues, and of evil spirits; and unto many that were blind he gave sight.**
>
> **Luke 7:21**

"In that same hour" implies that for nearly an hour, Jesus didn't answer John the Baptist's disciples, but He performed all of these healings and miracles. Then He told these disciples to go back and tell John the Baptist what they had just seen and heard. That's a major difference from Matthew's account where it seems like Jesus immediately answered their question by telling them to go back and tell John what they have seen and heard.

Notice how specific Luke was in mentioning each type of miracle Jesus performed. Later on we'll see just how important this was. But for now, Jesus spent around an hour performing all these miracles before telling John's disciples to go back and tell him all that they'd seen and heard.

> **And as they** [John's disciples] **departed, Jesus began to say unto the multitudes concerning John.**
>
> **Matthew 11:7, brackets mine**

Out of Earshot

Luke's account records it slightly differently, saying,

> **And when the messengers of John were** [past tense] **departed, he began to speak unto the people concerning John.**
>
> **Luke 7:24, brackets mine**

Instead of "as they departed," Jesus actually waited until after John the Baptist's disciples had already departed before He started saying all these complimentary things about John.

So, by comparing both Matthew and Luke's two accounts of this one incident, we can see that Jesus didn't even answer John the Baptist's disciples for about an hour. Instead of giving them a straight answer right away, what He did was go out and open up blind eyes, raise people from the dead, cast demons out of folks, and cause the lame to walk and the deaf to hear. He did all of these miracles in the space of one hour!

I've seen blind eyes open, people raised from the dead, and folks come out of wheelchairs. I've seen many miracles happen, but I've never seen all of that happen in one hour's time. I've seen multiple miracles within a short period of time, but the Lord crammed raising people from the dead, blind eyes opening, deaf ears hearing, and the lame walking, all into one hour. Imagine the impact this would have had on you!

Then, after John the Baptist's disciples were out of earshot and they couldn't take back to him what Jesus was about to say, then the Lord began to say these things that—at least to my way of thinking—would have actually been more beneficial to John than the answer He gave.

In John's Shoes

Put yourself in John's shoes. There you are, one of the central figures in the nation. People are looking to you for leadership. At one time, hundreds of thousands of people were saying that you were the most important figure in the entire nation. You had that kind of following. Here you are, in your darkest crisis hour, doubting the very truths that made you the instrument God used in such a mighty way. You are at your lowest. In prison, it looks like you are going to be executed at any time. (As it turned out, John the Baptist was beheaded.) During this low period of time, you send word to the person who has taken your place and succeeded you. This is the same person whom you promoted and actually pushed to the forefront. You're the one who drew all of the crowds, but then you told them to follow Him. You drew all the people together and then turned them over to Him.

So, in this crisis moment, John the Baptist sent disciples to Jesus asking for help, but it didn't even seem like the Lord helped these disciples at first. He ignored them and performed these miracles. Then He told them,

> **Go your way, and tell John what things ye have seen and heard; how that the blind see, the lame walk, the lepers are cleansed, the deaf hear, the dead are raised, to the poor the gospel is preached. And blessed is he, whosoever shall not be offended in me.**
>
> **Luke 7:22-23**

When I first read these passages of Scripture, I actually felt sorry for John. I thought, *Jesus didn't really do much to help John the Baptist here.* Think about it. John the Baptist had been separated to the Gospel from his mother's womb. He didn't have a normal childhood. He didn't have a wife or children. The Word says he was in the deserts until the day he began his ministry (Luke 1:80). This means he had been separated unto God. There was no Plan B or Plan C. He never had any other enjoyments outside of his calling. This man was totally separated and completely focused on this from his mother's womb.

A Huge Mistake?

If Jesus wasn't the Christ, then John the Baptist had squandered the anointing that was on his life. He had said of Jesus,

> **Behold the Lamb of God, which taketh away the sin of the world.**
>
> **John 1:29**

John's own disciples had come and wanted to follow Jesus, but they were torn in their allegiance. John said,

> **He must increase, but I must decrease.**
>
> **John 3:30**

John the Baptist sent his own disciples to follow after Jesus. If Jesus wasn't the Messiah, then John had made a huge personal mistake that rendered his whole life a failure and a waste. Not only that, but he had taken this anointing he had, which nobody else in the history of the world had ever had, and sent his disciples, the entire nation, and multiple neighboring nations after the wrong man. He could have been an instrument of the devil instead of the instrument of God that he was separated to be. This wasn't just a flippant doubt that John the Baptist had; this was a crisis situation unlike any other in his life.

How did Jesus respond? He said, "Go tell him what you've seen and heard." The Lord didn't even answer John's messengers at first but told them after an hour of curing people, "Go tell him what you've seen and heard." Then, after John's disciples had departed, Jesus...

> **...began to speak unto the people concerning John, What went ye out into the wilderness for to see? A reed shaken with the wind?**
>
> **Luke 7:24**

Jesus was asking, "What drew the thousands, perhaps hundreds of thousands, of people out into the desert to listen to this man? Was it the reeds blowing in the wind?" No, the reeds had been out there for hundreds of years, and the crowds had never come. It wasn't nature. It wasn't because the desert was so beautiful. The crowds came because there was a man out there who was on fire for God.

On Fire for God

If you catch on fire for God, the whole world will come watch you burn.

John the Baptist was a man who was on fire for God. He was anointed by God. God's words were in his mouth. The Lord was giving John a great compliment, acknowledging that he had drawn huge crowds into the desert.

> **But what went ye out for to see? A man clothed in soft raiment? Behold, they which are gorgeously apparelled, and live delicately, are in kings' courts.**
>
> **Luke 7:25**

Was it John the Baptist's flashy clothes or patent leather shoes that drew everybody there? Was it his Pentecostal hairdo or his expensive suits that attracted the crowds? No, he didn't have any of those things. John the Baptist was clothed with camel's hair. The only thing that smells worse than camel's hair is wet camel's hair. John the Baptist wore camel's hair and spent half his time in the Jordan River baptizing people. So, this guy was definitely not a fashion statement.

On top of that, John the Baptist had a long beard. He ate locusts and wild honey. I could just see his beard matted with honey with a dismembered locust leg stuck in it somewhere. Jesus was simply saying that it wasn't John's hair or clothes that drew people out into the wilderness.

> **But what went ye out for to see? A prophet? Yea, I say unto you, and much more than a prophet. This is he, of whom it is written, Behold, I send my messenger before thy face, which shall prepare thy way before thee.**
>
> **Luke 7:26-27**

That's a quotation from Malachi 3:1, and it was universally understood to pertain to the prophet who was to prepare the way for the Messiah—a very high position of authority and leadership. Jesus was making it very clear that John the Baptist was this man who was prophesied about in the Old Testament.

Greater

> **For I say unto you, Among those that are born of women there is not a greater prophet than John the Baptist: but he that is least in the kingdom of God is greater than he.**
>
> **Luke 7:28**

Jesus said that John the Baptist was greater than any Old Testament figure, including Moses, Elijah, Elisha, Isaiah, Jeremiah, etc. Those were some pretty powerful words to be spoken by a man who was the most popular figure in the nation at that time.

There John the Baptist was—rotting in prison, feeling lonely, and wondering, *What about me? I had a six-month ministry, and since then, I've been rotting in prison for years. Does anybody remember me? Does anyone even care?*

What would it be like if you were in John's position, and you sent to the most popular, influential religious figure in the nation, asking for help? How do you think it would help you if He were to stand up in His pulpit and begin talking about you? How would you feel if He started saying on radio and television that you're the greatest prophet who has ever lived? Greater than Abraham, Moses, or Elijah—greater than anyone? If you were struggling the way John the Baptist was, you'd probably find such words to be very encouraging.

At least, that's what I thought. When I saw this crisis situation that John the Baptist was in and how the Lord treated his disciples—ignoring them for an hour, healing these other people, and then sending them back with that message—I thought, *God, that just doesn't seem to meet the need. Then, after John's disciples had gone, You give all of these compliments. Why didn't You say that while his disciples were still there? Wouldn't that have blessed John more?*

A Crisis Situation
LESSON 7 – OUTLINE

I. As John the Baptist wrestled with doubt, he sent two of his disciples to Jesus to ask if He really was the Christ.

   A. Matthew's account of this instance simply recorded John's disciples asking their question and Jesus answering them (Matt. 11:2-6).

   B. However, here in Luke's account, we see that before Jesus answered John the Baptist's disciples (Luke 7:20-23), He performed many miracles.

      In that same hour he cured many of their infirmities and plagues, and of evil spirits; and unto many that were blind he gave sight.

      Luke 7:21

   C. **"In that same hour"** implies that for nearly an hour, Jesus didn't answer John the Baptist's disciples, but He performed all of these healings and miracles.

   D. Then He told these disciples to go back and tell John the Baptist what they had just seen and heard.

   E. I've seen multiple miracles within a short period of time, but the Lord crammed raising people from the dead, blind eyes opening, deaf ears hearing, and the lame walking, all into one hour.

   F. Imagine the impact this would have had on you!

II. If Jesus wasn't the Christ, then John the Baptist had squandered the anointing that was on his life, which nobody else in the history of the world had ever had.

   A. He could have been an instrument of the devil instead of the instrument of God that he was separated to be.

   B. This wasn't just a flippant doubt that John the Baptist had; this was a crisis situation unlike any other in his life.

   C. How did Jesus respond? "Go tell him what you've seen and heard."

III. Then, after John's disciples had departed, Jesus said that John the Baptist was greater than any Old Testament figure, including Moses, Elijah, Elisha, Isaiah, Jeremiah, etc.

A. Those were some pretty powerful words to be spoken by a man who was the most popular figure in the nation at that time.

B. There John the Baptist was—rotting in prison, feeling lonely, and wondering, *What about me? I had a six-month ministry, and since then, I've been rotting in prison for years. Does anybody remember me? Does anyone even care?*

C. When I saw this crisis situation that John the Baptist was in and how the Lord treated his disciples—ignoring them for an hour, healing these other people, and then sending them back with that message—I thought, *God, that just doesn't seem to meet the need. Then, after John's disciples had gone, You began to give all of these compliments. Why didn't You say that while his disciples were still there? Wouldn't that have blessed John more?*

A Crisis Situation
LESSON 7 – TEACHER'S GUIDE

1. As John the Baptist wrestled with doubt, he sent two of his disciples to Jesus to ask if He really was the Christ. Matthew's account of this instance simply recorded John's disciples asking their question and Jesus answering them (Matt. 11:2-6). However, here in Luke's account (Luke 7:20-23), we see that before Jesus answered John the Baptist's disciples, **"in that same hour he cured many of their infirmities and plagues, and of evil spirits; and unto many that were blind he gave sight"** (Luke 7:21). **"In that same hour"** implies that for nearly an hour, Jesus didn't answer John the Baptist's disciples, but He performed all of these healings and miracles. Then He told these disciples to go back and tell John the Baptist what they had just seen and heard. I've seen multiple miracles within a short period of time, but the Lord crammed raising people from the dead, blind eyes opening, deaf ears hearing, and the lame walking, all into one hour. Imagine the impact this would have had on you!

2. If Jesus wasn't the Christ, then John the Baptist had squandered the anointing that was on his life, which nobody else in the history of the world had ever had. He could have been an instrument of the devil instead of the instrument of God that he was separated to be. This wasn't just a flippant doubt that John the Baptist had; this was a crisis situation unlike any other in his life. How did Jesus respond? "Go tell him what you've seen and heard."

1. A. Read Matthew 11:2-6. What did John the Baptist send two of his disciples to ask Jesus? (If He really was the Christ)
   B. Read Luke 7:20-23. What information does Luke's account imply that Matthew's doesn't? (That for nearly an hour, Jesus didn't answer John the Baptist's disciples, but He performed all of these healings and miracles)
2. A. If Jesus wasn't the Christ, what had John the Baptist squandered? (The anointing that was on his life, which nobody else in the history of the world had ever had)
   B. Jesus told John's disciples to tell him not only what they had seen but also what they had _____. (Heard)

3. Then, after John's disciples had departed, Jesus said that John the Baptist was greater than any Old Testament figure, including Moses, Elijah, Elisha, Isaiah, Jeremiah, etc. Those were some pretty powerful words to be spoken by a man who was the most popular figure in the nation at that time. There John the Baptist was—rotting in prison, feeling lonely, and wondering, *What about me? I had a six-month ministry, and since then, I've been rotting in prison for years. Does anybody remember me? Does anyone even care?* When I saw this crisis situation that John the Baptist was in and how the Lord treated his disciples—ignoring them for an hour, healing these other people, and then sending them back with that message—I thought, *God, that just doesn't seem to meet the need. Then, after John's disciples had gone, You began to give all of these compliments. Why didn't You say that while his disciples were still there? Wouldn't that have blessed John more?*

3. A. What did Jesus say after John's disciples had departed? (That John the Baptist was greater than any Old Testament figure, including Moses, Elijah, Elisha, Isaiah, Jeremiah, etc.)
   B. What did Andrew think about Jesus' response to John's disciples? (*God, that just doesn't seem to meet the need. Then, after John's disciples had gone, You began to give all of these compliments. Why didn't You say that while his disciples were still there? Wouldn't that have blessed John more?*)

A Crisis Situation
LESSON 7 – ADDITIONAL INFORMATION

I'd like to encourage you to check out my *Life for Today Study Bible and Commentary*: the Gospels Edition. This hardbound book has over six hundred pages containing all four Gospels in their entirety, commentary, cross-references, footnotes, and other great study tools. In addition to all this, one unique and very important feature is that the four Gospel accounts are organized chronologically event by event. This means that all the scriptures in Matthew, Mark, Luke, and John concerning each Gospel incident have been conveniently laid out together on one page. This allows you to gain a comparative understanding of the Gospels and see the slight differences of recorded details that shed important additional light on certain events. You might not normally see these by reading them apart from each other. By putting the exact same story, as recorded by the different Gospel authors, together side by side, you can see noticeable differences. Nothing contradicts; new information is simply added to paint a fuller picture of what actually happened. Whether you use the *Life for Today Study Bible and Commentary*: the Gospels Edition for devotional or study purposes, it would be a worthwhile investment and powerful addition to your spiritual tool belt. In fact, it will help you more easily see the very truths I discuss in this **Lesson**.

A Crisis Situation

LESSON 7 – DISCIPLESHIP QUESTIONS

1. Read Matthew 11:2-7. What did John's disciples see and hear?

2. Who did Jesus say was blessed?

3. Read Luke 7:20-28. What did the people go out to the wilderness to see?

4. Who prepared Jesus' way?

5. According to Luke 1:80, John the Baptist waxed (grew) strong in what?
   A. Spirit
   B. Battle
   C. Odor
   D. All of the above
   E. None of the above

6. How long was he in the deserts?

7. Read John 1:29. The Lamb of God takes away whose sins?
   A. The twelve disciples'
   B. Those who plead the blood of Jesus
   C. Only those in Judea, Galilee, and Samaria
   D. The world's
   E. Those who deserve it

8. Read John 3:30. Who must increase?

9. According to Malachi 3:1, God's messenger prepares the way before Him with his what?

10. In whom would the people delight?

A Crisis Situation
LESSON 7 – ANSWER KEY

1. The blind received their sight, the lame walked, the lepers were cleansed, the deaf heard, the dead were raised up, and the poor had the Gospel preached to them
2. The person who is not offended in Him
3. A prophet, and much more than a prophet
4. John the Baptist
5. A. Spirit
6. Until the day of his showing (appearance) in Israel
7. D. The world's
8. Jesus
9. Message
10. The messenger of the Covenant

A Crisis Situation
LESSON 7 – SCRIPTURES

MATTHEW 11:2-7
Now when John had heard in the prison the works of Christ, he sent two of his disciples, [3] And said unto him, Art thou he that should come, or do we look for another? [4] Jesus answered and said unto them, Go and shew John again those things which ye do hear and see: [5] The blind receive their sight, and the lame walk, the lepers are cleansed, and the deaf hear, the dead are raised up, and the poor have the gospel preached to them. [6] And blessed is he, whosoever shall not be offended in me. [7] And as they departed, Jesus began to say unto the multitudes concerning John, What went ye out into the wilderness to see? A reed shaken with the wind?

LUKE 7:20-28
When the men were come unto him, they said, John Baptist hath sent us unto thee, saying, Art thou he that should come? or look we for another? [21] And in that same hour he cured many of their infirmities and plagues, and of evil spirits; and unto many that were blind he gave sight. [22] Then Jesus answering said unto them, Go your way, and tell John what things ye have seen and heard; how that the blind see, the lame walk, the lepers are cleansed, the deaf hear, the dead are raised, to the poor the gospel is preached. [23] And blessed is he, whosoever shall not be offended in me. [24] And when the messengers of John were departed, he began to speak unto the people concerning John, What went ye out into the wilderness for to see? A reed shaken with the wind? [25] But what went ye out for to see? A man clothed in soft raiment? Behold, they which are gorgeously apparelled, and live delicately, are in kings' courts. [26] But what went ye out for to see? A prophet? Yea, I say unto you, and much more than a prophet. [27] This is he, of whom it is written, Behold, I send my messenger before thy face, which shall prepare thy way before thee. [28] For I say unto you, Among those that are born of women there is not a greater prophet than John the Baptist: but he that is least in the kingdom of God is greater than he.

LUKE 1:80
And the child grew, and waxed strong in spirit, and was in the deserts till the day of his shewing unto Israel.

JOHN 1:29
The next day John seeth Jesus coming unto him, and saith, Behold the Lamb of God, which taketh away the sin of the world.

JOHN 3:30
He must increase, but I must decrease.

MALACHI 3:1
Behold, I will send my messenger, and he shall prepare the way before me: and the LORD, whom ye seek, shall suddenly come to his temple, even the messenger of the covenant, whom ye delight in: behold, he shall come, saith the LORD of hosts.

"Don't Quit!"
LESSON 8

When I was young in the ministry and just getting started, I pastored a church in Seagoville, Texas. People were staying away from my church by the thousands. It was just amazing the crowds that didn't come. I was struggling and not seeing very much happen.

I went to a conference being held at Calvary Cathedral in Fort Worth, Texas. Bob Nichols was the pastor there, and the guest speakers included all kinds of big names like Kenneth Hagin, Kenneth Copeland, and others. They were all sitting on the front. Gifts of the Holy Spirit were flowing, and they were prophesying and encouraging one another in the Lord.

There were 2,000 people in the auditorium, and nobody knew who I was. I was sitting dead center in the middle of one of these long, twenty- or thirty-seat rows, right in the center of the auditorium. I was literally just a speck in this huge crowd. There I was, feeling so insignificant and thinking, *There's all those leaders up there getting words of encouragement. Nobody in this auditorium needs to be encouraged more than I do.* I felt loneliness and several other negative emotions. Anyway, somebody at the front said, "Go around, shake someone's hand, and encourage them."

I had met the pastor of this church once before. Without going into the details, it wasn't a very good first meeting. It's only because Bob was a gracious person that he even liked me after that first meeting. It wasn't good, and it's not something I'm proud of. Yet there I was, in the middle of the clump of all these people. Bob Nichols got down off that platform, pushed his way through all those folks, worked his way all the way down the aisle, and found me. It was obvious he was looking specifically for me. Bob just started hugging me and saying, "Don't quit. Don't quit! Hold on! God loves you. Don't quit." He didn't know me, or my situation. I knew God had singled me out from all of those thousands of people there. In my time of need, that really blessed and encouraged me.

As I read the story about John the Baptist, I wondered, *Why didn't Jesus do something like that for John? While John's disciples were there, why didn't He say all of these complimentary things about him being the greatest person who had ever lived in history up until that time? Seems to me like that would have been more beneficial than simply performing some miracles and then instructing the messengers to go back and tell John what they had seen and heard and that he'll be blessed if he's not offended.* I struggled with this for years.

Connected

Finally, one day I was reading through Scripture in Isaiah. These questions I had about Matthew 11 weren't forgotten, but they certainly weren't in the forefront of my mind. As I was reading, I came across a prophecy that was given to the messenger who would come before Jesus and prepare His way. This is what these scriptures told this messenger who would prepare the way for the Messiah:

> **Strengthen ye the weak hands, and confirm the feeble knees. Say to them that are of a fearful heart, Be strong, fear not: behold, your God will come with vengeance, even God with a recompence; he will come and save you. Then the eyes of the blind shall be opened, and the ears of the deaf shall be unstopped. Then shall the lame man leap as an hart, and the tongue of the dumb sing: for in the wilderness shall waters break out, and streams in the desert.**
>
> **Isaiah 35:3-6**

All of a sudden, the Holy Spirit reminded me of what Jesus had said to John's disciples and how He'd spent an hour doing these miracles.

> **Jesus answered and said unto them, Go and shew John again those things which ye do hear and see: The blind receive their sight, and the lame walk, the lepers are cleansed, and the deaf hear, the dead are raised up, and the poor have the gospel preached to them. And blessed is he, whosoever shall not be offended in me.**
>
> **Matthew 11:4-6**

In an instant, the Holy Spirit connected these two passages of Scripture for me.

Just Believe!

Jesus waited to say all of these emotional, complimentary things about John the Baptist until after his disciples were gone. While they were present, the answer He gave them was to perform all these miracles right before their eyes. Then He said, "Go tell John what you have heard and seen."

> **The blind receive their sight, and the lame walk, the lepers are cleansed, and the deaf hear, the dead are raised up, and the poor have the gospel preached to them.**
>
> **Matthew 11:5**

Basically, Jesus fulfilled the Messianic prophecy of Isaiah 35:5-6 right in front of their eyes. He opened blind eyes, unstopped deaf ears, enabled the lame to leap, and the tongue of the dumb to sing. These were the very miracles Jesus performed and then told John's disciples to go back and tell him about. In one hour's time, Jesus did everything that was prophesied concerning the miracles He would do. Plus, He added raising someone from the dead.

Then Jesus told John's disciples to go back to him and tell him He had done all of these things and that he'll be blessed if he would just believe. Just believe!

Doubts Drowned Out

John the Baptist knew the Scriptures. When the Pharisees came to him and asked "Who are you? Are you the Christ?" he answered, "No, I'm not the Christ."

> **I am the voice of one crying in the wilderness, Make straight the way of the Lord, as said the prophet Esaias** [Isaiah].
>
> **John 1:23, brackets mine**

That was a quote from Isaiah 40, just five chapters after Isaiah 35.

> **The voice of him that crieth in the wilderness, Prepare ye the way of the LORD, make straight in the desert a highway for our God.**
>
> **Isaiah 40:3**

In fact, John had quoted from a number of passages all around this part of Isaiah. Back then, they didn't have Bibles like we have today with chapters and verses. They had scrolls of paper. It was hard to find a certain sentence or passage because they weren't divided into chapters and verses. What we call the book of Isaiah was just one letter.

So, for John the Baptist to quote from what we call Isaiah 40, which was very close in that letter to what we call Isaiah 35, I believe it is proof positive that he had read these verses. He knew what God had prophesied the Messiah would come and do.

John the Baptist's messengers may not have understood. But they went back to John and said, "Well, He didn't answer our question directly, whether He was the Christ. However, He made us wait an hour, during which time He opened up blind eyes and healed deaf ears. People who couldn't talk, talked, and people who couldn't walk, walked. Then He told us to come back and tell you what He had done and that you'd be blessed if you would just believe."

When John's disciples delivered that message to him, I believe the Holy Spirit connected what Isaiah had prophesied about the Messiah and what Jesus had just done. The light came on as John realized, *How could I doubt that this was the Messiah? He has performed everything the Word of God prophesied He would do. No other man has opened up blind eyes, unstopped deaf ears, enabled the lame to walk, and caused dumb tongues to sing—especially not in one hour's time. He even raised the dead.* I believe the Holy Spirit came in like a flood and washed away all of John the Baptist's doubts. Jesus appealed to John's knowledge of the Word, not just his emotions. When the truth of God's Word drowned out John the Baptist's doubts, I believe he began to praise and thank God.

Victor or Victim?

Jesus wasn't dishonoring John by not giving him emotional compliments. He didn't just tell him something to tide him over. It was just the opposite. Jesus honored John so much, He refused to give him an emotional response. Instead, He referred him back to the Word of God. That's powerful!

You might want an emotional boost like having somebody put their arm around you and cry with you. That might make you feel good temporarily and help you over a hump, but it's not going to help you long-term. I'm not saying no one should show you compassion. However, in the long-term, you need to know the truth. You need to get a hold of the Word of God. Faith comes by hearing the Word of God (Rom. 10:17). God's Word is the sword of the Spirit (Eph. 6:17). That's how you fight off depression, discouragement, and despair. Yet many people simply wallow in their tears, wanting God to come down to their level and help them by saying, "It's really bad!"

A friend of mine was ministering encouragement at one of our *Ministers' Conferences.* He'd called forward people who were discouraged, and he was going to pray for them. You didn't have to ask this one couple who came up for prayer if they were discouraged. Their body language had discouragement written all over it. They were stooped over, crying, and looked miserable. As they stood in front of my friend, he just looked at them and declared, "Thus says the Lord, 'Don't feel bad. If I wasn't God, I would be discouraged too.'" When he said that, it encouraged me. In fact, I thought it was hilarious. However, I'm not sure that couple rejoiced over it that much.

Perhaps some of you honestly think your problem is so bad that even God is wringing His hands and wondering how He's going to take care of it. The truth is, your problem is nothing to God. Yet many times, we want God to come down and cry with us, saying, "I know it's so hard. I'm grieving with you." But that's not true. The Lord has already conquered. He's victorious. Now, He does have compassion and love toward you if you're discouraged. I'm not discounting that. But instead of wanting something emotional that will make you feel good today, but then tomorrow you'll need another emotional fix, you need to take the truth of God's Word. Whether you feel like it or not, stand up and start saying, "I am an overcomer in Christ Jesus. I don't care what I feel like, what somebody else has said, or what has happened to me. I'm going to rise again. I am a victor and not a victim." Start taking God's Word and applying it to your situation.

But thanks be to God, which giveth us the victory through our Lord Jesus Christ.

1 Corinthians 15:57

This is the victory that overcometh the world, even our faith.

1 John 5:4

You start speaking the Word, and build yourself up.

Eyes on the Truth

In a sense, that's what Jesus did for John the Baptist. Instead of giving him all of these compliments, He referred him back to the prophecies he had known—that God had used to call him to the ministry and that had put him on the right path. At one time, the Word of God had motivated John, and for thirty years, these prophecies kept him focused and on track. But in a crisis situation, he took his eyes off of the Word and started looking at his surroundings. He was in prison, and it looked like he was going to die. Because of this, John became discouraged.

As long as Peter looked at Jesus—the Author and Finisher of his faith—he walked on water (Matt. 14:28-31). He did something that no other person outside of the Lord had ever done. It was miraculous. But when Peter took his eyes off of Jesus and began to look at the wind and waves, he started to sink.

John the Baptist had taken his eyes off of the Word, off of the truths that God had instilled in his heart. He was looking at his prison and the fact that he was facing death. It appeared that this tyrant, Herod, was prevailing and that he was losing. John was looking at these things and had lost sight of what the Word of God said. Jesus referred him back to the Word, the Word that he was well acquainted with.

When that happened, I believe the Holy Spirit rose up on the inside of him. The Scripture doesn't tell us what John's response was, but we know he remained faithful to the end.

Eventually, Herod beheaded him. But there was no whimpering, crying, or renouncing his beliefs. John the Baptist stayed strong. I personally believe that when Jesus responded to him this way, he recognized, *How could I have doubted? This is what the Word says.* Regardless of how his emotions made him feel, he got his thoughts back on the truth.

That really encourages me. If I were to go by my emotions, there are times when I feel like running away. There are times when I feel like giving up and quitting. But I've learned to go by the Word and not by how I feel. This truth has changed me, and it's worked in my life for decades.

Raised from the Dead

I remember receiving a phone call at 4:15 a.m. and being told that my son had died. Jamie and I immediately got up and got dressed. It took us an hour and fifteen minutes to drive from our house to the hospital in Colorado Springs. We live so far out that our cell phones didn't work. During that period of time, I didn't have any way to call the hospital.

When I received that call, I declared, "The first report is not the last report." I spoke my faith. Then my wife and I agreed and prayed. We called our son back to life. He had been dead for nearly five hours by that time. It was absolutely miraculous.

From the time we got the call until we arrived at the hospital and saw that he had been raised from the dead, I began having some negative thoughts and feelings—grief and things like that. I just praised God. It's not really to my credit. It's the Holy Spirit, and He's spent a lot of time teaching and training me. But when I started having these negative thoughts, I cried out to God, and He started sharing His Word with me. He brought me back to scriptures and reminded me of truths. Because of that, God's Word rose up on the inside of me, and I literally went against those negative feelings. I didn't care how I felt.

Imagine if someone told you your son was dead. How would you feel? What kinds of thoughts would run through your mind? Well, I had everything going through me that probably would go through you. But the Word of God rose up within me, and by the grace of God, I never spoke anything contrary to what the Word said. In fact, as I began to praise God, my emotions turned around and started agreeing with God. I actually began to rejoice and praise the Lord.

I'm sharing this to encourage you. Even though your emotions are pulling you one way, you know what the Word of God says. You can come to the place where God's Word is more real to you than what you feel. That's what the Bible calls faith. That's what the Word calls maturity.

Stand on the Word

For many Christians, all the devil has to do is give them a thought that brings an emotion contrary to what the Word says, and they fold up like a two-dollar suitcase and fall apart. The Bible says you have love, joy, and peace (Gal. 5:22), but all somebody has to do is just say the slightest little thing and criticize you. Maybe your pastor didn't speak to you as he walked down the hall. You feel neglected and ignored. Perhaps someone said something about you or didn't give you the attention you need. Pull your thumb out of your mouth and grow up!

We need to recognize that the Word of God is what's supposed to work in our lives. What if you were in a crisis situation and doubting the way John the Baptist was? Would you be asking the Lord to give you something emotional, to have an angel appear, for a goose bump to go up and down your spine? Would you want someone to call you and say, "I think you're awesome"? If you're looking for those kinds of responses, you're looking in the wrong place. You need to go to the Word of God.

Are you doing what God has told you to do? Do you have a promise? Has He led you to move in a direction? If He has, then you take the Word of God and stand in faith. It doesn't matter how you feel or if it hair lips every demon in hell; just keep doing what God told you to do. Don't back off of it. Get to where the Word of God becomes absolute authority in your life, and you aren't going to back off of it regardless of what anybody has or hasn't done. When you get that kind of attitude and the Word of God begins to dominate you, then you will overcome doubt. You'll be walking in faith.

Faith is seldom a feeling. Very seldom do you just feel this surge of boldness. At times, you will walk in a gift of faith. However, most times, when I've seen great things happen in my life, I've stepped out in faith. My emotions were wavering, but I just chose not to go by them. I decided not to be bound by them. I knew what God's Word says and ministered it from my heart. Then I stood on what the Word of God said, sometimes with my knees shaking. But that's faith.

Some people think faith is having an absence of any problems, doubts, or fears. That's not true. It's just learning how to reject those things and not let them control you as you take a stand on the Word of God.

"Don't Quit!"
LESSON 8 – OUTLINE

I. One day I was reading through Scripture in Isaiah:

> **Strengthen ye the weak hands, and confirm the feeble knees. Say to them that are of a fearful heart, Be strong, fear not: behold, your God will come with vengeance, even God with a recompence; he will come and save you. Then the eyes of the blind shall be opened, and the ears of the deaf shall be unstopped. Then shall the lame man leap as an hart, and the tongue of the dumb sing: for in the wilderness shall waters break out, and streams in the desert.**
>
> **Isaiah 35:3-6**

A. All of a sudden, the Holy Spirit reminded me of what Jesus had said to John's disciples and how He'd spent an hour doing these miracles.

B. In one hour's time, Jesus did everything that was prophesied concerning the miracles He would do.

C. Plus, He added raising someone from the dead.

D. Then Jesus told John's disciples to go back to him and tell him He had done all of these things and that he'll be blessed if he would just believe.

II. John the Baptist knew the Scriptures.

A. He had quoted from a number of passages all around this part of Isaiah (Is. 40:3).

B. When John's disciples delivered Jesus' message to him, I believe the Holy Spirit connected what Isaiah had prophesied about the Messiah and what Jesus had just done.

C. The light came on as John realized, *How could I doubt that this was the Messiah? He has performed everything the Word of God prophesied He would do. No other man has opened up blind eyes, unstopped deaf ears, enabled the lame to walk, and caused dumb tongues to sing—especially not in one hour's time. He even raised the dead.*

D. I believe the Holy Spirit came in like a flood and washed away all of John the Baptist's doubts.

III. You might want an emotional boost like having somebody put their arm around you and cry with you.

A. I'm not saying no one should show you compassion.

B. But instead of wanting something emotional that will make you feel good today, but then tomorrow you'll need another emotional fix, you need to take the truth of God's Word.

C. Whether you feel like it or not, stand up and start saying, "I am an overcomer in Christ Jesus. I don't care what I feel like, what somebody else has said, or what has happened to me. I'm going to rise again. I am a victor and not a victim."

D. Start taking God's Word and applying it to your situation.

E. You start speaking the Word, and build yourself up.

IV. John the Baptist had taken his eyes off of the Word, off of the truths that God had instilled in his heart.

A. Jesus referred him back to the Word, the Word that he was well acquainted with.

B. Eventually, Herod beheaded him.

C. But there was no whimpering, crying, or renouncing his beliefs.

D. John the Baptist stayed strong.

E. Regardless of how his emotions made him feel, he got his thoughts back on the truth.

V. That really encourages me.

A. If I were to go by my emotions, there are times when I feel like running away.

B. There are times when I feel like giving up and quitting.

C. But I've learned to go by the Word and not by how I feel.

D. This truth has changed me, and it's worked in my life for decades.

E. When you get that kind of attitude and the Word of God begins to dominate you, then you will overcome doubt.

F. You'll be walking in faith.

VI. Faith is seldom a feeling.

   A. Very seldom do you just feel this surge of boldness.

   B. At times, you will walk in a gift of faith.

   C. However, most times, when I've seen great things happen in my life, I've stepped out in faith.

   D. My emotions were wavering, but I just chose not to go by them.

   E. I knew what God's Word says and ministered it from my heart.

   F. Then I stood on what the Word of God said, sometimes with my knees shaking.

   G. But that's faith.

VII. Some people think faith is having an absence of any problems, doubts, or fears.

   A. That's not true.

   B. It's just learning how to reject those things and not let them control you as you take a stand on the Word of God.

"Don't Quit!"
LESSON 8 – TEACHER'S GUIDE

1. One day I was reading through Scripture in Isaiah (Is. 35:3-6). All of a sudden, the Holy Spirit reminded me of what Jesus had said to John's disciples and how He'd spent an hour doing these miracles. In one hour's time, Jesus did everything that was prophesied concerning the miracles He would do. Plus, He added raising someone from the dead. Then Jesus told John's disciples to go back to him and tell him He had done all of these things and that he'll be blessed if he would just believe.

2. John the Baptist knew the Scriptures. He had quoted from a number of passages all around this part of Isaiah (Is. 40:3). When John's disciples delivered Jesus' message to him, I believe the Holy Spirit connected what Isaiah had prophesied about the Messiah and what Jesus had just done. The light came on as John realized, *How could I doubt that this was the Messiah? He has performed everything the Word of God prophesied He would do. No other man has opened up blind eyes, unstopped deaf ears, enabled the lame to walk, and caused dumb tongues to sing—especially not in one hour's time. He even raised the dead.* I believe the Holy Spirit came in like a flood and washed away all of John the Baptist's doubts.

3. We might want an emotional boost like having somebody put their arm around us and cry with us. I'm not saying no one should show us compassion. But instead of wanting something emotional that will make us feel good today, but then tomorrow we'll need another emotional fix, we need to take the truth of God's Word. Whether we feel like it or not, we need to stand up and start saying, "I am an overcomer in Christ Jesus. I don't care what I feel like, what somebody else has said, or what has happened to me. I'm going to rise again. I am a victor and not a victim." We need to start taking God's Word and applying it to our situations. Let's start speaking the Word and building ourselves up.

1. A. Read Isaiah 35:3-6. What did Jesus do in one hour's time? (Everything that was prophesied concerning the miracles He would do)
   B. Is that all He did? (No, He added raising someone from the dead)
2. A. What does Andrew believe the Holy Spirit did when John's disciples delivered Jesus' message to him? (That the Holy Spirit connected what Isaiah had prophesied about the Messiah and what Jesus had just done)
   B. What else does he believe? (That the Holy Spirit came in like a flood and washed away all of John the Baptist's doubts)
3. A. Whether we feel like it or not, we should stand up and start saying what? ("I am an overcomer in Christ Jesus. I don't care what I feel like, what somebody else has said, or what has happened to me. I'm going to rise again. I am a victor and not a victim")
   B. We need to take God's Word and do what with it? (Start applying it to our situations)
   C. Let's start doing what? (Speaking the Word and building ourselves up)

4. John the Baptist had taken his eyes off of the Word, off of the truths that God had instilled in his heart. Jesus referred him back to the Word, the Word that he was well acquainted with. Eventually, Herod beheaded him. But there was no whimpering, crying, or renouncing his beliefs. John the Baptist stayed strong. Regardless of how his emotions made him feel, he got his thoughts back on the truth.

5. That really encourages me. If I were to go by my emotions, there are times when I feel like running away. There are times when I feel like giving up and quitting. But I've learned to go by the Word and not by how I feel. This truth has changed me, and it's worked in my life for decades. When we get that kind of attitude and the Word of God begins to dominate us, then we will overcome doubt. We'll be walking in faith.

6. Faith is seldom a feeling. Very seldom do we just feel this surge of boldness. At times, we will walk in a gift of faith. However, most times, when I've seen great things happen in my life, I've stepped out in faith. My emotions were wavering, but I just chose not to go by them. I knew what God's Word says and ministered it from my heart. Then I stood on what the Word of God said, sometimes with my knees shaking. But that's faith.

7. Some people think faith is having an absence of any problems, doubts, or fears. That's not true. It's just learning how to reject those things and not let them control us as we take a stand on the Word of God.

4. A. What had John the Baptist taken his eyes off of? (The Word, off of the truths that God had instilled in his heart)
   B. Was there any whimpering, crying, or renouncing his beliefs when Herod beheaded John? (No)
5. A. What has Andrew learned? (To go by the Word and not by how he feels)
   B. What will happen when we get that kind of attitude and the Word of God begins to dominate us? (We will overcome doubt. We'll be walking in faith)
6. Seldom is faith a _____. (Feeling)
7. A. Faith is not the absence of any _____. (Problems, doubts, or fears)
   B. It's learning how to what? (Reject those things and not let them control us as we take a stand on the Word of God)

“Don’t Quit!”
LESSON 8 – DISCIPLESHIP QUESTIONS

1. Read Isaiah 35:3-6. What kind of heart should hear these things?

2. What shall break out in the wilderness?
   A. A reed
   B. Waters
   C. Fiery serpents
   D. A cloud by day
   E. A sale

3. Read Matthew 11:4-6. Who was the Gospel preached to?

4. According to John 1:23, John was **“the _____ of one crying in the wilderness.”**

5. Read Isaiah 40:3. What was to be made straight in the desert?

6. Read Romans 10:17. **“Faith cometh by hearing”** just anything?

7. According to Ephesians 6:17, take salvation for a _____.

8. **“The sword of the _____, which is the _____ of God.”**

9. Read 1 Corinthians 15:57. Who is the victory through?

10. Read 1 John 5:4. When you are born of God, you overcome what?

11. Read Matthew 14:28-31. When Peter cried out to the Lord to save him, when did Jesus stretch forth His hand?

12. After Peter walked on the water and began to sink, what kind of faith did Jesus say he had?
    A. Little faith
    B. Mustard seed faith
    C. Great faith
    D. All of the above
    E. None of the above

13. According to Galatians 5:22, **“the _____ of the Spirit is love, joy, peace, longsuffering, gentleness, goodness, faith.”**

"Don't Quit!"
LESSON 8 – ANSWER KEY

1. A fearful heart
2. B. Waters
3. The poor
4. **"Voice"**
5. A highway for our God
6. No, **"hearing by the word of God"**
7. Helmet
8. **"Spirit," "word"**
9. Our Lord Jesus Christ
10. The world
11. Immediately
12. A. Little faith
13. **"Fruit"**

"Don't Quit!"
LESSON 8 – SCRIPTURES

ISAIAH 35:3-6
Strengthen ye the weak hands, and confirm the feeble knees. [4] Say to them that are of a fearful heart, Be strong, fear not: behold, your God will come with vengeance, even God with a recompence; he will come and save you. [5] Then the eyes of the blind shall be opened, and the ears of the deaf shall be unstopped. [6] Then shall the lame man leap as an hart, and the tongue of the dumb sing: for in the wilderness shall waters break out, and streams in the desert.

MATTHEW 11:4-6
Jesus answered and said unto them, Go and shew John again those things which ye do hear and see: [5] The blind receive their sight, and the lame walk, the lepers are cleansed, and the deaf hear, the dead are raised up, and the poor have the gospel preached to them. [6] And blessed is he, whosoever shall not be offended in me.

JOHN 1:23
He said, I am the voice of one crying in the wilderness, Make straight the way of the Lord, as said the prophet Esaias.

ISAIAH 40:3
The voice of him that crieth in the wilderness, Prepare ye the way of the LORD, make straight in the desert a highway for our God.

ROMANS 10:17
So then faith cometh by hearing, and hearing by the word of God.

EPHESIANS 6:17
And take the helmet of salvation, and the sword of the Spirit, which is the word of God.

1 CORINTHIANS 15:57
But thanks be to God, which giveth us the victory through our Lord Jesus Christ.

1 JOHN 5:4
For whatsoever is born of God overcometh the world: and this is the victory that overcometh the world, even our faith.

MATTHEW 14:28-31
And Peter answered him and said, Lord, if it be thou, bid me come unto thee on the water. [29] **And he said, Come. And when Peter was come down out of the ship, he walked on the water, to go to Jesus.** [30] **But when he saw the wind boisterous, he was afraid; and beginning to sink, he cried, saying, Lord, save me.** [31] **And immediately Jesus stretched forth his hand, and caught him, and said unto him, O thou of little faith, wherefore didst thou doubt?**

GALATIANS 5:22
But the fruit of the Spirit is love, joy, peace, longsuffering, gentleness, goodness, faith.

A More Sure Word
LESSON 9

When I first began seeking the Lord, I had come from a background that didn't believe that God did miracles today. There wasn't any such thing as angelic visitations, the audible voice of God, or supernatural unctions from the Lord. Those things didn't exist to us. When I became baptized in the Holy Spirit and began to study the Word under the inspiration of the Holy Spirit, I realized that those things didn't pass away with the apostles. I started listening to other people's testimonies and began seeking to see an angel or have God speak to me in an audible voice.

One of the ministers I listened to a lot back then would often have a burning sensation in the palms of his hands. When ministering to people, he would lay both of his hands on them. If the burning in his hand jumped, then it was a healing. If it didn't jump but just burned in his hands, then it was a deliverance. This supernatural manifestation of God's power caused an actual physical manifestation he could perceive.

So, I began to pray and seek the Lord for things like that. I started asking God questions like, "How come I've never had any of these kinds of supernatural things happen to me?" Then the Lord showed me this truth about how Jesus helped John the Baptist overcome his doubts. He revealed to me that the reason Jesus didn't respond to him on an emotional level but used God's Word to raise him up to the level of speaking the Word to him was because of His respect for him. It's because He honored him so much, not because He honored him so little, that He referred him back to the Word. I began to see that believing the Word of God is actually the highest way to respond to the Lord.

Once I understood this, I turned the other direction and prayed, "God, I want Your best. If it honors You more for me to just take Your Word and trust Your Word than to have a vision, for You to quicken Scripture to me and have that be the way I hear from You instead of hearing an audible voice or an angelic messenger, then I'll be glad to go that way." So, I quit praying for something special.

Now, I've had the Lord give me dreams before. The Scriptures speak of what's called a night vision. I've had dreams that I really felt God had given me. But I've never had what people call an open vision—where you're awake and your eyes are open, but you're seeing into the supernatural realm. I've never heard an audible voice from God. I've never had most of the things many people claim to have seen or heard. Neither am I discrediting them. I'm just saying I have learned to relate to the Lord through His Word and that I honestly believe that's His best.

A Higher Level

Satan can also appear in an angelic form (2 Cor. 11:14). You can see and hear things that could lead you astray. But if you go through the Word of God, you'll be safe. The devil can't discredit God's Word. The Word of God is the acid test for everything supernatural. It's the number-one way of hearing from God.

However, you need to realize that the Lord may not have answered your prayer in the way you've been asking, because He has something better for you. You may have been wanting Him to come down and cry with you, saying, "It's really bad!" You may have been asking for an emotional response that would make you feel better. The Lord may not have answered you that way, because He loves you so much—not because He loves you so little. It may be that He's trying to bring you up to a higher level of maturity. He wants you to get beyond just an emotional level and learn to receive from Him through His Word.

In 2 Peter 1, the Apostle Peter was saying that he realized he was close to his death. Therefore, he felt an urgency to remind the believers of the truths he had shared with them before. This was his purpose in writing this second letter.

> **Wherefore I will not be negligent to put you always in remembrance of these things, though ye know them, and be established in the present truth. Yea, I think it meet, as long as I am in this tabernacle, to stir you up by putting you in remembrance; Knowing that shortly I must put off this my tabernacle, even as our Lord Jesus Christ hath shewed me. Moreover I will endeavour that ye may be able after my decease to have these things always in remembrance.**
>
> **2 Peter 1:12-15**

Special Manifestation

He continued by saying,

> **For we have not followed cunningly devised fables, when we made known unto you the power and coming of our Lord Jesus Christ, but were eyewitnesses of his majesty. For he received from God the Father honour and glory, when there came such a voice to him from the excellent glory, This is my beloved Son, in whom I am well pleased. And this voice which came from heaven we heard, when we were with him in the holy mount.**
>
> **2 Peter 1:16-18**

Peter was saying, "These things I'm telling you aren't things I dreamed up. This wasn't something that came as a result of eating pizza before bed. They didn't just come out of my own heart. These truths were imparted to me by God." Then to verify that, he said, "We saw the glory of God when Jesus was on the Mount of Transfiguration. The glory of God came out of Jesus so brightly that it was like the sun. Not only that, but we saw a cloud come over Jesus—the glory cloud that used to inhabit the Old Testament tabernacle. Out of this cloud came a voice from heaven, saying, 'This is My beloved Son, in whom I am well pleased.'"

The reason Peter was saying all of this was to tell them, "Look, these aren't our own ideas. We didn't dream this up. We experienced it. We saw it and heard it." He was validating his message, declaring, "I know what I'm saying is from God."

This compares to me coming to your city to hold a series of meetings. If I came on the television to advertise these meetings by saying "I was caught up to heaven and given a message from the Lord. I have a message from God, and I'll be in your city on Friday to deliver it. Be there at 7:00 p.m.," the amount of people attending would increase dramatically. But when I come on television and say, "We're coming to your city to preach God's Word. I'm going to share with you the truths that the Lord has shared with me," we don't get nearly as many people respond as if I said, "I've had a vision. God has given me a word for this city."

A couple of decades ago, a certain woman claimed to have feathers fall down from heaven at her meetings. After a while, someone actually videotaped her pulling these feathers out from her sleeve. Other people have claimed that their hands will sweat anointing oil. Some people will claim that gold flakes have manifested in the meetings and that they get them in their Bibles. I've actually had people show them to me, saying, "This just makes the Word of God so much more real." If I were to come up with some physical, tangible thing like that, there are many people who would say, "Let's go!" But when I say "I'm going to come and share the Word of God," not as many people are excited about that. Yet that's the wrong attitude. Actually, hearing God through His Word is better than gold dust, feathers, anointing oil, goose bumps, glory clouds, angelic visitations, or anything else. Nothing trumps or supersedes the Word of God. We need to change our thinking in this area.

If you were to unveil two doors, one saying "the Word of God" and the other "some special manifestation," most people would want this "special manifestation."

Something Better

So, in 2 Peter 1, the Apostle Peter was saying, "I know I'm going to be dying soon. I want you to remember these things because we didn't just follow cunningly devised fables. These aren't old wives' tales or stories we dreamed up. We have seen and heard the visible and audible presence of God. We were with Jesus when He was transfigured." He's saying all this to validate his message and get the people to receive as authoritative everything he's been saying.

Then Peter added this in verse 19:

> **We have also a more sure word of prophecy.**

Peter had just talked about how that he saw Jesus radiate light. He saw the glory cloud of God overshadow Him. He heard an audible voice out of heaven, saying, "This is my beloved Son" (Matt. 17:1-9). He had seen Jesus raise Lazarus from the dead and open Bartimaeus' blind eyes (John 11:43-44 and Mark 10:46-52). He had seen the power of the Lord heal the lame man and make him walk (Acts 3:6-8). Peter had seen all of these things. He was recounting it, saying, "This proves that what we've seen and heard is real." But then he said, "We have something better than all of this." What could be better than seeing the visible presence of God and hearing His audible voice? What could be better than seeing Jesus perform all of these miracles?

2 Peter 1:19-21 says,

> **We have also a more sure word of prophecy...Knowing this first, that no prophecy of the scripture is of any private interpretation. For the prophecy came not in old time by the will of man: but holy men of God spake as they were moved by the Holy Ghost.**

Putting all of this together, Peter was saying, "We have something better than a visible representation of God, something better than an audible voice from God, something better than all of the physical, tangible miracles. The most authoritative thing I could possibly share with you to validate the truth is the Word of God. The Word of God is greater than any other way to hear from God." Therefore, the Word of God is the strongest, most powerful way that we have to counter our fears and unbelief.

Backward

That ought to be obvious. Yet in my dealings with people, most folks just want you to put your arm around them and say something encouraging. They'd like a little note with a chocolate from you. They'd like this or that. They have the Word with them, but they don't care what it says. They wouldn't say it that way. But they do come up to me and ask, "Would you pray for me and give me a word?"

"Well, you have ten thousand words right there under your arm, on your night stand, or wherever your Bible is. Why don't you open it up and use it?"

The problem is, most people don't honor the written Word of God the way they would honor a prophecy or word of encouragement from a person, or some audible or visible sign. That's backward, and it's precisely the reason we have so much doubt.

The Lord will meet you where your faith is. God has spoken to many people through these different external ways. I'm not against them. I know many people who have had them, and the testimony of what they heard, saw, and experienced lines up with the Word. I don't doubt that's God. I'm just saying that if you are more insistent, more desirous of a sign, an audible voice, a visible representation, something miraculous that will help you—that's just a temporary fix. Those things don't last very long. Circumstances change. Satan can come along and give you negative signs and such. But if you would go to the Word of God, making it your absolute authority and viewing it as God speaking to you, then the Word will overcome any doubt you have. God's Word will confirm everything you need to know. It's the highest and best way of hearing from Him.

Physical, Tangible Proof

When one of the Lord's disciples, Thomas (often called "Doubting Thomas"), heard that Jesus was raised from the dead, he responded,

> **Except I shall see in his hands the print of the nails, and put my finger into the print of the nails, and thrust my hand into his side, I will not believe.**
>
> **John 20:25**

In other words, "Unless it comes out of the spirit realm and manifests itself in the physical realm, I'm not going to believe. I need physical, tangible proof." That's the way most people are today.

Finally, eight days later, Jesus showed up. Thomas was present this time. After inviting Thomas to inspect His hands and side, the Lord said to him,

> **Be not faithless, but believing.**
>
> **John 20:27**

Thomas answered, **"My Lord and my God"** (John 20:28). Then Jesus said to him,

> **Thomas, because thou hast seen me, thou hast believed: blessed are they that have not seen, and yet have believed.**
>
> **John 20:29**

Jesus put the greater blessing on believing because of the Word than believing because of physical experience.

Step Up

That may not sound exciting, because you look at the Word of God as being lifeless, dead, and dry. That's because you haven't gotten sincere and serious enough to have the Holy Spirit quicken it to you. But I tell you, God's Word is alive. It's living. It's powerful (Heb. 4:12). It's the most sure word of prophecy (2 Pet. 1:19). A greater blessing and anointing would be released in your life if you could take the truths of God's Word by faith and say, "I believe this is God speaking to me. I've had it revealed to me by the Holy Spirit, and I don't have to have three goose bumps and two visions to confirm it. This is what God's Word says." If you would get that attitude and start believing and basing your life on the Word of God, there is a greater anointing and manifestation of faith through that than there is through all these other things people pursue.

God wants to bring you up to this higher level. The very reason He may not have answered your pleas, cries, and begging for a dream, an angelic visitation, or someone to call out your name and prophesy directly to you is because He loves you so much. God doesn't want to keep you on the bottom rung of the ladder; He wants you to take a step up higher and begin to trust Him through His Word.

In 1978, my wife and I and our two boys went out to California to a *West Coast Believers' Convention* with Kenneth Copeland. At the time, I was pastoring a little church, so this was a major vacation for us. We pooled all the resources we had. I went there expecting to hear from God.

The Lord had been speaking to me about making a change in my ministry. I had always pastored churches up until that time, and the Lord was speaking to me about starting to travel and minister much the way I do now. This was a huge step of faith for me, so I went out to this conference really believing I was going to receive a prophetic word from God.

There were thousands of people at this convention. We sat way up in the balcony—in the nosebleed section. We were so far away, I'm not even sure Kenneth Copeland could have seen us from the platform. Yet, in my heart, I was putting a draw on him and saying, "I'm believing for a word. O God, give me a prophecy."

"Why Don't You Trust Me?"

Right in the midst of me praying and asking God for a prophecy, Kenneth started prophesying. He was standing way down there on the stage, but it looked like he was pointing right at me. I was shocked. I thought, *It worked! God is speaking to me!*

This prophecy was basically along the lines of, "Just do what I've told you to do. I've told you to get up and go for it. I'm going to provide for your needs. Take this step of faith. There's a change coming. You have to leave where you are and go out into this promised land that God has given you," and some other powerful things.

Everything Kenneth Copeland was saying matched exactly, almost word for word, what God had spoken in my heart. I was just so excited. I thought, *It worked! God is speaking directly to me!* Then, at the end of the prophecy, Kenneth said, "Did you hear that, Ed? That's for you." I looked down below and saw a man named Ed standing up downstairs on the main floor. Kenneth Copeland was actually prophesying to him. While I was praying and asking God for a word, I missed the first part of that. So, when I heard him say Ed's name, my heart just sank. I thought, *O God, I thought You were talking to me.*

Then the Lord spoke to my heart and said, "If that prophecy had been for Andrew Wommack, would you have learned anything that I haven't already told you? Would you have received any new piece of information that I hadn't already revealed to you as you studied the Word and prayed?"

I answered, "No."

"Then why don't you trust Me instead of having to have all of these other things? Why don't you get to where My Word is sufficient?"

"Father, That's It!"

The Lord was lovingly rebuking me. So based on that, I said, "Father, that's it! I'm not going to need three confirmations. I know what You've said to me in my heart." I made a decision. So, right after that, we left that church and I started traveling. It was a major change of direction in my life and ministry.

Most of us don't want to just take the Word. We're too insecure. We don't have confidence in God's Word alone and the Holy Spirit quickening it to us. We want to have everybody come and give us ten confirmations so there is zero doubt. That's not how it usually happens.

The Word of God is a more sure word of prophecy than anything else you could ever get. If you would take God's Word, begin to meditate on it, let the Holy Spirit make direct application to your situation, and then act on it—that's the highest form of faith you can possibly have. That's faith based entirely on God's Word alone.

If you would take these wonderful truths and apply them to your life, you'll be transformed.

A More Sure Word
LESSON 9 – OUTLINE

I. When I became baptized in the Holy Spirit and began to study the Word under the inspiration of the Holy Spirit, I realized that angelic visitations, the audible voice of God, and supernatural unctions from the Lord didn't pass away with the apostles.

   A. I started asking God questions like, "How come I've never had any of these kinds of supernatural things happen to me?"

   B. Then the Lord showed me this truth about how Jesus didn't respond to John the Baptist on an emotional level, but used God's Word to raise him up to the level of speaking the Word to him because of His respect for him.

   C. It's because He honored him so much, not because He honored him so little, that He referred him back to the Word.

   D. I began to see that believing the Word of God is actually the highest way to respond to the Lord.

   E. Once I understood this, I turned the other direction and prayed, "God, I want Your best. If it honors You more for me to just take Your Word and trust Your Word than to have a vision, for You to quicken Scripture to me and have that be the way I hear from You instead of hearing an audible voice or an angelic messenger, then I'll be glad to go that way."

II. Satan can also appear in an angelic form (2 Cor. 11:14).

   A. You can see and hear things that could lead you astray.

   B. But if you go through the Word of God, you'll be safe.

   C. The Word of God is the acid test for everything supernatural.

III. You need to realize that the Lord may not have answered your prayer in the way you've been asking, because He has something better for you—because He loves you so much, not because He loves you so little.

   A. It may be that He's trying to bring you up to a higher level of maturity.

   B. He wants you to get beyond just an emotional level and learn to receive from Him through His Word.

IV. In 2 Peter 1, the Apostle Peter was saying that he realized he was close to his death and therefore felt an urgency to remind the believers of the truths he had shared with them before.

A. Peter talked about how that he saw Jesus radiate light.

B. He saw the glory cloud of God overshadow Him.

C. He heard an audible voice out of heaven, saying, "This is my beloved Son" (Matt. 17:1-9).

D. But then he said, "We have something better than all of this."

E. What could be better than seeing the visible presence of God and hearing His audible voice?

> **Knowing this first, that no prophecy of the scripture is of any private interpretation. For the prophecy came not in old time by the will of man: but holy men of God spake as they were moved by the Holy Ghost.**
>
> **2 Peter 1:20-21**

F. Peter said, "The most authoritative thing I could possibly share with you to validate the truth is the Word of God. The Word of God is greater than any other way to hear from God."

G. Therefore, the Word of God is the strongest, most powerful way that we have to counter our fears and unbelief.

V. The problem is, most people don't honor the written Word of God the way they would honor a prophecy or word of encouragement from a person, or some audible or visible sign.

A. That's backward, and it's precisely the reason we have so much doubt.

B. The Lord will meet you where your faith is.

C. God has spoken to many people through different external ways.

D. I'm not against them.

E. I'm just saying that if you are more insistent, more desirous of a sign, an audible voice, a visible representation, something miraculous that will help you—that's just a temporary fix. Circumstances change.

F. But if you would go to the Word of God, making it your absolute authority and viewing it as God speaking to you, then the Word will overcome any doubt you have.

G. God's Word will confirm everything you need to know.

VI. That may not sound exciting, because you look at the Word of God as being lifeless, dead, and dry.

A. That's because you haven't gotten sincere and serious enough to have the Holy Spirit quicken it to you.

B. But I tell you, God's Word is alive. It's powerful (Heb. 4:12).

C. A greater blessing and anointing would be released in your life if you could take the truths of God's Word by faith and say, "I believe this is God speaking to me. I've had it revealed to me by the Holy Spirit, and I don't have to have three goose bumps and two visions to confirm it. This is what God's Word says" (John 20:29).

VII. The Word of God is a more sure word of prophecy than anything else you could ever get.

A. If you would take God's Word, begin to meditate on it, let the Holy Spirit make direct application to your situation, and then act on it—that's the highest form of faith you can possibly have.

B. That's faith based entirely on God's Word alone.

A More Sure Word
LESSON 9 – TEACHER'S GUIDE

1. When I became baptized in the Holy Spirit and began to study the Word under the inspiration of the Holy Spirit, I realized that angelic visitations, the audible voice of God, and supernatural unctions from the Lord didn't pass away with the apostles. I started asking God questions like, "How come I've never had any of these kinds of supernatural things happen to me?" Then the Lord showed me this truth about how Jesus didn't respond to John the Baptist on an emotional level, but used God's Word to raise him up to the level of speaking the Word to him because of His respect for him. It's because He honored him so much, not because He honored him so little, that He referred him back to the Word. I began to see that believing the Word of God is actually the highest way to respond to the Lord. Once I understood this, I turned the other direction and prayed, "God, I want Your best. If it honors You more for me to just take Your Word and trust Your Word than to have a vision, for You to quicken Scripture to me and have that be the way I hear from You instead of hearing an audible voice or an angelic messenger, then I'll be glad to go that way."

2. Satan can also appear in an angelic form (2 Cor. 11:14). We can see and hear things that could lead us astray. But if we go through the Word of God, we'll be safe. The Word of God is the acid test for everything supernatural.

3. We need to realize that the Lord may not have answered our prayers in the way we've been asking, because He has something better for us—because He loves us so much, not because He loves us so little. It may be that He's trying to bring us up to a higher level of maturity. He wants us to get beyond just an emotional level and learn to receive from Him through His Word.

1. A. Jesus used God's Word to do what? (To raise John the Baptist up to the level of speaking the Word to him because of His respect for him)
   B. It was because He _____ him so much. (Honored)
   C. Once Andrew understood that believing the Word of God is actually the highest way to respond to the Lord, what did he do? (He turned the other direction and prayed, "God, I want Your best. If it honors You more for me to just take Your Word and trust Your Word than to have a vision, for You to quicken Scripture to me and have that be the way I hear from You instead of hearing an audible voice or an angelic messenger, then I'll be glad to go that way")
2. A. Read 2 Corinthians 11:14. How can Satan also appear? (In an angelic form)
   B. What is the acid test for everything supernatural? (The Word of God)
3. A. The Lord may not have answered our prayers the way we've been asking because of what? (Because He has something better for us—because He loves us so much, not because He loves us so little)
   B. What may the Lord be trying to bring us to? (A higher level of maturity)

4. In 2 Peter 1, the Apostle Peter was saying that he realized he was close to his death and therefore felt an urgency to remind the believers of the truths he had shared with them before. Peter talked about how that he saw Jesus radiate light. He saw the glory cloud of God overshadow Him. He heard an audible voice out of heaven, saying, "This is my beloved Son" (Matt. 17:1-9). But then he said, "We have something better than all of this." What could be better than seeing the visible presence of God and hearing His audible voice? Peter said, "The most authoritative thing I could possibly share with you to validate the truth is the Word of God. The Word of God is greater than any other way to hear from God" (2 Pet. 1:20-21). Therefore, the Word of God is the strongest, most powerful way that we have to counter our fears and unbelief.

5. The problem is, most people don't honor the written Word of God the way they would honor a prophecy or word of encouragement from a person, or some audible or visible sign. That's backward, and it's precisely the reason we have so much doubt. The Lord will meet us where our faith is. God has spoken to many people through different external ways. I'm not against them. I'm just saying that if we are more insistent, more desirous of a sign, an audible voice, a visible representation, something miraculous that will help us—that's just a temporary fix. Circumstances change. But if we would go to the Word of God, making it our absolute authority and viewing it as God speaking to us, then the Word will overcome any doubt we have. God's Word will confirm everything we need to know.

6. That may not sound exciting, because we look at the Word of God as being lifeless, dead, and dry. That's because we haven't gotten sincere and serious enough to have the Holy Spirit quicken it to us. But I tell you, God's Word is alive. It's powerful (Heb. 4:12). A greater blessing and anointing would be released in our lives if we could take the truths of God's Word by faith and say, "I believe this is God speaking to me. I've had it revealed to me by the Holy Spirit, and I don't have to have three goose bumps and two visions to confirm it. This is what God's Word says" (John 20:29).

4. A. What did Peter say after he talked about how that he saw Jesus radiate light, saw the glory cloud of God overshadow Him, and heard an audible voice out of heaven, saying, "This is my beloved Son"? ("We have something better than all of this")
   B. What was he saying is the most authoritative thing he could possibly share with us to validate the truth? (The Word of God)
5. A. Most people don't honor _____ the way they would honor a prophecy or word of encouragement from a person, or some audible or visible sign. (The written Word of God)
   B. If we would go to the Word of God, making it our absolute authority and viewing it as God speaking to us, what would the Word do? (It would overcome any doubt we have)
   C. What will it confirm? (Everything we need to know)
6. A. Read Hebrews 4:12. What is God's Word? (Alive and powerful)
   B. We need to take the truths of God's Word by faith and say what? ("I believe this is God speaking to me. I've had it revealed to me by the Holy Spirit, and I don't have to have three goose bumps and two visions to confirm it. This is what God's Word says")

7. The Word of God is a more sure word of prophecy than anything else we could ever get. If we would take God's Word, begin to meditate on it, let the Holy Spirit make direct application to our situations, and then act on it—that's the highest form of faith we can possibly have. That's faith based entirely on God's Word alone.

7. If we would take God's Word, begin to meditate on it, let the Holy Spirit make direct application to our situations, and then act on it, what is that? (That's the highest form of faith we can possibly have)

A More Sure Word
LESSON 9 – ADDITIONAL INFORMATION

There's a balance to what I'm emphasizing in this **Lesson**. That's why I encourage you to check into my teaching entitled *How to Hear God's Voice* for additional information. In it, I deal with other important aspects of hearing God's voice that I'm not able to cover in this **Study Guide**.

A More Sure Word

LESSON 9 – DISCIPLESHIP QUESTIONS

1. Read 2 Corinthians 11:14. Who is transformed into an angel of light?

2. Read 2 Peter 1:12-21. Peter thought it was meet (right) to stir you up by putting you in what?
   A. Condemnation
   B. A new convertible
   C. Remembrance
   D. All of the above
   E. None of the above

3. What had Peter not followed?

4. The prophecy came not by what?

5. Read Matthew 17:1-9. Jesus was _____ before them.

6. His face shined like what?

7. What was his raiment [clothing] white as?

8. What did the voice out of the cloud say?
   A. "This is my beloved Son, in whom I am well pleased; hear [listen to] him"
   B. "This is my beloved Son, in whom I am well pleased; hear [listen to] Me"
   C. "This is my beloved Son, in whom I am well pleased; hear [listen to] the angels sing"
   D. "This is my beloved Son, in whom I am well pleased; hear [listen to] the Law of Moses"
   E. "This is my beloved Son, in whom I am well pleased; hear [listen to] each other"

9. What did Jesus charge Peter, James, and John?
   A. A fee for seeing His glory.
   B. He told them not to tell anyone the vision they saw until He had risen from the dead.
   C. He told them to proclaim the matter freely.
   D. All of the above
   E. None of the above

10. According to John 11:43-44, what happened when Jesus cried with a loud voice **"Lazarus, come forth?"**

11. Read Mark 10:46-52. Did blind Bartimaeus keep silent after many charged him?

12. What did Jesus do?

13. What did Jesus ask Bartimaeus?

14. Read Acts 3:6-8. Peter said, **"Such as _____ have."**

15. According to John 20:25, Thomas told the disciples, **"Except I shall see in his hands the print of the nails, and put my finger into the print of the nails, and thrust my hand into his side, I _____ not believe."**

16. According to John 20:27-29, Thomas called Jesus what?

17. Who are blessed?

18. Read Hebrews 4:12. What does the Word of God pierce and divide asunder?

19. It is a discerner of what?

A More Sure Word
LESSON 9 – ANSWER KEY

1. Satan himself
2. C. Remembrance
3. Cunningly devised fables
4. The will of man
5. Transfigured
6. The sun
7. The light
8. A. **"This is my beloved Son, in whom I am well pleased; hear** [listen to] **him"**
9. B. He told them not to tell anyone the vision they saw until He had risen from the dead
10. He who was dead came forth, bound hand and foot with grave clothes
11. No
12. He stood still and commanded him to be called
13. **"What wilt thou that I should do unto thee?"**
14. **"I"**
15. **"Will"**
16. His Lord and his God
17. Those who have not seen (Jesus) and yet have believed
18. Soul and spirit
19. The thoughts and intents of the heart

A More Sure Word
LESSON 9 – SCRIPTURES

2 CORINTHIANS 11:14
And no marvel; for Satan himself is transformed into an angel of light.

2 PETER 1:12-21
Wherefore I will not be negligent to put you always in remembrance of these things, though ye know them, and be established in the present truth. [13] **Yea, I think it meet, as long as I am in this tabernacle, to stir you up by putting you in remembrance;** [14] **Knowing that shortly I must put off this my tabernacle, even as our Lord Jesus Christ hath shewed me.** [15] **Moreover I will endeavour that ye may be able after my decease to have these things always in remembrance.** [16] **For we have not followed cunningly devised fables, when we made known unto you the power and coming of our Lord Jesus Christ, but were eyewitnesses of his majesty.** [17] **For he received from God the Father honour and glory, when there came such a voice to him from the excellent glory, This is my beloved Son, in whom I am well pleased.** [18] **And this voice which came from heaven we heard, when we were with him in the holy mount.** [19] **We have also a more sure word of prophecy; whereunto ye do well that ye take heed, as unto a light that shineth in a dark place, until the day dawn, and the day star arise in your hearts:** [20] **Knowing this first, that no prophecy of the scripture is of any private interpretation.** [21] **For the prophecy came not in old time by the will of man: but holy men of God spake as they were moved by the Holy Ghost.**

MATTHEW 17:1-9
And after six days Jesus taketh Peter, James, and John his brother, and bringeth them up into an high mountain apart, [2] **And was transfigured before them: and his face did shine as the sun, and his raiment was white as the light.** [3] **And, behold, there appeared unto them Moses and Elias talking with him.** [4] **Then answered Peter, and said unto Jesus, Lord, it is good for us to be here: if thou wilt, let us make here three tabernacles; one for thee, and one for Moses, and one for Elias.** [5] **While he yet spake, behold, a bright cloud overshadowed them: and behold a voice out of the cloud, which said, This is my beloved Son, in whom I am well pleased; hear ye him.** [6] **And when the disciples heard it, they fell on their face, and were sore afraid.** [7] **And Jesus came and touched them, and said, Arise, and be not afraid.** [8] **And when they had lifted up their eyes, they saw no man, save Jesus only.** [9] **And as they came down from the**

mountain, Jesus charged them, saying, Tell the vision to no man, until the Son of man be risen again from the dead.

JOHN 11:43-44

And when he thus had spoken, he cried with a loud voice, Lazarus, come forth. [44] **And he that was dead came forth, bound hand and foot with graveclothes: and his face was bound about with a napkin. Jesus saith unto them, Loose him, and let him go.**

MARK 10:46-52

And they came to Jericho: and as he went out of Jericho with his disciples and a great number of people, blind Bartimaeus, the son of Timaeus, sat by the highway side begging. [47] **And when he heard that it was Jesus of Nazareth, he began to cry out, and say, Jesus, thou Son of David, have mercy on me.** [48] **And many charged him that he should hold his peace: but he cried the more a great deal, Thou Son of David, have mercy on me.** [49] **And Jesus stood still, and commanded him to be called. And they call the blind man, saying unto him, Be of good comfort, rise; he calleth thee.** [50] **And he, casting away his garment, rose, and came to Jesus.** [51] **And Jesus answered and said unto him, What wilt thou that I should do unto thee? The blind man said unto him, Lord, that I might receive my sight.** [52] **And Jesus said unto him, Go thy way; thy faith hath made thee whole. And immediately he received his sight, and followed Jesus in the way.**

ACTS 3:6-8

Then Peter said, Silver and gold have I none; but such as I have give I thee: In the name of Jesus Christ of Nazareth rise up and walk. [7] **And he took him by the right hand, and lifted him up: and immediately his feet and ankle bones received strength.** [8] **And he leaping up stood, and walked, and entered with them into the temple, walking, and leaping, and praising God.**

JOHN 20:25

The other disciples therefore said unto him, We have seen the Lord. But he said unto them, Except I shall see in his hands the print of the nails, and put my finger into the print of the nails, and thrust my hand into his side, I will not believe.

JOHN 20:27-29

Then saith he to Thomas, Reach hither thy finger, and behold my hands; and reach hither thy hand, and thrust it into my side: and be not faithless, but believing. [28] **And Thomas answered and said unto him, My Lord and my**

God. [29] **Jesus saith unto him, Thomas, because thou hast seen me, thou hast believed: blessed are they that have not seen, and yet have believed.**

HEBREWS 4:12

For the word of God is quick, and powerful, and sharper than any twoedged sword, piercing even to the dividing asunder of soul and spirit, and of the joints and marrow, and is a discerner of the thoughts and intents of the heart.

Read with Your Heart
LESSON 10

I knew that God had awesome plans for my life and that there needed to be a tremendous amount of growth and change in me, but I just didn't know how to get started. I didn't know how to get from where I was to where I saw in my heart God wanted me to go. As I was seeking Him, the Lord specifically spoke the parables in Mark 4 to me. They made a profound impact on me and set me on a course. They actually gave me a track to run on. I still use them almost daily. They've become woven into the very fabric of my life.

On the same day that He ministered the parable of the sower, Jesus taught ten parables about how the kingdom of God works. This is actually the most recorded information in one day of the life of Jesus that we have in all of the Word of God. You can see this by taking all the scriptures from Matthew, Mark, Luke, and John, and putting them side by side chronologically, like they are in my *Life for Today Study Bible and Commentary:* the Gospels Edition. It's really helpful to be able to see all of the Gospel accounts of one event on one page.

> **And he began again to teach by the sea side: and there was gathered unto him a great multitude, so that he entered into a ship, and sat in the sea; and the whole multitude was by the sea on the land. And he taught them many things by parables, and said unto them in his doctrine.**
>
> **Mark 4:1-2**

Then Jesus began to teach what I call the parable of the sower sowing the seed.

> **Hearken; Behold, there went out a sower to sow: And it came to pass, as he sowed, some fell by the way side, and the fowls of the air came and devoured it up. And some fell on stony ground, where it had not much earth; and immediately it sprang up, because it had no depth of earth: But when the sun was up, it was scorched; and because it had no root, it withered away. And some fell among thorns, and the thorns grew up, and choked it, and it yielded no fruit. And other fell on good ground, and did yield fruit that sprang up and increased; and brought forth, some thirty, and some sixty, and some an hundred. And he said unto them, He that hath ears to hear, let him hear.**
>
> **Mark 4:3-9**

Four Types of Ground

Jesus gave this parable about a man who went out and sowed seed. He didn't dig furrows and plant the seeds one by one. Back then, a person would carry some kind of a sack that would have all of the seed in it. He would just walk through the fields, throwing the seed and letting it land anywhere and everywhere. According to the parable, there were basically four different types of ground that this seed fell on.

Verse 4 reveals the first type of ground by saying,

> **Some fell by the way side, and the fowls of the air came and devoured it up.**

In other words, the seed never even got below the surface of the ground. The birds came and ate it before it ever took root.

The seed did begin to get beneath the surface of the second type of ground, but there was too much rock (Mark 4:5-6). There was so much stone, there was no depth of earth, so the seed simply didn't produce properly.

The third type of ground had a good depth of earth. It began to produce, but there were weeds that choked the seed and prevented it from bearing fruit (Mark 4:7).

The fourth type of ground brought forth fruit—up to a one-hundred-fold return on the seed that was sown (Mark 4:8).

That's this parable in a nutshell.

Spiritually Dull

After Jesus gave the parable, His disciples came and asked Him for an interpretation. They thought this parable was just about someone sowing seed and how that seed germinates and produces fruit. They knew there had to be some spiritual application, but they didn't know what it was. So, they asked Him for the interpretation of this parable. They also asked Him, "Why do You speak to these people in parables?" (Matt. 13:10).

> **He answered and said unto them, Because it is given unto you to know the mysteries of the kingdom of heaven, but to them it is not given. For whosoever hath, to him shall be given, and he shall have more abundance: but whosoever hath not, from him shall be taken away even that he hath. Therefore speak I**

to them in parables: because they seeing see not; and hearing they hear not, neither do they understand.

Matthew 13:11-13

People have become so hardened toward God. They can't understand spiritual truth, because their thinking is so inconsistent with the way God intended it to be. They're spiritually dull.

For this people's heart is waxed gross, and their ears are dull of hearing, and their eyes they have closed; lest at any time they should see with their eyes, and hear with their ears, and should understand with their heart, and should be converted, and I should heal them.

Matthew 13:15

Although Jesus made this amazing statement to a group of people 2,000 years ago, it's also quite descriptive of our day and age. He said, **"This people's heart is waxed gross."** This is literally speaking of a step-by-step, incremental progression. A person's heart doesn't just instantly turn against God and become insensitive and unable to hear from Him; it's a process.

Spiritual Code

This word "waxed" literally refers to the way some wax candles are made. They take a wick and dip it into hot wax. They keep dipping it again and again, putting on layer upon layer of wax until they have a candle.

That's the way our hearts have become. Through a process of being dominated by the things of this world, we've become spiritually insensitive. These things don't even have to be ungodly. They can simply be natural things. We're just so focused on all of the tragedy, news, entertainment, etc., that layer after layer, we've insulated ourselves against spiritual thinking. We live and move in a physical world. Not many people really spend much time in the Word of God, in communion with Him, and allowing their hearts to listen and learn spiritual things. We've become so consumed with physical things that after a while, layer after layer of neglect accumulates and literally hinders the way we think.

So, one of the reasons the Lord taught in parables is because people's hearts have become so dull. They've "waxed gross." Their ears have become hard of hearing. They have eyes but can't see. The Lord can't speak to a lot of people today, because they're so carnal. There isn't any spiritual sensitivity in them that allows them to be able to receive.

Inside of every person, there's a spark. There's the potential for spiritual perception and receiving from God, but it must be developed. Since most people spend virtually no time focused on the things of the Lord, they've become spiritually dull. Because there's no way the Lord can speak plainly to such people, He puts spiritual truths in parables.

Jesus went on to say that these disciples had a special anointing from God that enabled them to decipher and learn these spiritual truths. This is the second purpose of the Lord speaking in parables. Parables were like a spiritual code: The truths were hidden from people who didn't have ears to hear. To those who didn't seek God and didn't have hearts for Him, parables seemed foolish, and they rejected them. But to those who have hearts for God, the Holy Spirit has been given to specifically decode and explain these truths.

> **But blessed are your eyes, for they see: and your ears, for they hear. For verily I say unto you, That many prophets and righteous men have desired to see those things which ye see, and have not seen them; and to hear those things which ye hear, and have not heard them. Hear ye therefore the parable of the sower.**
>
> **Matthew 13:16-18**

"What Does It Mean?"

Jesus was explaining that they had a special anointing. First John 2:20 says that...

> **...ye have an unction from the Holy One, and ye know all things.**

The Holy Spirit is sent to you specifically to teach you and explain things that you can't know with just your natural mind (John 14:26 and 16:13-15). The Lord used parables as physical, natural examples that people could understand. This was an agricultural society, so they were used to seeing people sow seed. In a sense, they lived close to the ground. Yet there were spiritual truths hidden behind and embedded within each parable that the Holy Spirit was intended to reveal.

The same is true today. Some of us ask, "Why was the Word written this way? Why didn't the Lord just record everything He wanted to say to us in a straightforward manner?" The truth is, we don't have the ability in our physical minds alone to understand the spiritual truths God is trying to communicate to us. He had to put them in this form. However, the Holy Spirit has been given to every one of us to explain the Word of God.

Many of you may come against the Word, criticizing it, and saying, "The Bible is hard to understand." That's because you're reading it with your mind. If you're trying to figure things out with just your peanut-sized brain, then yes, the Word of God would be difficult. However, the Bible wasn't written to your head. Now, that doesn't mean it's not logical. It doesn't mean it's incorrect or senseless. God's Word is different than the natural things this world teaches you. It wasn't written to your carnal, natural mind; the Lord wrote the Word of God to your heart.

You can read God's Word with your heart. As you read the Word, you may not understand with your peanut brain something you're reading. But as you come across something like this, you can stop and pray, "Father, I don't understand this. What does it mean?" Then you start meditating on that scripture, opening your heart to listen to Him, and saying from your heart, "I want to know You. I want to know what Your Word has to say." God—through His Word—will begin speaking to you.

The Rosetta Stone

Perhaps you've already experienced this before, so you know what I'm talking about. You may not be able to verbalize it any better than I have, but you recognize there are things you now know that are beyond just the words that you read on a page. It's what God spoke to you in your heart.

Or perhaps you haven't experienced this before, so you're struggling to understand.

One of the greatest things in my Christian life is the ability to take the Word of God and read it with my mind. Yet, at the same time that I'm looking at the pages, I go beyond just my mind, and I let my heart listen. God speaks to me. His Word comes alive. Life is literally pumped into me through the Bible. If you haven't experienced that, you're missing one of the greatest experiences of all.

This parable of the sower sowing the seed transformed my life. These truths that I'll be sharing with you in the rest of this Study Guide are some of the most foundational truths God has ever shown me. If the sower sowing the seed isn't one of your favorite passages—one that has just transformed your life—then you're missing out on one of the most important keys to the Christian life.

As a matter of fact, after Jesus gave this parable, His disciples asked, "What does this parable mean?" The Lord answered,

Know ye not this parable? and how then will ye know all parables?

Mark 4:13

Jesus was saying, "If you don't understand this parable, then you can't understand any of My parables. If you can't get the interpretation and application to your personal life of this parable, then you can't understand My teaching." In other words, this is critical. I call it the Rosetta Stone of the Bible.

The Key

For a long time, archaeologists excavated in Egypt. They found all kinds of Egyptian hieroglyphics, but they didn't have a key to unlock what those writings meant. Nobody knew the language. There was a tremendous amount of information recorded by the ancient Egyptians, but it was all in hieroglyphics that no one knew how to read.

Then one day, they found this stone, which later became known as the Rosetta Stone. It had the exact same text written in three different languages, including the Egyptian hieroglyphics. Using the two known languages recorded on this stone enabled them to understand the previously unknown hieroglyphics. This Rosetta Stone became the key that unlocked the entire language. Since then, they've been able to read and understand all of these records that the ancient Egyptians left us in hieroglyphics.

This parable of the sower sowing the seed is the Rosetta Stone of the Bible. Our Lord was saying, "Don't you understand this parable? If you don't comprehend this parable, how will you understand any of them?" This is the key to understanding all of the parables—all of the teachings—Jesus gave. Christ Himself declared, "This is the key. If you understand this parable, you can understand any of them. If you don't understand this parable, you won't understand any of them." That's powerful!

This parable is a foundational teaching of Jesus. It's something that everyone who wants to prosper in the kingdom of God must learn. These are fundamental, foundational truths that we must operate in and base our daily lives upon.

So, if the scriptures of the parable of the sower sowing the seed (Matt. 13, Mark 4, and Luke 8) aren't some of the most important scriptures in your life—scriptures from which God has spoken to you—then that's one reason you don't have clear understanding of the Bible. That's one reason you don't know how the kingdom of God works, and you're dependent on going to someone else and asking them for help. It's because you have no ability on your own to understand—you're dependent on other people who have developed themselves spiritually and learned how to relate to the Lord.

If you will learn these scriptures, they'll change your life. It's not hard to understand the things of God. The hardest thing is getting people to listen with their hearts. You may be saying, "Enough already. You've sold me. Get on with it, and tell me these truths!"

Read with Your Heart
LESSON 10 – OUTLINE

I. I knew that God had awesome plans for my life and that there needed to be a tremendous amount of growth and change in me, but I just didn't know how to get started.

   A. As I was seeking Him, the Lord specifically spoke the parables in Mark 4 to me.

   B. They made a profound impact on me and set me on a course.

   C. I still use them almost daily.

   D. They've become woven into the very fabric of my life.

II. Jesus gave this parable about a man who went out and sowed seed (Mark 4:1-9).

   A. The disciples asked Jesus, "Why do You speak to these people in parables?"

   B. He said, **"This people's heart is waxed gross"** (Matt. 13:15).

   C. This is literally speaking of a step-by-step, incremental progression.

   D. A person's heart doesn't just instantly turn against God and become insensitive and unable to hear from Him; it's a process.

   E. Their ears have become hard of hearing.

   F. They have eyes but can't see.

   G. Inside of every person, there's the potential for spiritual perception and receiving from God, but it must be developed.

   H. Since most people spend virtually no time focused on the things of the Lord, they've become spiritually dull.

   I. Because there's no way the Lord can speak plainly to such people, He puts spiritual truths in parables.

III. Jesus went on to say that these disciples had a special anointing from God that enabled them to decipher and learn these spiritual truths (Matt. 13:16-18).

   A. This is the second purpose of the Lord speaking in parables.

B. Parables were like a spiritual code: To those who didn't seek God and didn't have hearts for Him, parables seemed foolish, and they rejected them. But to those who have hearts for God, the Holy Spirit has been given to specifically decode and explain these truths.

C. The Holy Spirit is sent to you specifically to teach you and explain things that you can't know with just your natural mind (John 14:26 and 16:13-15).

D. There were spiritual truths hidden behind and embedded within each parable that the Holy Spirit was intended to reveal.

IV. Many of you may come against the Word, criticizing it, and saying, "The Bible is hard to understand."

A. That's because you're reading it with your mind.

B. The Lord wrote the Word of God to your heart.

C. As you read the Word, you may not understand with your peanut brain something you're reading.

D. But you can stop and pray, "Father, I don't understand this. What does it mean?"

E. Then you start meditating on that scripture, opening your heart to listen to Him, and saying from your heart, "I want to know You. I want to know what Your Word has to say."

F. God—through His Word—will begin speaking to you.

V. One of the greatest things in my Christian life is the ability to take the Word of God and read it with my mind.

A. Yet, at the same time that I'm looking at the pages, I go beyond just my mind, and I let my heart listen.

B. God speaks to me.

C. His Word comes alive.

D. Life is literally pumped into me through the Bible.

E. If you haven't experienced that, you're missing one of the greatest experiences of all.

VI. If the sower sowing the seed isn't one of your favorite passages—one that has just transformed your life—then you're missing out on one of the most important keys to the Christian life.

> **Know ye not this parable? and how then will ye know all parables?**
>
> **Mark 4:13**

A. Jesus was saying, "If you don't understand this parable, then you can't understand any of My parables. If you can't get the interpretation and application to your personal life of this parable, then you can't understand My teaching."

B. Christ Himself declared, "This is the key. If you understand this parable, you can understand any of them."

C. That's powerful!

VII. So, if the scriptures of the parable of the sower sowing the seed (Matt. 13, Mark 4, and Luke 8) aren't some of the most important scriptures in your life—scriptures from which God has spoken to you—then that's one reason you don't have clear understanding of the Bible.

A. That's one reason you don't know how the kingdom of God works, and you're dependent on going to someone else and asking them for help.

B. It's because you have no ability on your own to understand.

C. It's not hard to understand the things of God.

D. The hardest thing is getting people to listen with their hearts.

Read with Your Heart
LESSON 10 – TEACHER'S GUIDE

1. I knew that God had awesome plans for my life and that there needed to be a tremendous amount of growth and change in me, but I just didn't know how to get started. As I was seeking Him, the Lord specifically spoke the parables in Mark 4 to me. They made a profound impact on me and set me on a course. I still use them almost daily. They've become woven into the very fabric of my life.

2. Jesus gave this parable about a man who went out and sowed seed (Mark 4:1-9). The disciples asked Jesus, "Why do You speak to these people in parables?" He said, **"This people's heart is waxed gross"** (Matt. 13:15). This is literally speaking of a step-by-step, incremental progression. A person's heart doesn't just instantly turn against God and become insensitive and unable to hear from Him; it's a process. Their ears have become hard of hearing. They have eyes but can't see. Inside of every person, there's the potential for spiritual perception and receiving from God, but it must be developed. Since most people spend virtually no time focused on the things of the Lord, they've become spiritually dull. Because there's no way the Lord can speak plainly to such people, He puts spiritual truths in parables.

3. Jesus went on to say that these disciples had a special anointing from God that enabled them to decipher and learn these spiritual truths (Matt. 13:16-18). This is the second purpose of the Lord speaking in parables. Parables were like a spiritual code: To those who didn't seek God and didn't have hearts for Him, parables seemed foolish, and they rejected them. But to those who have hearts for God, the Holy Spirit has been given to specifically decode and explain these truths. The Holy Spirit is sent to us specifically to teach us and explain things that we can't know with just our natural minds (John 14:26 and 16:13-15). There were spiritual truths hidden behind and embedded within each parable that the Holy Spirit was intended to reveal.

1. What has become woven into the very fabric of Andrew's life? (The parables of Mark 4)
2. A. Read Matthew 13:15. What is a process? (A person's heart turning against God and becoming insensitive and unable to hear from Him)
   B. Why does the Lord put spiritual truths in parables for most people? (Because there's no way He can speak to them)
3. A. Read Matthew 13:16-18. What is the second purpose of the Lord speaking in parables? (So that Holy Spirit could decode and explain these truths to those who have hearts for God)
   B. What are hidden behind and embedded within each parable? (Spiritual truths that the Holy Spirit was intended to reveal)

4. Many of us may come against the Word, criticizing it, and saying, "The Bible is hard to understand." That's because we're reading it with our minds. The Lord wrote the Word of God to our hearts. As we read the Word, we may not understand with our peanut brains something we're reading. But we can stop and pray, "Father, I don't understand this. What does it mean?" Then we start meditating on that scripture, opening our hearts to listen to Him, and saying from our hearts, "I want to know You. I want to know what Your Word has to say." God—through His Word—will begin speaking to us.

5. One of the greatest things in my Christian life is the ability to take the Word of God and read it with my mind. Yet, at the same time that I'm looking at the pages, I go beyond just my mind, and I let my heart listen. God speaks to me. His Word comes alive. Life is literally pumped into me through the Bible. If we haven't experienced that, we're missing one of the greatest experiences of all.

6. If the sower sowing the seed isn't one of our favorite passages—one that has just transformed our lives—then we're missing out on one of the most important keys to the Christian life. Jesus was saying, "If you don't understand this parable, then you can't understand any of My parables. If you can't get the interpretation and application to your personal life of this parable, then you can't understand My teaching" (Mark 4:13). Christ Himself declared, "This is the key. If you understand this parable, you can understand any of them." That's powerful!

7. So, if the scriptures of the parable of the sower sowing the seed (Matt. 13, Mark 4, and Luke 8) aren't some of the most important scriptures in our lives—scriptures from which God has spoken to us—then that's one reason we don't have clear understanding of the Bible. That's one reason we don't know how the kingdom of God works, and we're dependent on going to someone else and asking them for help. It's because we have no ability on our own to understand. It's not hard to understand the things of God. The hardest thing is getting people to listen with their hearts.

4. A. The Bible is hard to understand when we read it with our _____. (Minds)
   B. What did the Lord write the Word of God to? (Our hearts)
   C. When we start meditating on a scripture, opening our hearts to listen to God, and saying from our hearts "I want to know You. I want to know what Your Word has to say," what will happen? (God—through His Word—will begin speaking to us)
5. A. What does Andrew do besides read the Word of God with his mind? (He lets his heart listen)
   B. What comes alive as a result? (The Word)
   C. If we haven't experienced that, what are we missing? (One of the greatest experiences of all)
6. A. Read Mark 4:13. What was Jesus saying? ("If you don't understand this parable, then you can't understand any of My parables. If you can't get the interpretation and application to your personal life of this parable, then you can't understand My teaching")
   B. What did Christ declare? ("This is the key. If you understand this parable, you can understand any of them")
7. A. If the scriptures of the parable of the sower sowing the seed (Matt. 13, Mark 4, and Luke 8) aren't some of the most important scriptures in our lives—scriptures from which God has spoken to us—that is what? (It's one reason we don't have clear understanding of the Bible)
   B. What is the hardest thing to do with people? (Get them to listen with their hearts)

Read with Your Heart
LESSON 10 – DISCIPLESHIP QUESTIONS

1. Read Mark 4:1-9. Jesus taught the people many things by what?
   A. The seaside
   B. Parables
   C. The temple
   D. A. and B.
   E. B. and C.

2. What did the fowls of the air devour?

3. What happened to the seed sown on the stony ground?

4. What did the thorns do to the plant?

5. What happened after the seed fell on the good ground?

6. Read Matthew 13:10-13. To whom was it given to know the mysteries of the kingdom of God?

7. What will happen to the person who has?

8. What will happen to the person who does not have?

9. According to Matthew 13:15-18, what are you supposed to do with your heart?

10. Who desired to see and hear the things the disciples did?

11. According to 1 John 2:20, you have an _____ from the Holy One.

12. Read John 14:26. What shall the Holy Spirit teach you?

13. What shall He bring to your remembrance?

14. According to John 16:13-15, what will the Spirit of Truth guide you into?
    A. All circumstances
    B. All emotion
    C. All facts
    D. All truth
    E. All power

15. Whom will He glorify?

16. Read Mark 4:13. Jesus expected His disciples to _____ this parable.

Read with Your Heart
LESSON 10 – ANSWER KEY

1. D. A. and B.

2. The seed by the wayside

3. It sprang up immediately because it had no depth of earth, but when the sun was up, the plant was scorched and, because it had no root, withered away

4. They grew up and choked it, and the plant yielded no fruit

5. The plant sprang up, increased, and brought forth fruit—some thirty, some sixty, and some a hundred

6. The disciples

7. To them shall be given, and they shall have more in abundance

8. Even what they have shall be taken away

9. Understand

10. Many prophets and righteous men

11. Unction

12. All things

13. What Jesus has said

14. D. All truth

15. Jesus

16. Know

Read with Your Heart
LESSON 10 – SCRIPTURES

MARK 4:1-9
And he began again to teach by the sea side: and there was gathered unto him a great multitude, so that he entered into a ship, and sat in the sea; and the whole multitude was by the sea on the land. [2] And he taught them many things by parables, and said unto them in his doctrine, [3] Hearken; Behold, there went out a sower to sow: [4] And it came to pass, as he sowed, some fell by the way side, and the fowls of the air came and devoured it up. [5] And some fell on stony ground, where it had not much earth; and immediately it sprang up, because it had no depth of earth: [6] But when the sun was up, it was scorched; and because it had no root, it withered away. [7] And some fell among thorns, and the thorns grew up, and choked it, and it yielded no fruit. [8] And other fell on good ground, and did yield fruit that sprang up and increased; and brought forth, some thirty, and some sixty, and some an hundred. [9] And he said unto them, He that hath ears to hear, let him hear.

MATTHEW 13:10-13
And the disciples came, and said unto him, Why speakest thou unto them in parables? [11] He answered and said unto them, Because it is given unto you to know the mysteries of the kingdom of heaven, but to them it is not given. [12] For whosoever hath, to him shall be given, and he shall have more abundance: but whosoever hath not, from him shall be taken away even that he hath. [13] Therefore speak I to them in parables: because they seeing see not; and hearing they hear not, neither do they understand.

MATTHEW 13:15-18
For this people's heart is waxed gross, and their ears are dull of hearing, and their eyes they have closed; lest at any time they should see with their eyes, and hear with their ears, and should understand with their heart, and should be converted, and I should heal them. [16] But blessed are your eyes, for they see: and your ears, for they hear. [17] For verily I say unto you, That many prophets and righteous men have desired to see those things which ye see, and have not seen them; and to hear those things which ye hear, and have not heard them. [18] Hear ye therefore the parable of the sower.

1 JOHN 2:20
But ye have an unction from the Holy One, and ye know all things.

JOHN 14:26
But the Comforter, which is the Holy Ghost, whom the Father will send in my name, he shall teach you all things, and bring all things to your remembrance, whatsoever I have said unto you.

JOHN 16:13-15
Howbeit when he, the Spirit of truth, is come, he will guide you into all truth: for he shall not speak of himself; but whatsoever he shall hear, that shall he speak: and he will shew you things to come. [14] He shall glorify me: for he shall receive of mine, and shall shew it unto you. [15] All things that the Father hath are mine: therefore said I, that he shall take of mine, and shall shew it unto you.

MARK 4:13
And he said unto them, Know ye not this parable? and how then will ye know all parables?

The Seed
LESSON 11

Jesus interpreted the parable of the sower for His disciples, saying,

> **The sower soweth the word. And these are they by the way side, where the word is sown; but when they have heard, Satan cometh immediately, and taketh away the word that was sown in their hearts. And these are they likewise which are sown on stony ground; who, when they have heard the word, immediately receive it with gladness; And have no root in themselves, and so endure but for a time: afterward, when affliction or persecution ariseth for the word's sake, immediately they are offended. And these are they which are sown among thorns; such as hear the word, And the cares of this world, and the deceitfulness of riches, and the lusts of other things entering in, choke the word, and it becometh unfruitful. And these are they which are sown on good ground; such as hear the word, and receive it, and bring forth fruit, some thirtyfold, some sixty, and some an hundred.**
>
> **Mark 4:14-20**

Jesus was talking about a man who took seed and started throwing it everywhere. (That's the way they sowed seed in those days.) As he threw this seed, it landed on four different types of ground. He continued talking about how these four different types of ground responded by allowing seed to germinate or not. That's what the parable is about.

Simple

The real purpose of this parable isn't to teach you how to sow seed or be a farmer; Jesus simply took something natural that we could relate to and used it to illustrate a spiritual truth.

Mark 4:14 is the key to this entire parable:

> **The sower soweth the word.**

Luke 8:11 communicates it this way:

> **Now the parable is this: The seed is the word of God.**

The seed being sown is the Word of God. So, this whole parable isn't really about how to be a farmer and get a crop; it's about how the kingdom of God works, and it works off of the Word of God.

People are always looking for something deeper and more complex, but this is so simple that you're going to have to have somebody help you misunderstand it. The whole kingdom of God—the Christian life, your victory, your success as a believer—is as simple as taking the Word of God and sowing it in your heart. If you will just cooperate with it and let the Word of God germinate, you will change effortlessly.

Disappointed and Surprised

There are very specific reasons that Jesus chose to use a seed to illustrate the way the Word of God works. That's because there is a great comparison between the way a physical seed operates in the natural realm and the way God's Word works in your life.

In the natural realm, we'd call anyone "crazy" who expects a garden to grow without the ground being tilled or seeds being planted or watered. If we didn't do any of these necessary things to grow a garden, we wouldn't be surprised when a garden doesn't grow. Yet, in the spiritual realm, people are constantly surprised at this outcome.

People who never planted any seeds are disappointed and surprised that they don't have a garden. They wonder, *Why am I not healed? How come I haven't been prospered? Why hasn't God answered this prayer? How come my relationships are falling apart? Why can't I hold down a job? How come nothing in my life ever seems to work?* They've been praying and asking God, but they haven't taken His Word and the promises therein and sown those truths in their lives.

Many of these people have come to me and said, "I prayed and asked God to heal me." I've asked them, "What scriptures are you standing on for being healed? What promise or promises—seed from God's Word—have you sown into your life to produce that healing?"

They've answered, "I don't know what the Word says; I just know it's God's will. I believe that God wants to heal me." But they don't have a scripture to stand on. They don't have a promise. They haven't sown His Word into their hearts.

Physical Healing Promised

There's benefit in knowing the addresses of promises in the Word of God. For instance, Isaiah 53:4-5 says,

Surely he hath borne our griefs, and carried our sorrows: yet we did esteem him stricken, smitten of God, and afflicted. But he was wounded for our transgressions, he was bruised for our iniquities: the chastisement of our peace was upon him; and with his stripes we are healed.

Then in Matthew 8:16-17, this is interpreted:

When the even was come, they brought unto him many that were possessed with devils: and he cast out the spirits with his word, and healed all that were sick: That it might be fulfilled which was spoken by Esaias [Isaiah] **the prophet, saying, Himself took our infirmities, and bare our sicknesses.**

Brackets mine

This reveals that Isaiah wasn't just talking about a spiritual, emotional type of healing. Since what Jesus did in Matthew 8 fulfilled what Isaiah 53 prophesied, it's clear that we've also been promised physical healing through His Atonement.

Number-One Reason

It's important to know where those verses are because it helps you. Specifically, it helps you to be able to share these truths with other people.

However, I will compromise on this point. You may not know the exact place in Scripture. You may not have the address memorized. You may have to refresh your memory and look something up. But those truths—those revelations—ought to be yours.

When you have symptoms of sickness in your body and you're lying on your bed, ready to puke your guts out, it's not sufficient to cry out to God, saying, "I know that somewhere in the Bible, it says that You want to heal me." That's not the way the kingdom works. That's like a person who hasn't planted a garden but is praying for a harvest. It's not going to happen.

The number-one reason people aren't receiving from God is because they literally haven't taken the truths of His Word and planted them in their hearts. This is why people aren't experiencing the victory they are praying for and desiring, and begging and pleading with God to give them. This is why the Lord used this kind of a parable. He wants you to understand how His kingdom works. The sower sows the Word of God. The seed He's talking about is not a physical seed. Rather, the Word of God is like a seed.

If you want healing in your life, take the scriptures that talk about healing and meditate on them. Look up every scripture in the Bible on healing. Study the examples where people were healed.

Tight, but Right

Proverbs 4:22 says that God's words are...

> **...life unto those that find them, and health to all their flesh.**

If you'll take God's Word like a seed and begin to plant it in your heart, it will literally start releasing supernatural healing into your life.

Psalm 107:20 says that God...

> **Sent his word, and healed them, and delivered them from their destructions.**

God's Word will bring healing and deliverance to you.

I'm not scolding anyone. I'm just trying to be forceful with this because so many people are missing it big time. The kingdom of God works from this truth that the Word of God is a seed.

Just like in the natural realm, you must plant seeds to produce a crop. You can't have a forest without planting many seeds. You can't have victory in your life without the Word of God being planted in your heart. That's tight, but it's right. It's simple, but it's true. This is how the kingdom of God works.

Quality and Quantity

If you humble yourself and receive this truth, it would provide you with an answer to why you aren't seeing more victory in your life than you are. It's why you aren't seeing more of the power of God work. The average person isn't meditating in the Word of God. They aren't spending time—both quality and quantity amounts of time—in God's Word. The average person doesn't have a good understanding of the Word of God.

I can say that because I deal with thousands of people on a regular basis. Nearly every person comes to me with their sad story. I'm not trying to demean or make fun of anyone. Yet they come to me, crying and complaining. You could take their knowledge of God's Word and put it in a thimble, and it would be nearly empty. They don't know what the Word of God says. Or they might say, "My pastor said..." or "I believe the Bible says this somewhere." That's not going to get you healed! The Word of God must beome revelation to you. It has to be alive in you. You have to take the promises like a seed, plant them in your heart, and meditate on them to see the Word of God work.

You're wondering, *Why isn't God answering my prayer?* He's given us these seeds! That's like someone praying over their ground and saying, "God, how come You haven't let this garden grow?" You didn't plant the seeds!

God has established natural laws, and He's not going to break them. He's also established spiritual laws, and He won't break them either. The Lord has sent His Word and healed us and delivered us from all our destructions (Ps. 107:20). All through the Word are promises revealing God as our Healer and Provider and how He wants to prosper us, but to see His healing and provision, we must take God's Word and start planting it in our lives.

One reason the Lord used this parable about a man sowing seed is because the process of germination is a natural system, not a social system. Social—man-made or man-operated—systems can be broken or manipulated. Most of us have been through school, but we didn't really study for our tests the way we should. We goofed off with our friends and waited until the last minute. Then, the night before the exam, we stayed up all night and crammed for the final. We were able to pass the test, get a grade, and graduate, but we broke the system. We didn't learn the material. It's not retained in our long-term memory. We just circumvented things. But we can't do that with a natural system.

"I Don't Understand!"

A certain man who attended a Bible study I used to hold was probably one of the worst sinners in that whole county. He was a drunk and a womanizer. He did anything and everything. Then he was miraculously born again and baptized in the Holy Spirit. Just as much as he had served the devil, he turned around and served God with all his heart. Everybody in this county was aware of what had happened to this man. He couldn't go anywhere—the post office, grocery store, or gas station—without people recognizing the transformation. So, he had many opportunities to be a witness. He started talking to everybody about the Lord. This man opened his home and had me come in to teach the Word. Sixty or seventy people were coming to this Bible study just to see the change in this man.

This brother had tremendous zeal, but he made some serious mistakes because he didn't have very much knowledge of the Word. He started traveling and giving his testimony in many different meetings on top of all he was doing in his church. So, he just didn't have time to plant his crops the way he normally did. This guy owned so much land that he counted it in sections. Each section was 640 acres. He didn't have time to plant his wheat crop, because he was too busy giving his testimony for the Lord and being a witness to people. Since his desire and heart was right—he was loving the Lord, and all these things were good—this fellow just supposed that God would supernaturally bless him with a crop even though he didn't take time to sow it.

Finally, it was about three weeks or so before everybody else harvested their crops. Their wheat was up, had already started turning golden in color, and they were getting ready to harvest. About that time, this man went out and borrowed $500,000 to buy wheat seed. (That will tell you how much land he had to plant!) He spent weeks planting half a million dollars' worth of wheat just days before the harvest was supposed to come. He thought that God would just grant him a supernatural harvest because he had been out doing "the Lord's work."

Of course, it didn't happen. He lost all of this money he'd spent. He was in jeopardy of going bankrupt. This man came to me, wanting prayer. He was angry, saying, "I don't understand why God didn't give me this harvest!"

I had to tell him, "That isn't the way the kingdom works. You have to plant your seed at a certain time and give it time to grow and mature. These are just natural laws."

He countered, saying, "I know that's the way it works. I've been doing this for years. But I thought that since I was in the spirit, things would just work differently."

Learn and Cooperate

This man was just verbalizing what many people think. They think in the natural realm that they're bound by these physical, natural laws, and certain things have to happen. But in the spiritual realm, they just think that if they're sincere, really in need, and mean it with all of their hearts, they can expect positive results to come.

This parable says that in the same way there are laws that govern how a physical, natural seed has to be planted and germinate, there are laws that govern the spiritual realm. One of these laws is that the Word of God is a seed. If you want results in your life, you must plant the Word of God in your heart. If you desire certain kingdom fruit in your marriage, relationships, finances, health, emotions—whatever you need—take the seeds (promises in God's Word that speak about those specific things) and plant them in your life. If you will give them the proper nourishment and take care of them the way this parable tells you to, then it's inevitable that you will reap the fruit you want. This is so simple that you have to have somebody help you misunderstand it!

However, most people don't follow this pattern. They wait until they're already in a crisis situation and then pray, wanting God to pull them out by a miracle. They get offended, upset, and fall into disbelief if they don't see the right results. Pardon me for being blunt, but that's just as stupid as the farmer who waits to plant their crop a week before it's due to harvest, and then gets upset with God because "the laws didn't work."

No, there's nothing wrong with the natural laws; you just have to cooperate with them. There's nothing wrong with the spiritual laws either; you just have to learn what they are and cooperate with them.

If I want results in my life, I go to the Word of God. I take seeds—promises that talk about the fruit I want to produce—and I start meditating on them. Over time, it comes to pass, and I receive the harvest. That's one of the truths this parable teaches.

The Seed
LESSON 11 – OUTLINE

I. Jesus interpreted the parable of the sower for His disciples.

A. The seed being sown is the Word of God (Mark 4:14).

B. So, this whole parable isn't really about how to be a farmer and get a crop; it's about how the kingdom of God works, and it works off of the Word of God.

C. The whole kingdom of God—the Christian life, your victory, your success as a believer—is as simple as taking the Word of God and sowing it in your heart.

D. If you will just cooperate with it and let the Word of God germinate, you will change effortlessly.

II. If we didn't do any necessary things to grow a garden, we wouldn't be surprised when a garden doesn't grow.

A. Yet, in the spiritual realm, people are constantly surprised at this outcome.

B. They've been praying and asking God, but they haven't taken His Word and the promises therein and sown those truths in their lives.

C. They don't have a scripture to stand on.

D. They don't have a promise.

III. There's benefit in knowing the addresses of promises in the Word of God.

A. Specifically, it helps you to be able to share these truths with other people.

B. You may have to refresh your memory and look something up.

C. But those truths—those revelations—ought to be yours.

D. When you have symptoms of sickness in your body and you're lying on your bed, ready to puke your guts out, it's not sufficient to cry out to God, saying, "I know that somewhere in the Bible, it says that You want to heal me."

IV. I'm just trying to be forceful with this because so many people are missing it big time.

A. The average person isn't meditating in the Word of God.

B. They aren't spending time—both quality and quantity amounts of time—in God's Word.

C. The average person doesn't have a good understanding of the Word of God.

D. Or they might say, "My pastor said..." or "I believe the Bible says this somewhere."

E. The Word of God must become revelation to you.

F. It has to be alive in you.

G. You have to take the promises like a seed, plant them in your heart, and meditate on them to see the Word of God work.

V. God has established spiritual laws, and He won't break them.

A. One reason the Lord used this parable about a man sowing seed is because the process of germination is a natural system, not a social system that can be broken or manipulated.

B. This parable says that in the same way there are laws that govern how a physical, natural seed has to be planted and germinate, there are laws that govern the spiritual realm.

C. If you desire certain kingdom fruit in your marriage, relationships, finances, health, emotions—whatever you need—take the seeds (promises in God's Word that speak about those specific things) and plant them in your life.

D. If you will give them the proper nourishment and take care of them the way this parable tells you to, then it's inevitable that you will reap the fruit you want.

E. This is so simple that you have to have somebody help you misunderstand it!

VI. Most people don't follow this pattern.

A. They wait until they're already in a crisis situation and then pray, wanting God to pull them out by a miracle.

B. Pardon me for being blunt, but that's just as stupid as the farmer who waits to plant their crop a week before it's due to harvest, and then gets upset with God because "the laws didn't work."

C. There's nothing wrong with the spiritual laws; you just have to learn what they are and cooperate with them.

D. That's one of the truths this parable teaches.

The Seed
LESSON 11 – TEACHER'S GUIDE

1. Jesus interpreted the parable of the sower for His disciples. The seed being sown is the Word of God (Mark 4:14). So, this whole parable isn't really about how to be a farmer and get a crop; it's about how the kingdom of God works, and it works off of the Word of God. The whole kingdom of God—the Christian life, our victory, our success as believers—is as simple as taking the Word of God and sowing it in our hearts. If we will just cooperate with it and let the Word of God germinate, we will change effortlessly.

2. If we didn't do any necessary things to grow a garden, we wouldn't be surprised when a garden doesn't grow. Yet, in the spiritual realm, people are constantly surprised at this outcome. They've been praying and asking God, but they haven't taken His Word and the promises therein and sown those truths in their lives. They don't have a scripture to stand on. They don't have a promise.

3. There's benefit in knowing the addresses of promises in the Word of God. Specifically, it helps us to be able to share these truths with other people. We may have to refresh our memories and look something up. But those truths—those revelations—ought to be ours. When we have symptoms of sickness in our bodies and we're lying on our beds, ready to puke our guts out, it's not sufficient to cry out to God, saying, "I know that somewhere in the Bible, it says that You want to heal me."

1. A. Read Mark 4:14. In the parable of the sower, what is the Word of God? (The seed)
   B. What is as simple as taking the Word of God and sowing it in our hearts? (The kingdom of God—the Christian life, our victory, our success as believers)
2. A. If we didn't do any necessary things to grow a garden, what wouldn't we be surprised at? (That a garden didn't grow)
   B. Yet, in the spiritual realm, what are people? (Constantly surprised at this outcome)
3. A. What is there benefit in? (Knowing the addresses of the promises in the Word of God)
   B. What ought to be ours? (Those truths—those revelations)

4. I'm just trying to be forceful with this because so many people are missing it big time. The average person isn't meditating in the Word of God. They aren't spending time—both quality and quantity amounts of time—in God's Word. The average person doesn't have a good understanding of the Word of God. Or they might say, "My pastor said…" or "I believe the Bible says this somewhere." The Word of God must become revelation to us. It has to be alive in us. We have to take the promises like a seed, plant them in our hearts, and meditate on them to see the Word of God work.

5. God has established spiritual laws, and He won't break them. One reason the Lord used this parable about a man sowing seed is because the process of germination is a natural system, not a social system that can be broken or manipulated. This parable says that in the same way there are laws that govern how a physical, natural seed has to be planted and germinate, there are laws that govern the spiritual realm. If we desire certain kingdom fruit in our marriages, relationships, finances, health, emotions—whatever we need—we need to take the seeds (promises in God's Word that speak about those specific things) and plant them in our lives. If we will give them the proper nourishment and take care of them the way this parable tells us to, then it's inevitable that we will reap the fruit we want. This is so simple that we have to have somebody help us misunderstand it!

6. Most people don't follow this pattern. They wait until they're already in a crisis situation and then pray, wanting God to pull them out by a miracle. Pardon me for being blunt, but that's just as stupid as the farmer who waits to plant their crop a week before it's due to harvest, and then gets upset with God because "the laws didn't work." There's nothing wrong with the spiritual laws; we just have to learn what they are and cooperate with them. That's one of the truths this parable teaches.

4. A. The Word of God must become _____ to us. (Revelation)
   B. What do we have to do? (We have to take the promises like a seed, plant them in our hearts, and meditate on them to see the Word of God work)
5. A. If we desire fruit in our marriages, relationships, finances, health, emotions—whatever we need—what do we need to do? (We need to take the seeds [promises in God's Word that speak about those specific things] and plant them in our lives)
   B. What will happen if we will give them the proper nourishment and take care of them the way this parable tells us to? (Then it's inevitable that we will reap the fruit we want)
6. A. What do most people do? (They wait until they're already in a crisis situation and then pray, wanting God to pull them out by a miracle)
   B. There's nothing wrong with the spiritual laws, but what do we have to do? (Learn what they are and cooperate with them)

The Seed
LESSON 11 – ADDITIONAL INFORMATION

For more scriptures concerning healing, please refer to the "Healing Scriptures" audio CD or the section entitled "Is It Always God's Will to Heal?" located in the back of my book and **Study Guide** *God Wants You Well.*

The Seed
LESSON 11 – DISCIPLESHIP QUESTIONS

1. Read Mark 4:14-20. What happens where the Word is sown by the wayside?

2. Why are those offended who represent the stony ground?

3. What chokes the Word in those among the thorns?

4. Read Luke 8:11. The seed is the _____ of God.
   A. Letter
   B. Spirit
   C. Word
   D. All of the above
   E. None of the above

5. According to Isaiah 53:4-5, even though Jesus bore our griefs and carried our sorrows, what did we do?

6. **"But he was wounded for _____ transgressions."**

7. With what are we healed?

8. According to Matthew 8:16-17, Jesus cast out the spirits with what?

9. He healed _____ that were sick.

10. By this, Jesus fulfilled the prophecy from which book?

11. According to Proverbs 4:22, if you find God's words, what are they?

12. Read Psalm 107:20. What two things did God do for you?
    A. Blessed and cursed me
    B. Healed and delivered me
    C. Smote and spurned me
    D. Afflicted and wounded me
    E. Gave and took away from me

The Seed
LESSON 11 – ANSWER KEY

1. Satan comes immediately and takes away the Word that was sown in their hearts
2. Because affliction and persecution arose for the Word's sake in their lives
3. The cares of this world, the deceitfulness of riches, and the lusts of other things
4. C. Word
5. We esteemed Him stricken, smitten of God, and afflicted
6. **"Our"**
7. His stripes
8. His word
9. All
10. Isaiah
11. Life and health to all my flesh
12. B. Healed and delivered

The Seed
LESSON 11 – SCRIPTURES

MARK 4:14-20

The sower soweth the word. [15] And these are they by the way side, where the word is sown; but when they have heard, Satan cometh immediately, and taketh away the word that was sown in their hearts. [16] And these are they likewise which are sown on stony ground; who, when they have heard the word, immediately receive it with gladness; [17] And have no root in themselves, and so endure but for a time: afterward, when affliction or persecution ariseth for the word's sake, immediately they are offended. [18] And these are they which are sown among thorns; such as hear the word, [19] And the cares of this world, and the deceitfulness of riches, and the lusts of other things entering in, choke the word, and it becometh unfruitful. [20] And these are they which are sown on good ground; such as hear the word, and receive it, and bring forth fruit, some thirtyfold, some sixty, and some an hundred.

LUKE 8:11

Now the parable is this: The seed is the word of God.

ISAIAH 53:4-5

Surely he hath borne our griefs, and carried our sorrows: yet we did esteem him stricken, smitten of God, and afflicted. [5] But he was wounded for our transgressions, he was bruised for our iniquities: the chastisement of our peace was upon him; and with his stripes we are healed.

MATTHEW 8:16-17

When the even was come, they brought unto him many that were possessed with devils: and he cast out the spirits with his word, and healed all that were sick: [17] That it might be fulfilled which was spoken by Esaias the prophet, saying, Himself took our infirmities, and bare our sicknesses.

PROVERBS 4:22

For they are life unto those that find them, and health to all their flesh.

PSALM 107:20

He sent his word, and healed them, and delivered them from their destructions.

Understanding
LESSON 12

The seed produces the fruit, not the ground. It's the Word that brings forth the results. This was one of the first truths God ministered to me out of this parable of the sower sowing the seed.

Now, the ground does have a part to play. It can either allow the seed to produce to its fullest potential, or it can hinder, choke, and stop the Word of God from working. However, it's not the ground itself that produces the fruit; it's the seed.

Dirt

We are the ground. With our hearts, we can either allow the Word of God to have its complete rule, or we can let the Word be choked by the cares of this life, the deceitfulness of riches, and the lust for other things. Our hearts can become hardened toward God to not give His seed a place to germinate. Our hearts can do those things, but it's the seed—the Word of God—that brings forth fruit. All I am is the ground (Gen. 2:7). I'm just dirt—a place for the seed to germinate. I provide warmth and nutrients, but it's the Word that produces the fruit.

I may not have all of the natural things that other people have going for them—the education, the talents, the personality, or good looks—but it's the Word of God that will change my life and other people's lives through my ministry. God revealed this truth to me through this parable, and it continues impacting me deeply to this day.

That's why my radio and television programs are the way they are. We come on with a ten- or twenty-second tease in the beginning where I introduce the subject for the day. Then we have ten seconds of time where my wife and I are walking through the aspen trees while the announcer says, "Welcome to *Gospel Truth*." And within thirty seconds, you're getting the Word of God. I'm talking the Word, quoting Scripture, and teaching what the Word of God says. I'm not saying this to compare myself with or to criticize others; I'm just saying that the Lord has given me this revelation that it's not who I am, what I look like, or any of these other natural things; it's the Word of God that changes people's lives.

It's the same in my monthly letters, teaching articles, and books. Everything I put out is chock full of the Word of God. If you poke me, God's Word comes out. Everything in my life is centered on the Word of God, and it's working.

This is the attitude this parable teaches. The Word of God has to be planted in your heart for you to effectively change. If you would do it that way, change is as normal and natural as when a seed is planted in the ground and grows up. If you would take the Word of God and meditate in it day and night, it would change you. The Word would transform your life.

Hearts

In the parable of the sower, the four different types of ground where the seed was sown correspond to four different types of people's hearts. The Word of God has to be sown in your heart. The ground is representative of your heart. Out of these four different types of ground, only one really began to produce fruit.

It's estimated that in most churches, it's only about 25 percent of the people that do all of the giving and serving that make the church work. Three-fourths of the people just come, watch, and partake of the ministry being given, but they aren't actual players in the kingdom of God. This would correspond directly to what this parable is teaching. One in four types of people that had the Word sown in their hearts actually begins to produce fruit.

I've observed the same thing happening in my Bible college. About 25 percent of the people really take the Word of God to heart and go out and change their world with it. Now, many more people graduate and go out and affect the world to some degree. But here at Charis Bible College, it's about one in four that this experience and teaching just changes their life, and then they go out and change other people's lives through God's Word as well.

I would venture to say that this is about the same in any organization: It's about 25 percent of the people who really carry the load and make things work.

Although only 25 percent of the seed that was sown actually brought forth fruit, it wasn't the seed that was the problem.

Incorruptible

God's Word is an incorruptible seed.

> **Being born again, not of corruptible seed, but of incorruptible, by the word of God, which liveth and abideth for ever.**
>
> **1 Peter 1:23**

If you sow seed in the ground, sometimes you just get bad seed. The seed has been tainted or became rotten. For one reason or another, it's lost the life in it. In the natural realm, it's possible to get seed, plant it, and not produce the desired results because the seed was bad. However, in the spiritual realm, God's Word is the seed—and it's incorruptible.

The Word of God will work the same for anyone. The seed wasn't the variable in any of these four instances of the parable of the sower; it was the ground. Now, that's very, very important.

Sometimes, I'll hear people say, "I took the Word of God and meditated on it. I confessed the Word, but it just didn't work for me." What they're saying is that the seed was corruptible—that the seed doesn't work the same for everybody. This parable teaches exactly the opposite.

God's Word is an incorruptible seed. It's never the Word that fails to work; it's the people who fail to work it. It's the people's hearts who don't allow the Word to generate and release its fullest potential. As I continue going through this parable, you'll see some of the things that can hinder the Word of God from working in your life. But you need to take this truth, establish it in your heart, and never deviate from it. It's nonnegotiable. You never question it. This is just an actual fact that you never think contrary to: God's Word is incorruptible. It always works. God's Word never fails. You may fail to understand and properly apply it. You may fail to do the corresponding actions it tells you to do. But God's Word never fails.

Immediately

As a very young Christian just getting started, this truth came alive in my heart and ignited my faith. As I meditated on this parable, I saw and believed with all of my heart that God's Word would change my life. All I had to do was take the Word of God and meditate in it, and the Word would do the rest because I believed it's an incorruptible seed. Through this, my life has totally transformed. In my finances, I'm a totally different person than I used to be. I'm walking in health in my physical body, and I've seen other people miraculously healed because of the Word I've meditated on. In my emotions, I'm a different person because of God's Word. It's changed my relationships with people. I can trace back everything God has done in my life to His Word. That's powerful and it's what the parable of the sower is teaching.

The Lord describes the first type of soil in Mark 4:15, saying,

> **These are they by the way side, where the word is sown; but when they have heard, Satan cometh immediately, and taketh away the word that was sown in their hearts.**

Once the Word is sown, the devil comes immediately to steal the seed that was planted in your heart.

When some people hear about how the Word of God is a seed and that they will see miraculous results if they will just take the Word and plant it in their hearts, they think, *This is the answer! All I have to do is take the Word of God, and all my problems will be over.* Not exactly. It's actually more accurate to say that once you take the Word, commit yourself to it, and start meditating in it and getting to know the Word of God for yourself, all of your problems have just begun. You may not like what I'm saying, but it's true.

Satan isn't really against you personally. He knows that on your own, you're a zero. You aren't going to be a threat to him or anybody else. It doesn't matter who you think you are or what you think you have: Apart from the Lord and His Word, you are never going to truly change this world and have a powerful impact for God's kingdom. But if the Word of God ever starts taking root on the inside of you, and growing up and producing, the devil has had it. Satan is petrified of the Word! He's going to come against the Word of God immediately and try to steal it out of your heart.

Not Without a Fight

You may be tempted to say, "Well, if that's true, then I won't even get into the Word of God. I don't want to be a target for the devil." I'm not saying that you're going to lose. I'm winning, but it's not without a fight. Once you make a commitment to stand on the Word of God—that the Word is going to be number one in your life—don't be deceived into thinking that all of your problems are over; they've only just begun. However, if you will continue to stand on the Word of God and not give in, you'll win. You'll be a winner, but it won't be without a fight (1 Tim. 6:12 and Heb. 10:32).

Matthew 13:18-19 says,

> **Hear ye therefore the parable of the sower. When any one heareth the word of the kingdom, and understandeth it not, then cometh the wicked one, and catcheth away that which was sown in his heart. This is he which received seed by the way side.**

Matthew stated this just a little differently than Mark. The wayside means a place where many people have walked. In other words, the dirt has been packed down and compacted. Instead of being able to sink into the ground, germinate, and take root, the seed just laid on the surface. Just like a bird will come and eat seeds thrown on hard-packed ground, so Satan immediately steals the Word from people who didn't get God's Word down on the inside of them. If the Word doesn't penetrate and get down inside a person's heart, the devil comes immediately and steals that Word from them. Out of the four different types of people that the Lord described in this parable, this is the only one that Satan had total access to. The devil could easily steal the Word from this first type of person.

Notice what verse 19 reveals:

> **When any one heareth the word of the kingdom, and understandeth it not, then cometh the wicked one, and catcheth away that which was sown in his heart.**

In other words, understanding is what allows the seed of God's Word to sink down inside of you. Understanding allows the Word to penetrate your heart. It's the door that permits the Word to come into your life. If you lack understanding, then the Word is never going to germinate in your heart. So, the Word of God must be spoken in such a way that it's easy to understand.

The Doorway

I'm amazed at how some people have tried to make the Word so difficult. I've actually heard some preachers that think it helps their delivery to chase after all kinds of tangents and dig deep into the Hebrew and Greek. Of course, there's a place for these kinds of things. I use them myself at times. But some people have made the Word so complicated and intellectual that the average person can't understand it.

Jesus did just the opposite. In this very parable we're looking at, He took something that was easily understood by everyone. They were an agricultural society. Every one of them had sown seeds. They lived in this realm. Jesus took something very simple that people could relate to and used it to teach the Word.

Yet I see people all the time who think it's a sign of their intelligence if they can use words that nobody understands. They talk in such a way that someone has to go check a dictionary or believe God for an interpretation to understand what they've said. Some people actually think this is great ministry. I believe it's just the opposite. If they really understand something properly, then they should be able to explain it in a way that anybody can understand.

I don't know if I achieve that, but it's certainly one of my goals. Many people have written in and said that I make the Word of God so simple that they're able to understand it. They also mentioned that there are some other folks that they can't understand. People need to present God's Word to people in a way that the people can understand.

Understanding is the doorway that allows the Word to get into your heart. If there isn't understanding on your part, then the Word will be stolen from you immediately. Satan will come and take it away. The only people the devil can steal the Word from without any effort are the people who don't understand it. You must understand the Word in order to receive it.

Digest Your Food

As a minister of God's Word, the Apostle Paul also understood this. He said,

> **To the weak became I as weak, that I might gain the weak: I am made all things to all men, that I might by all means save some.**
>
> **1 Corinthians 9:22**

I try to do the same thing, especially when I'm ministering in another country or culture. I've been all over Europe, to Central America, and to certain countries in Africa and Asia. When I go into a different culture, I try to use things that are specific to their situation. I do whatever I can in an attempt to get people to understand.

Not understanding the Word is like me putting food in your mouth, but you not being able to chew or swallow it. It just stayed in your mouth, never getting down on the inside where you could begin to digest it. You could literally starve to death with food in your mouth if somehow or another you didn't get it down on the inside of you.

There are many people who have heard the Word of God, but they don't understand it. They hear scriptures, but they don't have a clue what they mean. There's no spiritual understanding on the inside. Therefore, the Word doesn't release any of its life—any of its nourishment—into their lives.

> **Wisdom is the principal thing; therefore get wisdom: and with all thy getting get understanding.**
>
> **Proverbs 4:7**

You not only have to have the right information, but you also have to have enough understanding to be able to apply and put it into practice in your life.

Satan Steals

This is where many people miss it. Are you someone who can hear somebody minister, and it sounds good to you, but thirty minutes or an hour later, you couldn't even tell someone else what the minister was talking about? You didn't get a thing out of it. One of two things happened: Either the minister isn't ministering properly, or you don't have the understanding to be able to take those truths and put them into practice in your life. So, Satan just steals the Word from you by the time you get out the back door of the church. That's not a good situation.

You need to get to where you have understanding of the Word of God in your life. This doesn't happen through a casual reading of the Bible or merely listening to someone's message; you have to focus on the Word.

Recently I was teaching on these exact same truths in a devotion time with my employees. I was emphasizing how important the Word of God is. Due to that, some people said they would like a Bible reading program. So, we now have a Bible reading program that our employees are going through. This past week, they've been reading through some scriptures in the neighborhood of Exodus 30. It's about the priests' garments, the way the tabernacle was to be built, colors of this and that, and all kinds of things that most people don't really find that interesting. As I was reading through this, I couldn't help but think that some of my employees are probably going to get bored reading this because it doesn't seem exciting to them. They'll just read through it without thinking about it, and probably won't understand it. When we don't understand the Word, Satan just steals that truth out of our lives.

Every Scripture Profitable

As I was reading through this, Exodus 30:12 stood out to me:

> **When thou takest the sum of the children of Israel after their number, then shall they give every man a ransom for his soul unto the Lord, when thou numberest them; that there be no plague among them, when thou numberest them.**

Now, that might not seem significant to you. But there are no insignificant verses in the Bible.

Second Timothy 3:16 says...

> **All scripture is given by inspiration of God, and is profitable for doctrine, for reproof, for correction, for instruction in righteousness.**

Every scripture can benefit us. We just need to slow down—maybe even stop—and think about what we're reading.

As I meditated on what I was reading in Exodus 30:12, I realized that this was the key that unlocks 2 Samuel 24 and 1 Chronicles 21. That's where David had numbered the people without meeting the requirements of Exodus 30:12, and a plague came from God. If you don't understand this truth from Exodus 30:12, you'll read through those other two chapters and wonder, *God, why did You send a plague upon the people?* Then you'll think, *God is so hard to understand.* That's because you don't take the scriptures and meditate on them until you understand.

You can read the Bible, yet if it's not something you're truly interested in at the moment, you can just let it go in one ear and out the other. Satan comes and steals the benefit. Or you can declare by faith, "Every scripture is profitable for doctrine and reproof (2 Tim. 3:16). There's something for me to learn in every single verse." You can take that scripture, open your heart, meditate on it, and let understanding come. Once you fit the pieces together, then Satan can't steal it from you.

Spiritual understanding enables you to connect the dots. It's when you don't just have disjointed pieces of information, but you're able to put them together in such a way that it begins to make sense, and it starts working in your life. Understanding comes from within. It's something that comes up from your spirit. The Spirit of God quickens it to you. This is why I believe we have children's ministries. The truth is the truth. You don't teach children different truths than the ones you teach adults. But you do have to reach them at a different level of understanding. You could say the most profound things, but if the children don't understand what you are telling them, then Satan will immediately steal those truths from them. I cannot overemphasize how important understanding is.

Understanding
LESSON 12 – OUTLINE

I. The seed produces the fruit, not the ground.

A. It's the Word that brings forth the results.

B. Now, the ground can either allow the seed to produce to its fullest potential, or it can hinder, choke, and stop the Word of God from working.

C. With our hearts, we can either allow the Word of God to have its complete rule, or our hearts can become hardened toward God to not give His seed a place to germinate.

D. All I am is dirt—a place for the seed to germinate (Gen 2:7).

E. The Word of God has to be planted in your heart for you to effectively change.

F. If you would do it that way, change is as normal and natural as when a seed is planted in the ground and grows up.

II. In the parable of the sower, out of these four different types of ground, only one really began to produce fruit.

A. Although, it wasn't the seed that was the problem.

B. In the natural realm, it's possible to get seed, plant it, and not produce the desired results because the seed was bad.

C. However, in the spiritual realm, God's Word is the seed—and it's incorruptible (1 Pet. 1:23).

D. It's never the Word that fails to work; it's the people who fail to work it.

III. The Lord describes the first type of soil:

> **Hear ye therefore the parable of the sower. When any one heareth the word of the kingdom, and understandeth it not, then cometh the wicked one, and catcheth away that which was sown in his heart. This is he which received seed by the way side.**
>
> **Matthew 13:18-19**

A. Understanding is the doorway that allows the Word to get into your heart.

B. The only people the devil can steal the Word from without any effort are the people who don't understand it.

C. You must understand the Word in order to receive it.

IV. Are you someone who can hear somebody minister, and it sounds good to you, but thirty minutes or an hour later, you couldn't even tell someone else what the minister was talking about?

A. One of two things happened: Either the minister isn't ministering properly, or you don't have the understanding to be able to take those truths and put them into practice in your life.

B. An understanding of the Word of God doesn't happen through a casual reading of the Bible or merely listening to someone's message; you have to focus on the Word.

V. Every scripture can benefit us.

A. We just need to slow down—maybe even stop—and think about what we're reading.

B. You can read the Bible, yet if it's not something you're truly interested in at the moment, you can just let it go in one ear and out the other.

C. Or you can declare by faith, "Every scripture is profitable for doctrine and reproof (2 Tim. 3:16). There's something for me to learn in every single verse."

D. You can take that scripture, open your heart, meditate on it, and let understanding come.

E. Once you fit the pieces together, then Satan can't steal it from you.

VI. Understanding comes from within.

A. It's something that comes up from your spirit.

B. The Spirit of God quickens it to you.

C. I cannot overemphasize how important understanding is.

Understanding
LESSON 12 – TEACHER'S GUIDE

1. The seed produces the fruit, not the ground. It's the Word that brings forth the results. Now, the ground can either allow the seed to produce to its fullest potential, or it can hinder, choke, and stop the Word of God from working. With our hearts, we can either allow the Word of God to have its complete rule, or our hearts can become hardened toward God to not give His seed a place to germinate. All I am is dirt—a place for the seed to germinate (Gen 2:7). The Word of God has to be planted in our hearts for us to effectively change. If we would do it that way, change is as normal and natural as when a seed is planted in the ground and grows up.

2. In the parable of the sower, out of these four different types of ground, only one really began to produce fruit. Although, it wasn't the seed that was the problem. In the natural realm, it's possible to get seed, plant it, and not produce the desired results because the seed was bad. However, in the spiritual realm, God's Word is the seed—and it's incorruptible (1 Pet. 1:23). It's never the Word that fails to work; it's the people who fail to work it.

3. The Lord describes the first type of soil (Matt. 13:18-19). Understanding is the doorway that allows the Word to get into our hearts. The only people the devil can steal the Word from without any effort are the people who don't understand it. We must understand the Word in order to receive it.

1. A. What produces the fruit? (The seed)
   B. What can the ground allow or hinder the seed to do? (It can allow the seed to produce to its fullest potential, or it can hinder, choke, and stop the Word of God from working)
   C. For us to effectively change, what has to happen? (The Word of God has to be planted in our hearts)
2. A. In the parable of the sower, out of the four types of ground, how many of them produced fruit? (Only one)
   B. Read 1 Peter 1:23. What is incorruptible? (God's Word)
   C. It's never the Word that fails to work, but it's what? (It's the people who fail to work it)
3. A. Read Matthew 13:18-19. Who are the only people the devil can steal the Word from? (The people who don't understand the Word)
   B. What do we have to do in order to receive the Word? (We have to understand it)

4. Are we people who can hear somebody minister, and it sounds good to us, but thirty minutes or an hour later, we couldn't even tell someone else what the minister was talking about? One of two things happened: Either the minister isn't ministering properly, or we don't have the understanding to be able to take those truths and put them into practice in our lives. An understanding of the Word of God doesn't happen through a casual reading of the Bible or merely listening to someone's message; we have to focus on the Word.

5. Every scripture can benefit us. We just need to slow down—maybe even stop—and think about what we're reading. We can read the Bible, yet if it's not something we're truly interested in at the moment, we can just let it go in one ear and out the other. Or we can declare by faith, "Every scripture is profitable for doctrine and reproof (2 Tim. 3:16). There's something for me to learn in every single verse." We can take that scripture, open our hearts, meditate on it, and let understanding come. Once we fit the pieces together, then Satan can't steal it from us.

6. Understanding comes from within. It's something that comes up from our spirits. The Spirit of God quickens it to us. I cannot overemphasize how important understanding is.

4. A. If we hear somebody minister, and it sounds good to us, but thirty minutes or an hour later, we couldn't even tell someone else what the minister was talking about, what happened? (One of two things: Either the minister isn't ministering properly, or we don't have the understanding to be able to take those truths and put them into practice in our lives)
   B. What doesn't happen through a casual reading of the Bible or merely listening to someone's message? (An understanding of the Word of God)
5. A. Read 2 Timothy 3:16. For every scripture to benefit us, what do we need to do? (We just need to slow down—maybe even stop—and think about what we're reading)
   B. When can't Satan take a scripture from us? (Once we take that scripture, open our hearts, meditate on it, and let understanding come)
6. What does the Spirit of God quicken to us? (Understanding)

Understanding

LESSON 12 – DISCIPLESHIP QUESTIONS

1. Read Genesis 2:7. What was breathed into the man?

2. Read 1 Peter 1:23. What were you born again of?

3. Does the Word of God only live forever?

4. Read Mark 4:15. Since the Word was sown in those by the wayside, this means it was sown _____.
   A. On accident
   B. Without care
   C. Without effort
   D. For a fee
   E. On purpose

5. According to 1 Timothy 6:12, you're supposed to **"fight the _____ fight of faith."**

6. What are you to lay hold of?

7. According to Hebrews 10:32, **"after ye were illuminated, ye _____ a great fight of afflictions."**
   A. "Lost"
   B. "Stopped"
   C. "Endured"
   D. All of the above
   E. None of the above

8. Read Matthew 13:18-19. The Word that is heard is the Word of what?

9. Does the wicked one come before a person doesn't understand or after?

10. According to 1 Corinthians 9:22, what did Paul become that by all means, he might save some?

11. According to Proverbs 4:7, what is the principal thing?

12. What else are you to get?

13. According to Exodus 30:12, for what reason was a person to give a ransom (a payment) for their soul?

14. Read 2 Timothy 3:16. What is Scripture profitable for?

Understanding
LESSON 12 – ANSWER KEY

1. The breath of life
2. Of incorruptible seed, by the Word of God
3. No, it also abides forever
4. E. On purpose
5. **"Good"**
6. Eternal life
7. C. **"Endured"**
8. The kingdom
9. After
10. All things to all people
11. Wisdom
12. Understanding
13. So that there would be no plague among the people when they were numbered
14. Doctrine, reproof, correction, and instruction in righteousness

Understanding
LESSON 12 – SCRIPTURES

GENESIS 2:7
And the LORD God formed man of the dust of the ground, and breathed into his nostrils the breath of life; and man became a living soul.

1 PETER 1:23
Being born again, not of corruptible seed, but of incorruptible, by the word of God, which liveth and abideth for ever.

MARK 4:15
And these are they by the way side, where the word is sown; but when they have heard, Satan cometh immediately, and taketh away the word that was sown in their hearts.

1 TIMOTHY 6:12
Fight the good fight of faith, lay hold on eternal life, whereunto thou art also called, and hast professed a good profession before many witnesses.

HEBREWS 10:32
But call to remembrance the former days, in which, after ye were illuminated, ye endured a great fight of afflictions.

MATTHEW 13:18-19
Hear ye therefore the parable of the sower. [19] When any one heareth the word of the kingdom, and understandeth it not, then cometh the wicked one, and catcheth away that which was sown in his heart. This is he which received seed by the way side.

1 CORINTHIANS 9:22
To the weak became I as weak, that I might gain the weak: I am made all things to all men, that I might by all means save some.

PROVERBS 4:7
Wisdom is the principal thing; therefore get wisdom: and with all thy getting get understanding.

EXODUS 30:12
When thou takest the sum of the children of Israel after their number, then shall they give every man a ransom for his soul unto the LORD, when thou numberest them; that there be no plague among them, when thou numberest them.

2 TIMOTHY 3:16
All scripture is given by inspiration of God, and is profitable for doctrine, for reproof, for correction, for instruction in righteousness.

Rooted and Established
LESSON 13

When I first started in ministry, I thought the results were all dependent on me. If I just ministered the Word properly, every person who sat under my ministry would be totally changed. So, I put a tremendous amount of effort into seeking the Lord, making sure I understood the truth correctly, and making sure I was clear and anointed in saying the truth.

Then, during the late 1970s, I did a circuit of six Bible studies a week in three different states (Oklahoma, New Mexico, and Colorado). I taught the exact same truth in each one of these Bible studies, trying to keep the people growing at the same rate and on the same page spiritually. I'd preach my heart out and see one person with an incurable disease receive the Word and be totally healed and set free. Yet the person sitting next to them would fall asleep and not get a thing out of it. One person would look bored to death, and the next would be getting their life changed by the revelation they were receiving.

After a while, my lightning-fast mind began to figure out that it couldn't be me producing such different results. They were all sitting in the same service and hearing the exact same words. Everything from me was the same, yet one was transformed and another fell asleep. One was healed and the other was bored. How could all of these things be happening from the same ministry of the Word? Then I began to realize that it's not just the Word I speak, but it's the condition of people's hearts.

Just like this first type of person Jesus described in the parable of the sower, I've seen this same response many times. I've preached my heart out, but the Word of God goes in one ear and out the other. It's like they had no heart for or understanding of the Word whatsoever. I quit taking that personally. I've realized that it's not just the way I speak—it's the way people hear.

Where Is Your Focus?

Are you one of those folks who say, "I never get anything out of the messages at church." It may not be the person who's speaking; it could be the way you're hearing, or should I say not hearing. It has to do with whether or not you're opening your heart and really desiring to know those truths.

Blessed are they which do hunger and thirst after righteousness: for they shall be filled.

Matthew 5:6

Is God's Word to you…

> **More to be desired…than gold, yea, than much fine gold: sweeter also than honey and the honeycomb.**
>
> **Psalm 19:10**

If you get to where you want to know the truth of God's Word more than you crave food, more than you desire wealth, you'll get it. The problem is that most only want this every once in a while. Maybe once a week or once a month, they have a little twinge of desire for five or ten minutes where they'd like to understand and be operating in more truth. But then they get occupied with everything else and that desire fades. If that's the way you are, you aren't ever going to have understanding. God isn't the one who determines the condition of your heart—you are.

It basically just boils down to where your focus is: If you are focused on the Lord and you're hungry and seeking after Him, you will be filled (Matt. 5:6).

If you're one of these first type of people depicted in the parable of the sower, the Word of God just doesn't mean anything to you: You can hear it, and it's gone before you even think about it. You just can't seem to retain God's Word. It's not time for you to pray and ask God to speak louder; it's time for you to change your heart and start focusing on the things of the Lord.

Progressive Steps

In Mark 4:16-17, Jesus began to teach from the parable of the sower about the second type of person that heard the Word of God:

> **And these are they likewise which are sown on stony ground; who, when they have heard the word, immediately receive it with gladness; And have no root in themselves, and so endure but for a time: afterward, when affliction or persecution ariseth for the word's sake, immediately they are offended.**

Now, before we look specifically into this second type of person, let me make another statement: This parable also describes progressive steps toward fruitfulness.

The Lord clearly gave four different types of people's hearts and how the Word of God interacted with their hearts to bring forth fruit (or not). I believe He was also describing four different stages toward fruitfulness.

First of all, you go through a stage where you hear the Word of God, but your heart isn't set on it. You aren't seeking after the things of God. The Word goes in one ear and out the other. That's the first type of person.

The second type of person gets excited about the Word, but doesn't have any root within. The end result is that there is no fruit.

Living off Others

The third type of person gets excited about the Word, and it takes root. The Word of God begins to germinate and start producing life in them. But then they get distracted by the things of this world.

> **And the cares of this world, and the deceitfulness of riches, and the lusts of other things entering in, choke the word, and it becometh unfruitful.**
>
> **Mark 4:19**

The fourth type of person is the one who really nurtures and takes care of the Word of God. This person focuses on it, isn't distracted by the things of this world, and therefore produces a bountiful harvest.

> **And these are they which are sown on good ground; such as hear the word, and receive it, and bring forth fruit, some thirtyfold, some sixty, and some an hundred.**
>
> **Mark 4:20**

Although I was genuinely born again as an eight-year-old, I was a typical kid. During church, I was focused on my friends in the church and what we were going to do after the service. So, I didn't really meditate on the Word of God and let it come into my life. I read my Bible every single day, but somehow or another, it just didn't penetrate. I suppose it did to a degree. I didn't get into a lot of the sin and other problems that many people do, so I'm not saying it had no effect. However, it didn't have the effect that it should have had on my life. It was like the Word was coming in one ear and out the other, just like this first person. I didn't understand the Word, and it wasn't impacting me.

Then I had this experience with the Lord on March 23, 1968, and I became excited about the Word of God. I don't think you've ever seen anybody more excited about God and His Word than I was. But there was a period of time when that Word wasn't rooted on the inside of me. I was living off of other people's revelation—their teaching about the Word—and not my own personal relationship. Even though I was excited and great things were happening on the inside, there still wasn't much fruit that came through my life.

Smoke and Mirrors

I was in this second stage when the Lord used this parable to really speak into my life. It was right around the time when Jamie and I were married in October 1972. Prior to our wedding, and then afterwards, the Lord made this teaching about the sower sowing the Word a revelation in my life.

> **And these are they likewise which are sown on stony ground; who, when they have heard the word, immediately receive it with gladness.**
>
> **Mark 4:16**

Now, I specifically related to that. After I had this experience on March 23, 1968, I fell head over heels in love with the Lord. The Word of God became powerful in my life. I was so excited over it. I couldn't open the Bible without hearing God talk directly to me through the Scriptures. Although I was excited about it, I was frustrated too. I could see the potential in my heart and what God wanted to do in my life, but I wasn't seeing it on the outside. Since there was frustration and I wasn't really bearing fruit, I began to relate to this second type of person that the Lord describes in this parable.

This second person gets excited over the Word of God and receives it with gladness, but they don't see it bring forth fruit.

Over time, I've observed a tendency among many people to be shallow. Some of them may be very demonstrative outwardly, but everything in their lives is outward. There isn't any depth in their personal lives. I don't understand all the reasons for this, but I see this in my dealings with people. Some folks are just shallow. Everything is all about the external. They don't have very much depth on the inside.

Because of this, I've seen many people in my meetings get so excited over the Word of God that it's easy to think, *This is awesome. They're totally transformed!* But I've come to realize that with some people, it's all show and no go. It's all just smoke and mirrors. There isn't any commitment in their hearts.

So, over the years, I've come to a place where I enjoy seeing people who are clearly being impacted by the Word. They take some time to really think about and deliberate on it. Of course, there are those who get so excited that they stand up, shout, and jump up and down in their chairs while I'm preaching. That's okay too. But I like to watch those who are being deliberate and thinking about the Word. It takes them a little bit of time before they really commit themselves. Sometimes these folks who are just so excited at first don't ever let the Word take root on the inside of them. There is a period of being rooted in the Word that's necessary for you to be able to produce fruit.

Two Terrariums

My sixth grade teacher put dirt in two identical large glass jars called terrariums. Then he planted tomato seeds in both of them on the same exact day as a part of our class project. He put them in the same place in our classroom, so they received the same light. He watered them exactly the same every day. One terrarium had about eight inches of soil, and the other had only one.

My teacher asked us questions like, "Which one do you think is going to grow? Which one do you think will produce fruit?" To my surprise, the tomato seed that was only in an inch of dirt sprang up first. It was probably a foot tall before the other tomato seed even began to start pushing up above the ground. At a glance, you'd think the one in less dirt was doing better. But when you only have a small amount of dirt, that seed has to put all of its energy into growing above the ground because it didn't have any room for roots. There wasn't enough soil to put roots down, so all of the life that was in that seed went into producing above ground. It looked good at first.

For many people, it's all about appearances. They don't really care about long-term results. They're short-term thinkers. They hear one message on healing and get excited, saying, "I've got it! I'll never have another problem." They think it's wonderful and are very demonstrative with it.

However, there really needs to be a period of time for that person to take those truths they've learned and, no matter how much the truths have excited them, let them take root on the inside.

The seed that only had an inch of dirt grew to nearly a foot tall before the other one even started poking out of the ground. But within a very short period of time, because there wasn't enough root to sustain the growth, it began to turn pale and then white. It wound up falling over and shriveling up. It died because it didn't have a root system to sustain the growth.

The tomato seed that started much slower above the ground—as far as what we could see—grew up into a full plant. We had to put a stake in there for support, as it began to produce many tomatoes.

Tiiiiiiiiime

Through that experiment, I learned a lesson: A seed must, first of all, grow underground. It has to start producing roots before it produces fruit.

In the spiritual realm, many people don't like the root stage. They don't like letting a truth from the Word of God take root on the inside of them and get established in their hearts. They just want to skip all this and get right to the fruit as quickly as they can. Therefore, they don't have very much depth of earth in their lives. Their hearts aren't totally committed to that truth. They may look like they're growing faster than somebody else, but in the end, they can't sustain that growth. Their commitment shrivels up and dies at the first little hardship that comes along. The Word isn't going to produce fruit in their lives.

If you want to be someone who really produces fruit and sees the Word of God work, it's not going to happen overnight. You can't microwave your miracle. It takes time. There is seed, time, and harvest. Actually, sometimes it is seed, tiiiiiiiiime, and then harvest. It takes a period of time.

You have to let God's Word stay rooted on the inside of you. You can't back off of it. You must keep digging and looking for greater revelation. Don't just take the surface revelation of what the Word of God says. Go back to those scriptures and ask, "Lord, have I received everything out of this scripture that I need to know? Please show me more." You must let that Word take root on the inside of you.

Failure to let the Word of God take root on the inside is probably the number-one reason people aren't seeing greater fruit manifest in their lives. They just aren't giving it time.

Many people know a scripture like 1 Peter 2:24, which says that by His stripes, we were healed. They spend five minutes thinking about that one little concept and conclude, "I've got it. Now I ought to be healed!" No, you need to meditate on that scripture, and meditate on that scripture some more. Spend days, weeks, months, and years focusing on that truth and applying it to your life, until it gets so rooted and established on the inside of you that nothing can pull it up.

Depth of Root

When I was a kid, we lived in a neighborhood, but our yard was a little over half an acre. We had twenty-three pecan trees in it. Every year, some of the pecans would fall, get stepped on, or otherwise find a way into the ground. Then they would germinate and start producing a plant. My job was to pull up these tiny little pecan trees that started to grow.

Like most kids, I didn't want to spend my time going around pulling up these little plants. We must have had hundreds of them! I'd see one, but I didn't want to stop playing to pull it up. So, I'd wait until that thing got tall enough that my parents could see it from inside the house. When they did, they'd say, "Andy, you need to go out there and pull up that pecan tree." That's how long I'd wait.

However, I learned pretty quickly that if I let a pecan tree get a foot tall, there would be about three feet of roots underneath the ground. There was three times as much growth underneath the ground as there was above the ground. If I waited until the pecan tree was a foot tall to get it, I'd have to get a shovel and dig it up. It would be so well rooted that I couldn't just pull it up. If I wanted to do it the easy way, I had to get those pecan trees when they were about an inch tall. Then I could just grab it and pull it out.

It's the same way with the seed of God's Word. Satan would love to get you to where you don't have any depth of root in your life. Then he can come against you and just steal the Word. He wants to pull it up before it ever gets rooted. However, if you grow a good root system, you'll be able to stand despite all the troubles, trials, and hardships that come in life.

Many people are just like this second type of ground that the Lord described. They can't bring forth fruit. It's not because they aren't excited about the Word of God. It's not because they don't love it. They do love it. It's just that they haven't taken time to let the Word take root on the inside of them.

Rooted and Established
LESSON 13 – OUTLINE

I. When I first started in ministry, I thought the results were all dependent on me.

   A. So, I put a tremendous amount of effort into seeking the Lord, making sure I understood the truth correctly, and making sure I was clear and anointed in saying the truth.

   B. I taught the exact same truth in six different Bible studies, trying to keep the people growing at the same rate and on the same page spiritually.

   C. One person would look bored to death, and the next would be getting their life changed by the revelation they were receiving.

   D. How could all of these things be happening from the same ministry of the Word?

   E. I began to realize that it's not just the Word I speak, but it's the condition of people's hearts.

   F. I've realized that it's not just the way I speak—it's the way people hear.

II. If you get to where you want to know the truth of God's Word more than you crave food, more than you desire wealth, you'll get it (Ps. 19:10).

   A. The problem is that most only want this every once in a while.

   B. If that's the way you are, you aren't ever going to have understanding.

   C. God isn't the one who determines the condition of your heart—you are.

   D. It's not time for you to pray and ask God to speak louder; it's time for you to change your heart and start focusing on the things of the Lord.

III. In Mark 4:16-17, Jesus began to teach from the parable of the sower about the second type of person that heard the Word of God:

> **And these are they likewise which are sown on stony ground; who, when they have heard the word, immediately receive it with gladness; And have no root in themselves, and so endure but for a time: afterward, when affliction or persecution ariseth for the word's sake, immediately they are offended.**

A. This person gets excited about the Word, but doesn't have any root within.

B. The end result is that there is no fruit.

C. In the spiritual realm, many people don't like letting a truth from the Word of God take root on the inside of them and get established in their hearts.

D. They just want to skip all this and get right to the fruit as quickly as they can.

E. Therefore, they don't have very much depth of earth in their lives.

F. Their hearts aren't totally committed to that truth.

G. They may look like they're growing faster than somebody else, but in the end, they can't sustain that growth.

H. Their commitment shrivels up and dies at the first little hardship that comes along.

IV. If you want to be someone who really produces fruit and sees the Word of God work, it's not going to happen overnight.

A. You can't microwave your miracle.

B. There is seed, tiiiiiiiiime, and then harvest.

C. You have to let God's Word stay rooted on the inside of you.

D. You can't back off of it.

E. You must keep digging and looking for greater revelation.

F. Don't just take the surface revelation of what the Word of God says.

G. Go back to those scriptures and ask, "Lord, have I received everything out of this scripture that I need to know? Please show me more."

H. Failure to let the Word of God take root on the inside is probably the number-one reason people aren't seeing greater fruit manifest in their lives.

I. They just aren't giving it time.

V. Satan would love to get you to where you don't have any depth of root in your life.

A. Then he can come against you and just steal the Word.

B. He wants to pull it up before it ever gets rooted.

C. However, if you grow a good root system, you'll be able to stand despite all the troubles, trials, and hardships that come in life.

Rooted and Established
LESSON 13 – TEACHER'S GUIDE

1. When I first started in ministry, I thought the results were all dependent on me. So, I put a tremendous amount of effort into seeking the Lord, making sure I understood the truth correctly, and making sure I was clear and anointed in saying the truth. I taught the exact same truth in six different Bible studies, trying to keep the people growing at the same rate and on the same page spiritually. One person would look bored to death, and the next would be getting their life changed by the revelation they were receiving. How could all of these things be happening from the same ministry of the Word? I began to realize that it's not just the Word I speak, but it's the condition of people's hearts. I've realized that it's not just the way I speak—it's the way people hear.

2. If we get to where we want to know the truth of God's Word more than we crave food, more than we desire wealth, we'll get it (Ps. 19:10). The problem is that most only want this every once in a while. If that's the way we are, we aren't ever going to have understanding. God isn't the one who determines the condition of our hearts—we are. It's not time for us to pray and ask God to speak louder; it's time for us to change our hearts and start focusing on the things of the Lord.

3. In Mark 4:16-17, Jesus began to teach from the parable of the sower about the second type of person that heard the Word of God. This person gets excited about the Word, but doesn't have any root within. The end result is that there is no fruit. In the spiritual realm, many people don't like letting a truth from the Word of God take root on the inside of them and get established in their hearts. They just want to skip all this and get right to the fruit as quickly as they can. Therefore, they don't have very much depth of earth in their lives. Their hearts aren't totally committed to that truth. They may look like they're growing faster than somebody else, but in the end, they can't sustain that growth. Their commitment shrivels up and dies at the first little hardship that comes along.

1. A. What happened when Andrew taught the exact same truth in six different Bible studies? (One person would look bored to death, and the next would be getting their life changed by the revelation they were receiving)
   B. What two things did Andrew realize? (That it's not just the Word he speaks, but it's the condition of people's hearts, and that it's not just the way he speaks—it's the way people hear)
2. A. Read Psalm 19:10. What will we get if want to know the truth of God's Word more than we crave food, more than we desire wealth? (Knowledge of the truth of God's Word)
   B. Does God determine the condition of our hearts? (No, we do)
3. A. What is the end result of the person who doesn't have root inside them? (They don't bear fruit)
   B. Many people may look like they're growing faster than somebody else, but what? (In the end, they can't sustain that growth)

4. If we want to be someone who really produces fruit and sees the Word of God work, it's not going to happen overnight. We can't microwave our miracles. There is seed, tiiiiiiiime, and then harvest. We have to let God's Word stay rooted on the inside of us. We can't back off of it. We must keep digging and looking for greater revelation. We shouldn't just take the surface revelation of what the Word of God says. We need to go back to those scriptures and ask, "Lord, have I received everything out of this scripture that I need to know? Please show me more." Failure to let the Word of God take root on the inside is probably the number-one reason people aren't seeing greater fruit manifest in their lives. They just aren't giving it time.

5. Satan would love to get us to where we don't have any depth of root in our lives. Then he can come against us and just steal the Word. He wants to pull it up before it ever gets rooted. However, if we grow a good root system, we'll be able to stand despite all the troubles, trials, and hardships that come in life.

4. A. We have to let God's Word _____ rooted on the inside of us. (Stay)
   B. We shouldn't just take the surface revelation, but we need to what? (We need to go back to those scriptures and ask, "Lord, have I received everything out of this scripture that I need to know? Please show me more")
   C. What is probably the number-one reason people aren't seeing greater fruit manifest in their lives? (Failure to let the Word of God take root on the inside)
5. A. What does Satan want to pull up before it ever gets rooted in our lives? (The Word)
   B. However, if we grow a good root system, what will we be able to do? (We'll be able to stand despite all the troubles, trials, and hardships that come in life)

Rooted and Established

LESSON 13 – DISCIPLESHIP QUESTIONS

1. Read Matthew 5:6. Why are those who hunger and thirst for righteousness blessed?

2. Read Psalm 19:10. **"More to be desired are they than gold, yea, than _____ fine gold."**

3. According to Mark 4:16-17, **"when they have heard the word, _____ receive it with gladness."**

4. **"Afterward, when affliction or persecution ariseth for the word's sake, _____ they are offended."**

5. According to Mark 4:19-20, what becomes unfruitful?
   A. The person
   B. The ground
   C. The Word
   D. All of the above
   E. None of the above

6. Once the ones on the good ground hear the Word, what do they do?

7. Read 1 Peter 2:24. Are you dead to sin, or is sin dead to you?
   A. I am dead to sin
   B. Sin is dead to me
   C. Both
   D. Neither
   E. That's not a fair question

Rooted and Established
LESSON 13 – ANSWER KEY

1. Because they shall be filled
2. **"Much"**
3. **"Immediately"**
4. **"Immediately"**
5. C. The Word
6. They receive it and bring forth fruit, some thirtyfold, some sixty, and some a hundred
7. A. I am dead to sin

Rooted and Established
LESSON 13 – SCRIPTURES

MATTHEW 5:6
Blessed are they which do hunger and thirst after righteousness: for they shall be filled.

PSALM 19:10
More to be desired are they than gold, yea, than much fine gold: sweeter also than honey and the honeycomb.

MARK 4:16-17
And these are they likewise which are sown on stony ground; who, when they have heard the word, immediately receive it with gladness; [17] **And have no root in themselves, and so endure but for a time: afterward, when affliction or persecution ariseth for the word's sake, immediately they are offended.**

MARK 4:19-20
And the cares of this world, and the deceitfulness of riches, and the lusts of other things entering in, choke the word, and it becometh unfruitful. [20] **And these are they which are sown on good ground; such as hear the word, and receive it, and bring forth fruit, some thirtyfold, some sixty, and some an hundred.**

1 PETER 2:24
Who his own self bare our sins in his own body on the tree, that we, being dead to sins, should live unto righteousness: by whose stripes ye were healed.

Persecution
LESSON 14

The parable Jesus gave in Mark 4 about the sower sowing the seed is one of the most foundational teachings of the Bible. In Mark 4:13, the Lord said, "If you don't understand this parable, you cannot understand any of the others." This passage is the key that unlocks the revelation of important foundational truths that you'll use every day for the rest of your Christian life. It's truly that important.

Jesus was using the illustration of a man sowing seed that fell on four different types of ground. The kingdom of God is likewise. God's Word is the seed that must be planted in our lives to bear good fruit. The Word of God is what brings change.

God's Word is never the variable; it has the same potential in every single person's life. What made the Word produce differently wasn't the seed itself, but rather the type of soil it found itself in. This parable illustrates four different types of hearts. The Word of God has the same potential to produce in every person's life, but the difference is how each person responds to the Word. This parable reveals that there's really only one type of response that will allow the seed of God's Word to fully produce its fruit.

No Small Stir

Let's continue looking at the second type of person who heard the Word:

> **And these are they likewise which are sown on stony ground; who, when they have heard the word, immediately receive it with gladness; And have no root in themselves, and so endure but for a time: afterward, when affliction or persecution ariseth for the word's sake, immediately they are offended.**
>
> **Mark 4:16-17**

When the Lord showed me this passage of Scripture and it really started having a major impact in my life, I was still in a denominational church that was against everything I was believing for. They acknowledged that there was such a thing as the baptism in the Holy Spirit and speaking in tongues, but they argued that it's the least of all the gifts and not really valid for today. They didn't emphasize these truths, and they certainly didn't emphasize righteousness and grace. I was in a situation where the Word of God I was hearing was constantly being persecuted.

My good friend Joe, who had a huge impact on my life, served as an associate minister of Kenneth Copeland Ministries at one time. He even traveled with him for a while. I used to attend Kenneth's meetings in Fort Worth, Texas, when he would rent the Will Rogers Auditorium. That place could seat up to 3,500 people. I remember Kenneth confessing and thanking God for that place to be full when he only had two hundred of us sitting down in the front. I was so green in faith and lacking understanding from the Word, that I didn't realize he was speaking forth his faith. I just figured he knew something I didn't and that maybe, there were some buses on the way or something.

I didn't know much then, but I'd go hear Kenneth Copeland speak the Word of God about righteousness. It would get me so fired up that I'd go back to this little denominational church and preach the very same things I'd heard. This was causing no small stir. People were getting healed, delivered, and set free. Good things were happening, but the leadership of the church was against what I was doing. They thought it was inaccurate compared to their interpretation of Scripture. So, because of this, they criticized me.

Offended

Notice that this is exactly what Mark 4:16-17 is saying. People who are like the stony ground have...

> **...no root in themselves, and so endure but for a time: afterward, when affliction or persecution ariseth for the word's sake, immediately they are offended.**

This is describing people who were excited about the Word when they heard it and would act on it to a degree but it didn't take root in them. When affliction, persecution, and criticism against the Word began to come, they became offended.

The word **"offended"** here doesn't mean that they quit believing or renounced the Word. I didn't renounce that God still heals today, that the baptism in the Holy Spirit and speaking in tongues is valid, and that miracles were of God. I still believed these truths, but I became offended, which means I lost my enthusiasm and excitement about them. The fire I had for these truths cooled off because of the criticism I received.

You need to recognize that Satan doesn't have to make you totally disavow your faith in the Word. If he can just get you to where you're cautious and afraid to speak, then you're hurt and offended, and now you aren't enthusiastic the way you used to be. If the devil can get you into that mode, he can stop the Word of God from working in your life.

This is exactly where I was when the Lord showed this to me. I'd hear Kenneth Copeland speak, I'd get all excited about the Word I'd heard, and then I'd go back to preaching truths like righteousness, faith, and grace in my denominational church. For a week or two, it would be really powerful. Then I'd receive so much criticism that I'd become introspective. I still believed the same truths, and was trying to say them and teach them in the classes I was leading, but they just weren't getting results like they had before. There wasn't any fruit coming from them.

Not Your Revelation

This happened so often that I began to recognize the cycle. I'd hear Kenneth Copeland speak and be okay for a week or two. Then I'd get to where I was trying to say and do the same things, but I just wasn't getting results. So, I'd have to go back and get my next Kenneth Copeland fix. This happened on a constant basis. When I began to see myself start running out of steam, I knew that the next time I taught just wouldn't be powerful the way it was before. I got to where I expected it. I didn't understand why it was happening, but I saw it happen so many times, and I could recognize it coming.

As I was studying this verse of Scripture, the Lord spoke to me. He said, "The problem is that the truths you are saying aren't your revelation; they're Kenneth Copeland's. You're simply saying things that you've heard somebody else say." Before God spoke this to me, I'd teach, saying "I heard this man Kenneth Copeland say..." and I'd quote him. I'd talk about what he taught, using his examples, his illustrations, and his jokes. People were being blessed by it because I was sharing truth—it just wasn't my truth. When the Lord showed this to me, a light switched on inside of me. I realized this was why I wasn't able to maintain and keep equilibrium. This was why I was up and down, sometimes excited about the Word and other times wondering, *What's going on?* It was because I didn't have root in myself. I was living off of another person's revelation. It was good revelation, but it wasn't mine.

I remember the Saturday night when the Lord showed this to Jamie and me. I discussed it with her, decided, and declared, "From now on, I am not going to say so-and-so said, and quote somebody else and tell people about someone else's revelation." As a matter of fact, you may watch my television program, listen by radio, or read my books, but this is the first time you've ever heard or seen me mention someone like Kenneth Copeland in this way. Really, I'm just speaking of him by way of testimony. That's because I totally got away from quoting what somebody else had to say. It started becoming God's Word to me.

I made a decision that I would stand no matter who came against the revelation that God had been speaking to me. I was going to keep that Word in my heart. I was going to get it rooted and grounded on the inside of me.

Mark 4:17 really ministered to me when I saw that the afflictions and persecutions come for the Word's sake. They don't come because of you or me personally; it's because of the Word. The Word of God has power in it. When you start speaking the Word to people, God uses it to bring conviction to them. It starts pressuring and motivating them to change. If a person doesn't want to change, then they have to do something with the conviction that they feel coming from you. They may not mentally be able to separate this and understand it, but that is really what's happening. They may think it's you they're upset with and it's you they're criticizing, but what they're really doing is criticizing God's Word coming through you. It's because of the Word's sake that affliction and persecution come. People are trying to resist and nullify this Word that you've spoken that's convicted them.

Revival or Riot

Spoken in truth, the Word of God will either bring a revival or a riot every time. That's what Jesus and the early apostles did (Acts 17:6 and Acts 19). Not everybody responded well to the Lord. His disciples came to Him and asked, "Don't You know that You offended these people?" He answered, "Leave them alone. If they're of God, they'll get over it. Every tree that My Father hasn't planted will be uprooted." Christ didn't take things personally.

Whenever Jesus spoke, He caused a revival or a riot. His disciples did the same when they ministered. It's naïve and incorrect for us to think that if we just walk in love, everybody will love us (Matt. 10:16-42). Jesus warned, "If they persecuted Me, they'll persecute you." You need to recognize that when you begin to stand on the Word without compromise, it starts to release its power. When you begin to declare "This is what the Word of God says and this is what I'm believing for—I don't care if it goes against our tradition or the way people have done things, this is what the Word says," God's Word will start putting pressure on people. Either they'll repent and love you for it, or they'll criticize you because of it.

Once I understood this, it made a huge difference in my life. It totally changed my expectation and enabled me to continue going on. When I began to get criticism, persecution, and affliction, I just recognized that this is what the Word of God will do. God's Word will divide and separate people (Matt. 10:34-36).

"Stay on Track!"

My friend Joe really helped me get started in the ministry. He had a very powerful influence in my life. I remember attending one of his meetings in a hotel where he called me out in front of all the people. Joe gave me a prophecy that has helped me to this day, saying,

"I see you like a runner on a track. You're running around this track and you're leading the pack. You're running the race and doing a good job. But the people in the grandstands are yelling at you. They're telling you that you're doing it all wrong. They're saying you should be doing this and doing that. I see you getting off of the track, running up into the grandstands, and arguing with the spectators. Even if you win the argument, you're going to lose the race. Stay on track. Get back in the race. Forget the grandstands!"

When the Lord spoke that through Joe, it was so descriptive of where I was at that time. Since then, that's been a word that has kept me on track for almost forty years. I'm not sure I do everything perfectly. I'm still green and growing. I may be better five or ten years from now, should the Lord tarry, but the reason I am still running the race is because of scriptures and words like this where God has shown me not to let the criticism of other people steal the Word from my heart.

If I get offended and become gun-shy about speaking the truth because of what people have to say, the Word of God will cease performing and producing in my life. I made a decision almost forty years ago that I wasn't going to let that happen. I've been trying to be bold and let the Word of God, rather than the opinions of man, rule and dominate me. It's become a habit and a lifestyle for me. I am this way because of Scripture. I may not be doing it perfectly, but I'm moving in this direction because of my conviction from the Word of God.

Persecution
LESSON 14 – OUTLINE

I. God's Word is never the variable; it has the same potential in every single person's life.

A. What made the Word produce differently in the parable of the sower wasn't the seed itself, but rather the type of soil it found itself in.

B. This parable illustrates four different types of hearts.

C. It reveals that there's really only one type of response that will allow the seed of God's Word to fully produce its fruit.

II. Let's continue looking at the second type of person who heard the Word (Mark 4:16-17).

A. The word **"offended"** here doesn't mean that they quit believing or renounced the Word.

B. You need to recognize that Satan doesn't have to make you totally disavow your faith in the Word.

C. If he can just get you to where you're cautious and afraid to speak, then you're hurt and offended, and now you aren't enthusiastic the way you used to be.

D. If the devil can get you into that mode, he can stop the Word of God from working in your life.

III. Mark 4:17 really ministered to me when I saw that the afflictions and persecutions come for the Word's sake.

A. They don't come because of you or me personally; it's because of the Word.

B. When you start speaking the Word to people, God uses it to bring conviction to them.

C. It starts pressuring and motivating them to change.

D. They may not mentally be able to separate this and understand it, but that is really what's happening.

E. They may think it's you they're upset with and it's you they're criticizing, but what they're really doing is criticizing God's Word coming through you.

IV. Whenever Jesus spoke, He caused a revival or a riot.

A. It's naïve and incorrect for us to think that if we just walk in love, everybody will love us.

B. You need to recognize that when you begin to stand on the Word without compromise, it starts to release its power.

C. Either people will repent and love you for it, or they'll criticize you because of it.

D. God's Word will divide and separate people (Matt. 10:34-36).

V. If I get offended and become gun-shy about speaking the truth because of what people have to say, the Word of God will cease performing and producing in my life.

A. I made a decision almost forty years ago that I wasn't going to let that happen.

B. I've been trying to be bold and let the Word of God, rather than the opinions of man, rule and dominate me.

C. It's become a habit and a lifestyle for me.

D. I may not be doing it perfectly, but I'm moving in this direction because of my conviction from the Word of God.

Persecution
LESSON 14 – TEACHER'S GUIDE

1. God's Word is never the variable; it has the same potential in every single person's life. What made the Word produce differently in the parable of the sower wasn't the seed itself, but rather the type of soil it found itself in. This parable illustrates four different types of hearts. It reveals that there's really only one type of response that will allow the seed of God's Word to fully produce its fruit.

2. Let's continue looking at the second type of person who heard the Word (Mark 4:16-17). The word **"offended"** here doesn't mean that they quit believing or renounced the Word. We need to recognize that Satan doesn't have to make us totally disavow our faith in the Word. If he can just get us to where we're cautious and afraid to speak, then we're hurt and offended, and now we aren't enthusiastic the way we used to be. If the devil can get us into that mode, he can stop the Word of God from working in our lives.

3. Mark 4:17 really ministered to me when I saw that the afflictions and persecutions come for the Word's sake. They don't come because of us personally; it's because of the Word. When we start speaking the Word to people, God uses it to bring conviction to them. It starts pressuring and motivating them to change. They may not mentally be able to separate this and understand it, but that is really what's happening. They may think it's us they're upset with and it's us they're criticizing, but what they're really doing is criticizing God's Word coming through us.

1. A. What has the same potential in every single person's life? (God's Word)
   B. What does the parable of the sower illustrate? (That there are four different types of hearts)
   C. What does it reveal? (That there's really only one type of response that will allow the seed of God's Word to fully produce its fruit)
2. A. Read Mark 4:16-17. Does the word **"offended"** mean that they quit believing or renounced the Word? (No)
   B. Where does Satan have to get us so he can stop the Word of God from working in our lives? (He has to get us to where we're cautious and afraid to speak, then hurt and offended, and unenthusiastic the way we used to be)
3. A. What happens when we start speaking the Word to people? (God uses it to bring conviction to them)
   B. If they start criticizing us for it, what are they really doing? (They're criticizing God's Word coming through us)

4. Whenever Jesus spoke, He caused a revival or a riot. It's naïve and incorrect for us to think that if we just walk in love, everybody will love us. We need to recognize that when we begin to stand on the Word without compromise, it starts to release its power. Either people will repent and love us for it, or they'll criticize us because of it. God's Word will divide and separate people (Matt. 10:34-36).

5. If I get offended and become gun-shy about speaking the truth because of what people have to say, the Word of God will cease performing and producing in my life. I made a decision almost forty years ago that I wasn't going to let that happen. I've been trying to be bold and let the Word of God, rather than the opinions of man, rule and dominate me. It's become a habit and a lifestyle for me. I may not be doing it perfectly, but I'm moving in this direction because of my conviction from the Word of God.

4. A. What did Jesus cause when He spoke? (Either a revival or a riot)
   B. If we think everybody will love us if we just walk in love, what is that? (Naïve and incorrect)
   C. Read Matthew 10:34-36. What will God's Word do? (Divide and separate)
5. A. Rather than the opinions of man, what does Andrew try to let rule and dominate him? (The Word of God)
   B. Why is Andrew moving in this direction? (Because of his conviction from the Word of God)

Persecution
LESSON 14 – DISCIPLESHIP QUESTIONS

1. According to Mark 4:13, what did Jesus expect His disciples to know (understand)?
   A. When it was time to eat
   B. The parable of the sower
   C. Seed, time, and harvest
   D. All of the above
   E. None of the above

2. Read Mark 4:16-17. These people received the Word _____.
   A. Reluctantly
   B. When they felt like it
   C. Out of fear
   D. With gladness
   E. As long as it lined up with their tradition

3. What do they do for a time?

4. According to Acts 17:6, Jason and certain brethren were those who what?

5. Read Matthew 10:16-42. Is Jesus saying these things to people who aren't His followers?

6. For whose sake would they be brought before governors and kings?

7. It is enough for the disciple to be like whom?

8. Who will Jesus confess before His Father in heaven?

9. **"He that findeth his life shall _____ it: and he that loseth his life for my sake shall _____ it."**

Persecution
LESSON 14 – ANSWER KEY

1. B. The parable of the sower
2. D. With gladness
3. Endure
4. Turned the world upside down
5. No
6. Jesus'
7. Their master
8. Those who confess Him before people
9. **"Lose," "find"**

Persecution
LESSON 14 – SCRIPTURES

MARK 4:13
And he said unto them, Know ye not this parable? and how then will ye know all parables?

MARK 4:16-17
And these are they likewise which are sown on stony ground; who, when they have heard the word, immediately receive it with gladness; [17] And have no root in themselves, and so endure but for a time: afterward, when affliction or persecution ariseth for the word's sake, immediately they are offended.

ACTS 17:6
And when they found them not, they drew Jason and certain brethren unto the rulers of the city, crying, These that have turned the world upside down are come hither also.

MATTHEW 10:16-42
Behold, I send you forth as sheep in the midst of wolves: be ye therefore wise as serpents, and harmless as doves. [17] But beware of men: for they will deliver you up to the councils, and they will scourge you in their synagogues; [18] And ye shall be brought before governors and kings for my sake, for a testimony against them and the Gentiles. [19] But when they deliver you up, take no thought how or what ye shall speak: for it shall be given you in that same hour what ye shall speak. [20] For it is not ye that speak, but the Spirit of your Father which speaketh in you. [21] And the brother shall deliver up the brother to death, and the father the child: and the children shall rise up against their parents, and cause them to be put to death. [22] And ye shall be hated of all men for my name's sake: but he that endureth to the end shall be saved. [23] But when they persecute you in this city, flee ye into another: for verily I say unto you, Ye shall not have gone over the cities of Israel, till the Son of man be come. [24] The disciple is not above his master, nor the servant above his lord. [25] It is enough for the disciple that he be as his master, and the servant as his lord. If they have called the master of the house Beelzebub, how much more shall they call them of his household? [26] Fear them not therefore: for there is nothing covered, that shall not be revealed; and hid, that shall not be known. [27] What I tell you in darkness, that speak ye in light: and what ye hear in the ear, that preach ye upon the housetops. [28] And fear not them which kill the body, but are not able

to kill the soul: but rather fear him which is able to destroy both soul and body in hell. [29] **Are not two sparrows sold for a farthing? and one of them shall not fall on the ground without your Father.** [30] **But the very hairs of your head are all numbered.** [31] **Fear ye not therefore, ye are of more value than many sparrows.** [32] **Whosoever therefore shall confess me before men, him will I confess also before my Father which is in heaven.** [33] **But whosoever shall deny me before men, him will I also deny before my Father which is in heaven.** [34] **Think not that I am come to send peace on earth: I came not to send peace, but a sword.** [35] **For I am come to set a man at variance against his father, and the daughter against her mother, and the daughter in law against her mother in law.** [36] **And a man's foes shall be they of his own household.** [37] **He that loveth father or mother more than me is not worthy of me: and he that loveth son or daughter more than me is not worthy of me.** [38] **And he that taketh not his cross, and followeth after me, is not worthy of me.** [39] **He that findeth his life shall lose it: and he that loseth his life for my sake shall find it.** [40] **He that receiveth you receiveth me, and he that receiveth me receiveth him that sent me.** [41] **He that receiveth a prophet in the name of a prophet shall receive a prophet's reward; and he that receiveth a righteous man in the name of a righteous man shall receive a righteous man's reward.** [42] **And whosoever shall give to drink unto one of these little ones a cup of cold water only in the name of a disciple, verily I say unto you, he shall in no wise lose his reward.**

My Revelation
LESSON 15

The parable of a grain of mustard seed is another parable Jesus told that day:

> **The kingdom of heaven is like to a grain of mustard seed, which a man took, and sowed in his field: Which indeed is the least of all seeds: but when it is grown, it is the greatest among herbs, and becometh a tree, so that the birds of the air come and lodge in the branches thereof.**
>
> **Matthew 13:31-32**

This is in the same chapter and the same context, on the same day, that the parable of the sower sowing the seed was given.

I remember one of my very first days as a U.S. soldier in Vietnam. I was on barracks duty while the rest of the people went through what was called "the CS chamber." It was a gas chamber, and they were teaching us how to put on our masks. They were using the equivalent of tear gas, which doesn't do any lasting damage, but it sure hurts and stings at first. It's a long story, but I had a very negative experience with that in basic training. Without overstating it, I nearly died.

At breakfast on the morning of this scheduled "training," they asked for a volunteer. One thing you learn very quickly in the Army is to never volunteer for anything. Nine times out of ten, you've made a mistake to do so. However, I figured that it didn't matter if they sent me to fight Vietcong by myself. It would be better than going through this gas chamber. That's how much I hated it.

So, I volunteered. It turned out that all they wanted me to do was sit there and guard the barracks while everybody else went through the gas chamber. It worked out great.

The Root System

While I sat there reading, I meditated on these scriptures in Matthew 13. I thought about how the kingdom of heaven is like a little grain of mustard seed—one of the smallest seeds. But when it is sown in the earth, it becomes this huge tree that the birds of the air come and lodge in.

As I was meditating on this, I remember thinking, *God, that's what I want my life to be. I want You to live through me so big that it affects millions of people. I want to see people's lives changed.*

While envisioning this, the Lord spoke to me, saying, "But your root is so small. The very first bird to land on a branch would cause the whole tree to fall over. The first breath of air to blow against it would knock it over." The Lord used this to paint a word picture for me.

I was more concerned about all of this growth above ground, which is the way most people are. They want visible results—something physical, something tangible. They desire to see lives being changed, people healed, and all kinds of other fruit. However, before all of this grows above ground, the vast majority of growth takes place underground in the root system. It's actually the root system that determines how big a plant or tree will be above ground.

If you neglect the root system, you might have a plant or tree grow up for a brief period of time, but it'll never produce the fruit. It won't live, because it'll never be able to withstand varying conditions like heat and drought. The root system is what enables the tree to really produce and withstand hardship.

This is what the Lord was speaking to me. I desired all of these great results, but I didn't want to take time to get rooted in the Word. He told me, "That's the big problem with most people." That was about 1970. I decided right then and there that I was going to be one of those in whom the Word of God would take root.

Seed Power

Once I made this decision, I actually quit worrying about the visible results to a large degree. Instead, I focused on taking the Word of God and keeping it in my heart. I knew that if I kept God's Word dwelling on the inside of me, instead of it coming in and out, it would literally begin to put down roots through every part of my being and start permeating me. This has been my focus since 1970.

I've taken the Word, meditated in it, gleaned truths from it, and applied my life toward those truths. Every good thing God has done in my life has come as the fruit of His Word. This includes the revelation He's shown me, the call to ministry He's given me, the people I've seen raised from the dead, the blind eyes and deaf ears I've seen opened, all kinds of other miracles, and the way God has abundantly met my needs. All the good in my life has come as the seed of God's Word has taken root in my heart and produced.

Once that seed has taken root, it just produces. What an awesome truth. I don't know about you, but this still gets me excited!

I have some huge boulders on my property. There's one I like to sit on sometimes that's over a hundred feet tall (that's more than one hundred feet above the ground). Yet, at the very top of this massive boulder, there's a little crack and a place where the wind has blown some leaves and debris in. Over time, it's made a little bit of soil. Somehow, a seed got up there on top of this boulder, took root, and a tree is growing out of that. Of course, the tree has outgrown that little bit of dirt that's on the top of this boulder, so it's sending roots down further, and it's splitting this huge boulder. There are several other boulders on my property that have literally been split in two by a tiny little seed taking root and growing up. The power that's in a seed is amazing!

A tiny little seed from God's Word can destroy any sickness, any disease, emotional issue, or financial problem if you would just take the Word of God, keep it in your heart, and let it dominate you. It's that powerful!

Meditate, Germinate, Release

But you must protect it. You have to let the Word take root in yourself. You can't go off of somebody else's revelation. You can't just tell people, "Andrew Wommack says..." That's not going to convince anybody. You need to take what I'm saying, meditate on it, and let the Lord bear witness to it in your heart. Once that revelation is yours, then you can go out and say, "God told me this truth. The Bible says in Mark 16..." and tell them directly what God spoke to you. It's not enough to know what I believe the Word of God says; it has to become personal revelation to you!

That is profound. Yet it's amazing how many people don't really have the Word of God rooted on the inside of them.

When the Lord first spoke this to me and it became a revelation, God convicted me that I was living off of somebody else's revelation. I remember saying to myself, "That will never happen again. In the name of Jesus, it's going to be my revelation. I may have heard somebody else say it, but I'm going to go to God and meditate on that word until it germinates and releases its life in me. It's going to be what God spoke to me!" There are thousands of things I've gleaned from the Word. Perhaps somebody else planted the seed, but it became my revelation as it took root on the inside of me.

My Revelation
LESSON 15 – OUTLINE

I. The parable of a grain of mustard seed is another parable Jesus told that day:

> **The kingdom of heaven is like to a grain of mustard seed, which a man took, and sowed in his field: Which indeed is the least of all seeds: but when it is grown, it is the greatest among herbs, and becometh a tree, so that the birds of the air come and lodge in the branches thereof.**
>
> **Matthew 13:31-32**

A. As I meditated on these scriptures, I remember thinking, *God, that's what I want life to be. I want You to live through me so big that it affects millions of people. I want to see people's lives changed.*

B. While envisioning this, the Lord spoke to me, saying, "But your root is so small. The very first bird to land on a branch would cause the whole tree to fall over. The first breath of air to blow against it would knock it over."

C. It's actually the root system that determines how big a plant or tree will be above ground.

D. I desired all of these great results, but I didn't want to take time to get rooted in the Word.

E. The Lord told me, "That's the big problem with most people."

II. I decided right then and there that I was going to be one of those in whom the Word of God would take root.

A. I actually quit worrying about the visible results to a large degree.

B. Instead, I focused on taking the Word of God and keeping it in my heart.

C. I knew that if I kept God's Word dwelling on the inside of me, instead of it coming in and out, it would literally begin to put down roots through every part of my being and start permeating me.

III. Every good thing God has done in my life has come as the fruit of His Word.

A. This includes the revelation He's shown me, the call to ministry He's given me, the people I've seen raised from the dead, the blind eyes and deaf ears I've seen opened, all kinds of other miracles, and the way God has abundantly met my needs.

B. Once that seed has taken root, it just produces.

C. I don't know about you, but this still gets me excited!

IV. A tiny little seed from God's Word can destroy any sickness, any disease, emotional issue, or financial problem if you would just take the Word of God, keep it in your heart, and let it dominate you.

A. It's that powerful!

B. But you must protect it.

C. You need to take what I'm saying, meditate on it, and let the Lord bear witness to it in your heart.

D. It's not enough to know what I believe the Word of God says; it has to become personal revelation to you!

E. That is profound.

V. When the Lord first spoke this to me and it became a revelation, God convicted me that I was living off of somebody else's revelation.

A. I remember saying to myself, "That will never happen again. In the name of Jesus, it's going to be my revelation. I may have heard somebody else say it, but I'm going to go to God and meditate on that word until it germinates and releases its life in me. It's going to be what God spoke to me!"

B. There are thousands of things I've gleaned from the Word.

C. Perhaps somebody else planted the seed, but it became my revelation as it took root on the inside of me.

My Revelation
LESSON 15 – TEACHER'S GUIDE

1. The parable of a grain of mustard seed is another parable Jesus told that day (Matt. 13:31-32). As I meditated on these scriptures, I remember thinking, *God, that's what I want my life to be. I want You to live through me so big that it affects millions of people. I want to see people's lives changed.* While envisioning this, the Lord spoke to me, saying, "But your root is so small. The very first bird to land on a branch would cause the whole tree to fall over. The first breath of air to blow against it would knock it over." It's actually the root system that determines how big the plant or tree will be above ground. I desired all of these great results, but I didn't want to take time to get rooted in the Word. The Lord told me, "That's the big problem with most people."

2. I decided right then and there that I was going to be one of those in whom the Word of God would take root. I actually quit worrying about the visible results to a large degree. Instead, I focused on taking the Word of God and keeping it in my heart. I knew that if I kept God's Word dwelling on the inside of me, instead of it coming in and out, it would literally begin to put down roots through every part of my being and start permeating me.

3. Every good thing God has done in my life has come as the fruit of His Word. This includes the revelation He's shown me, the call to ministry He's given me, the people I've seen raised from the dead, the blind eyes and deaf ears I've seen opened, all kinds of other miracles, and the way God has abundantly met my needs. Once that seed has taken root, it just produces. I don't know about you, but this still gets me excited!

1. A. What determines how big a plant or tree will be above ground? (Its root system)
   B. What is the big problem with most people? (They desire all of these great results, but they don't want to take time to get rooted in the Word)
2. A. What did Andrew quit worrying about to a large degree? (The visible results)
   B. What did he know? (That if he kept God's Word dwelling on the inside of him, instead of it coming in and out, it would literally begin to put down roots through every part of his being and start permeating him)
3. A. What has come as the fruit of God's Word? (Every good thing God has done in Andrew's life)
   B. What happens once the seed has taken root? (It just produces)

4. A tiny little seed from God's Word can destroy any sickness, any disease, emotional issue, or financial problem if you would just take the Word of God, keep it in your heart, and let it dominate you. It's that powerful! But you must protect it. You need to take what I'm saying, meditate on it, and let the Lord bear witness to it in your heart. It's not enough to know what I believe the Word of God says; it has to become personal revelation to you! That is profound.

5. When the Lord first spoke this to me and it became a revelation, God convicted me that I was living off of somebody else's revelation. I remember saying to myself, "That will never happen again. In the name of Jesus, it's going to be my revelation. I may have heard somebody else say it, but I'm going to go to God and meditate on that word until it germinates and releases its life in me. It's going to be what God spoke to me!" There are thousands of things I've gleaned from the Word. Perhaps somebody else planted the seed, but it became my revelation as it took root on the inside of me.

4. A. What can a tiny seed from God's Word do if we would just take the Word of God, keep it in our hearts, and let it dominate us? (It can destroy any sickness, any disease, emotional issue, or financial problem)
   B. What must we do with God's Word? (Protect it)
   C. Is it enough to know what Andrew believes the Word of God says? (No, it has to become personal revelation to us!)
5. Perhaps somebody else planted the seed, but as it took root on the inside of Andrew, what did it become? (His revelation)

My Revelation
LESSON 15 – DISCIPLESHIP QUESTIONS

1. Read Matthew 13:31-32. What kind of seed is the kingdom of heaven like?

2. Whose field did the man sow in?

3. What is a mustard seed among all the others?

4. What is it when it is grown?
   A. The smallest of shrubs
   B. A mulberry tree
   C. A juniper tree
   D. The greatest among herbs
   E. A fig tree

5. What does it become?

6. What is able to lodge in its branches?

My Revelation
LESSON 15 – ANSWER KEY

1. A mustard seed
2. His own
3. The least
4. D. The greatest among herbs
5. A tree
6. The birds of the air

My Revelation
LESSON 15 – SCRIPTURES

MATTHEW 13:31-32
Another parable put he forth unto them, saying, The kingdom of heaven is like to a grain of mustard seed, which a man took, and sowed in his field: [32] **Which indeed is the least of all seeds: but when it is grown, it is the greatest among herbs, and becometh a tree, so that the birds of the air come and lodge in the branches thereof.**

Choked!

LESSON 16

Now we come to the third type of person that heard God's Word, and how that person responded to it:

> **And these are they which are sown among thorns; such as hear the word, And the cares of this world, and the deceitfulness of riches, and the lusts of other things entering in, choke the word, and it becometh unfruitful.**
>
> **Mark 4:18-19**

In addition to the four different types of hearts that the Word of God was planted into, this parable also speaks about a progression. You first start out not having any desire for the Word of God at all. The Word is like water off a duck's back. It's in one ear and out the other. That's the first type.

The second type liked the Word of God and was excited about it, but there was no root in that person's heart.

The third type is someone who has learned God's truths enough that they are excited about the Word and have meditated in it enough that it's beginning to take root. There's a real life and vibrancy coming out of them. The Word of God is starting to produce results in their life, but then they get occupied with the cares of this life, the deceitfulness of riches, and the lusts of other things.

Personally, I feel that in my life, I've come through the first and second type of person. I believe that I'm moving out of the third type of person and into the fourth, where I am beginning to be productive. However, I still deal with some of these same things. I still get occupied with things other than what God has really called me to do. I believe that affects a lot of us.

Constantly Bombarded

In our day and age, we have access to information that previous generations never had. Most generations prior to the 1950s were basically isolated. It took a long time for news and information to get around. So, people lived in these smaller communities, and they didn't have all of the pressures and cares of this world inundating them the way we do. Today, if something happens on the other side of the globe, we hear about it nearly instantaneously. We can turn our televisions on and watch live coverage of it. We can literally take the problems of this world into our lives. Whereas, in previous generations, it would have taken weeks, or even a month, to find out what had happened. By that time, the situation would have been over, so it didn't cause the same level of anxiety, worry, or care.

Today we are being constantly bombarded, not only by news and the problems of this world, but also by all kinds of entertainment. We have an abundance of television, movies, and video games. Also, it seems that on the job, people are working harder than ever before. Americans are some of the biggest workaholics on the face of the earth. Individuals who work forty hours a week are the exception. Most workers put in more. People are just pouring themselves into all these worldly things, and it will choke the Word of God.

Now, don't get me wrong: I'm not saying God wants us all to leave life and enter monasteries so we can just sit there and study the Word twenty-four hours a day. That's not what I'm talking about. However, I am saying that meditating in the Word takes time. It takes quantity time, not just "quality" time, for the Word to take root on the inside of us. Many of our lifestyles today are not conducive to the Word of God taking root in our lives.

Sadhu Sundar Singh was a powerful Christian who lived in India in the early 1900s. He saw great miracles, including multiple people raised from the dead in one day. This brother had a tremendous ministry.

Around 1910, Sundar traveled by boat from India to New York City. It took him a month or two to get there because of the mode of travel. Due to this, he had a year's worth of meetings lined up in the United States. He got off the boat in New York City, spent thirty minutes walking around town, and then decided to get right back on the boat to return to India. He remarked that there was no point in ministering to the people in America, because their lifestyle would not allow the Word of God to take root in their hearts. And this was a hundred years ago! Yet it's the same truth I'm talking about right here. The cares of this world, the deceitfulness of riches, and the lusts of other things enter in and choke the Word (Mark 4:18-19).

Take Down Time

Busyness is not conducive to spirituality. There is a balance to this, but most people aren't walking in it. Most are far too occupied with other things than God and His Word. If you were to ask the average person how they're doing, the majority of their responses would have something to do with how busy they are. When I'm asked that question, I sometimes answer, "I'm busier than a one-armed wallpaper hanger!" Many people say, "I'm busier than I've ever been." That's pretty typical. Yet, according to Mark 4, it's busyness like this that will stop the Word of God from working in your life and producing fruit. You need time sitting and soaking in the Word of God for it to be able to release its power in your life.

Many people talk about having "devotion" times. To them, this means doing a little five-minute devotion in the morning when they first get up. I admit, there is some benefit to that. However, if you squeeze just five or ten minutes in, trying to hear the Lord's voice and stay your mind on the things of God, but the rest of the day you are running around at a frantic pace, you aren't going to have the Word of God produce itself in your life.

It takes some down time.

> **Be still, and know that I am God.**
>
> **Psalm 46:10**

You have to be still and quiet yourself. If I get really involved, busy, and going at a frantic pace, it takes a period of time for me to sit down, slow myself down, and get to where I can hear God from my heart. It just takes me awhile. If I've been preoccupied with something for a longer period of time—perhaps days or weeks—and I haven't had time to be still and know that He is God, then it takes me awhile to penetrate and break through that barrier to where I'm listening and tuned in to the spirit realm. If I have been spending lots of time with the Lord and am very sensitive to Him, I could get occupied and busy with something for an hour but then step out of that and go right back into the spirit realm almost immediately. But if it has been days or weeks that I've been preoccupied with something else, it takes me some time—not just quality, but quantity time—to quiet myself, get still, and allow the Word of God to work in my life.

One night I saw in a dream, "Psalm 46:10." I didn't see the words in that scripture. I just saw the Scripture reference. Even though I've ministered from that verse hundreds of times, when I woke up, I couldn't for the life of me think of what that verse said. So, I looked it up. Immediately, I recognized an old familiar friend, but I felt like it must have something more to say to me. So, I meditated on that verse all morning.

I don't believe that verse is only speaking of being physically still; I think it includes stilling our minds and emotions, and there are many other applications. But that afternoon, I decided I would literally sit still for one hour just to see what came of it. It was amazing. I didn't move anything but my eyes. I didn't rock in my chair or shift positions. I was as still as a stone. I had a deer walk right up to me. A chipmunk crawled up on my shoe. I was still.

And I noticed things all around me that I hadn't noticed before. I heard the wind blowing in the trees. It had been blowing all day, but my busyness had distracted me so that I didn't notice it until I was totally still. I counted dozens of chipmunks that I hadn't noticed before. There were thousands of ants, and before I was still, I never noticed. There was so much happening all around me that I had just missed because I was busy.

The Lord used that instance to speak to me that busyness with this natural world limits our perception of the spiritual world. Or, as Jesus put it, the cares of this life, the deceitfulness of riches, and the lust of other things choke the Word.

A lifestyle where you are going fast and frantic all the time will stop God's Word from working in your life. Even Jesus took down time (Mark 6:31). He was in such demand ministering to the people Him that sometimes, He didn't even have time to eat. So, He tried to separate Himself and His disciples, saying, "Let's go over into a desert place." Do you know why the Lord wanted to do that? Yes, His goal was to reach people. Yes, He desired to touch as many people's lives as He could. Yet, after He and His disciples had been out on this missionary tour, He was telling them to come apart, rest awhile, and go over to this desert place. Jesus did this because He realized that the cares of this life, the deceitfulness of riches, and the lusts of other things will choke the Word of God.

Separate Yourself

You need some time where you can separate yourself from all the busy activities of daily life and just spend time focused on God. Now, you don't necessarily have to have your nose buried in the Bible. To a degree, you will because you can't meditate on scriptures that you don't know. But if you've already been reading the Bible, you might be able to just go sit on the porch for a while and pray about what's been going on during that day. You could meditate on the scriptures He's been giving you and ask Him to show you things.

I do that a lot. I built a trail on my property, and walk on it an hour or two a day. I spend that time just meditating on the things of God, thinking about what He's leading me to do, and meditating on scriptures. We have a little swing out on our patio I like to sit on. You can't see another house from my place, so I like to sit out there and look at the mountains. I just look around, meditate, and think on things. That's an important time.

One of the things that will stop God's Word from working in your life is just being busy. If Satan came in a red suit with horns and a pitchfork, most of us would resist him, saying, "No way am I giving in to you!" Likewise, most of us would reject X-rated, even most R-rated material, or anything else that is just overtly of the devil. But there's nothing wrong with having a job, a career, and a family. Working your job and spending time with your family are good and right in their place, but it's not good if you cram so much into your life that you have very little or no time left for God and His Word. You may be occupying your life with decent things—things that aren't immoral of themselves—but if you have no time to sit and meditate on the things of the Lord, it will stop the Word of God from working in your life.

In my own personal life, God has dealt with me about a number of things. They aren't sin, but He's told me that I cannot afford to become preoccupied with them. I don't need another hobby. I don't need anything else to do, especially because of my personality. I have a compulsive type of personality, which means that everything I do, I do to an extreme. I've had some friends try to get me involved in doing certain things. They enjoy them and it's no problem for them. But I just don't have the time to devote to anything else. I have to keep the main thing the main thing!

I wish I could somehow or another make people understand this because Satan is really using this to hinder people's personal growth. He draws them into being so busy that they short-circuit God's provision for them to change. They just get so preoccupied that they don't take the time to be in the Word and in fellowship with Him. This hinders the change God wants to bring to pass.

Fellowshipping with God

If you are going to have effective change—the Word of God producing fruit in your life—you must start spending quantity time fellowshipping with God through the Word. You have to take these truths, plant them, and keep them in your heart. Some people don't like that, but it's just the way the kingdom works. This isn't necessarily the way we would have decided to have it done, but this is how the Lord said His kingdom operates. Since He's the Lord, it's going to work the way He says, not the way you choose.

This is something I have to deal with all the time. I constantly have to make time and force myself not to get too busy.

Although I'm not tempted to go out and do any of those things that the church calls "sin," God has to deal with me often about getting so preoccupied with ministry. It's the things concerning the ministry that crowd out my time of fellowship with God and study of His Word. The Lord has had to deal with me over that. And if I can become too preoccupied and busy with ministry—things that are good and that help other people—so that the Word of God is being choked and hindered in my life, what can happen in other people's lives who are occupied with pursuing their careers and running their kids all over town all week long?

Don't get me wrong: I'm not here to tell you what you can or cannot do. However, you may be one of these people who love God, place an importance on His Word, and want to see the fruit, but are so occupied with all kinds of "good" things that the seed of God's Word is being choked out in your life. Many Christians are simply involved in too many things. They're constantly taxiing their kids here, there, and yonder, and they're involved in everything the church has to offer. If you're not careful, these things will choke the Word of God and keep you from being productive. These things aren't bad—just natural.

Stay Home

While in Vietnam, I had a lot of time on my hands. I wasn't one of the "grunt" guys who were out in the field constantly hiking every day and engaging the enemy. I did see some action, and there was a lot of danger associated with being on that fire support base. However, to a large degree, it was boring just sitting there on a hill. I was a chaplain's assistant assigned to brigade headquarters. Yet I was on the battalion level. This means there was nobody directly over me because I reported back to people forty-five miles away. This is why I had such a huge amount of time on my hands.

So, I just started poring over the Word of God as much as fifteen or sixteen hours a day. I studied through the Bible all day long. I would go on bunker guard every single day and spend four hours praying and communicating with the Lord. After over thirteen months of just constantly being in the Word and praying, I returned home to the U.S.A., ready to go to church and be with other Christians again. Since I had a car, I became the taxi driver for some younger friends as we drove all over the Dallas-Fort Worth area. We often stayed out as late as one or two o'clock in the morning, attending prayer meetings, revival meetings, and even all-night prayer meetings.

Although that sounds good, after being back from Vietnam for about a month, I began to recognize my spiritual sensitivity to God was diminishing. My heart wasn't as focused on Him as before. I wasn't doing anything sinful or wrong, but the Lord spoke to me, saying, "Going to church every night is killing your relationship with Me."

Now, you may not understand that. In fact, you may be tempted right now to think I'm anti-church. Let me assure you, that's not the case. However, I was going to church every single night—seven nights a week. In the Dallas-Fort Worth area, there was always someplace you could go. Plus, we had prayer meetings in the morning and other meetings during the day. I was so involved in doing all of these things—godly things—that it was choking the Word of God out of my life. So, one of the things the Lord told me to do was to stay home at least two nights a week. He specifically instructed me NOT to go out with my friends to a revival meeting, convention, or prayer meeting, but to stay home, studying the Word and fellowshipping with Him. I needed to get back into the flow of personal relationship with Him.

Weeds

They're like weeds sprouting up all around the stalk of corn you planted. The soil (your heart) only has so much nourishment for the seed (God's Word). Those weeds will suck much of the moisture and nutrients out of the soil, which will keep the seed that you want to grow from really producing and bearing fruit. This is what happens to you if you get so occupied doing other things. It doesn't have to be bad things; it's just that you're so occupied with them that it saps your attention and energy. You don't really have any time to be able to focus on and fellowship with the Lord.

Honestly, do you fall asleep every time you try to get quiet and study the Word of God? Are you so busy that you aren't even getting a full night's sleep? Many people are cramming so much into their lives, and these things aren't improving the quality of their lives. These people have just become busy. That lifestyle needs to change.

Are you seeing the change in your life that you desire? Are you bearing the fruit that you know God wants you to bear? If not, I challenge you to start spending some quantity time just focused on the things of the Lord. I'm not going to put a certain amount on this, because it may vary from person to person. If you go from spending no time focused on God to spending thirty minutes a day—with everything else out of your mind—you'll see tremendous benefits. Perhaps you've already been spending time, and the Lord is drawing you deeper. You just need to make a decision that you are going to start taking away all of these things that choke the Word of God in your life.

CHOKED!
Lesson 16 – OUTLINE

I. Now we come to the third type of person that heard God's Word, and how that person responded to it:

> **And these are they which are sown among thorns; such as hear the word, And the cares of this world, and the deceitfulness of riches, and the lusts of other things entering in, choke the word, and it becometh unfruitful.**
>
> **Mark 4:18-19**

A. The third type is someone who has learned God's truths enough that they are excited about the Word and have meditated in it enough that it's beginning to take root.

B. There's a real life and vibrancy coming out of them.

C. The Word of God is starting to produce results in their life, but then they get occupied with the cares of this life, the deceitfulness of riches, and the lusts of other things.

II. Today we are being constantly bombarded, not only by news and the problems of this world, but also by all kinds of entertainment.

A. We have an abundance of television, movies, and video games.

B. Also, it seems that on the job, people are working harder than ever before.

C. They are just pouring themselves into all this, and it will choke the Word of God.

D. Busyness is not conducive to spirituality.

E. Most are far too occupied with other things than God and His Word.

III. If you squeeze just five or ten minutes in, trying to hear the Lord's voice and stay your mind on the things of God, but the rest of the day you are running around at a frantic pace, you aren't going to have the Word of God produce itself in your life.

A. You have to be still and quiet yourself (Ps. 46:10).

B. If I get really involved, busy, and going at a frantic pace, it takes a period of time for me to sit down, slow myself down, and get to where I can hear God from my heart.

C. If I have been spending lots of time with the Lord and am very sensitive to Him, I could get occupied and busy with something for an hour but then step out of that and go right back into the spirit realm almost immediately.

D. Busyness with this natural world limits our perception of the spiritual world.

IV. Even Jesus took down time (Mark 6:31).

A. Yes, His goal was to reach people.

B. Yes, He desired to touch as many people's lives as He could.

C. Yet, after He and His disciples had been out on this missionary tour, He was telling them to come apart, rest awhile, and go over to this desert place.

V. You need some time where you can separate yourself from all the busy activities of daily life and just spend time focused on God.

A. Now, you don't necessarily have to have your nose buried in the Bible.

B. To a degree, you will because you can't meditate on scriptures that you don't know.

C. But if you've already been reading the Bible, you might be able to just go sit on the porch for a while and pray about what's been going on during that day.

D. You could meditate on the scriptures He's been giving you and ask Him to show you things.

VI. Working your job and spending time with your family are good and right in their place, but it's not good if you cram so much into your life that you have very little or no time left for God and His Word.

A. I wish I could somehow or another make people understand this because Satan is really using this to hinder people's personal growth.

B. He draws them into being so busy that they short-circuit God's provision for them to change.

C. They just get so preoccupied that they don't take the time to be in the Word and in fellowship with Him.

D. This hinders the change God wants to bring to pass.

E. If I can become too preoccupied and busy with ministry—things that are good and that help other people—so that the Word of God is being choked and hindered in my life, what can happen in other people's lives who are occupied with pursuing their careers and running their kids all over town all week long?

VII. You may be one of these people who love God, place an importance on His Word, and want to see the fruit, but are so occupied with all kinds of "good" things that the seed of God's Word is being choked out in your life.

A. If you're not careful, these things will keep you from being productive.

B. They're like weeds sprouting up all around the stalk of corn you planted.

C. The soil (your heart) only has so much nourishment for the seed (God's Word).

D. Those weeds will suck much of the moisture and nutrients out of the soil, which will keep the seed that you want to grow from really producing and bearing fruit.

VIII. Many people are cramming so much into their lives, and these things aren't improving the quality of their lives.

A. That lifestyle needs to change.

B. Are you seeing the change in your life that you desire?

C. Are you bearing the fruit that you know God wants you to bear?

D. If not, I challenge you to start spending some quantity time just focused on the things of the Lord.

E. Perhaps you've already been spending time, and the Lord is drawing you deeper.

F. You just need to make a decision that you are going to start taking away all of these things that choke the Word of God in your life.

CHOKED!

Lesson 16 – TEACHER'S GUIDE

1. Now we come to the third type of person that heard God's Word, and how that person responded to it (Mark 4:18-19). The third type is someone who has learned God's truths enough that they are excited about the Word and have meditated in it enough that it's beginning to take root. There's a real life and vibrancy coming out of them. The Word of God is starting to produce results in their life, but then they get occupied with the cares of this life, the deceitfulness of riches, and the lusts of other things.

2. Today we are being constantly bombarded, not only by news and the problems of this world, but also by all kinds of entertainment. We have an abundance of television, movies, and video games. Also, it seems that on the job, people are working harder than ever before. They are just pouring themselves into all this, and it will choke the Word of God. Busyness is not conducive to spirituality. Most are far too occupied with other things than God and His Word.

3. If we squeeze just five or ten minutes in, trying to hear the Lord's voice and stay our minds on the things of God, but the rest of the day we are running around at a frantic pace, we aren't going to have the Word of God produce itself in our lives. We have to be still and quiet ourselves (Ps. 46:10). If I get really involved, busy, and going at a frantic pace, it takes a period of time for me to sit down, slow myself down, and get to where I can hear God from my heart. If I have been spending lots of time with the Lord and am very sensitive to Him, I could get occupied and busy with something for an hour but then step out of that and go right back into the spirit realm almost immediately. Busyness with this natural world limits our perception of the spiritual world.

4. Even Jesus took down time (Mark 6:31). Yes, His goal was to reach people. Yes, He desired to touch as many people's lives as He could. Yet, after He and His disciples had been out on this missionary tour, He was telling them to come apart, rest awhile, and go over to this desert place.

1. A. Read Mark 4:18-19. The third type is someone who what? (Who has learned God's truths enough that they are excited about the Word and have meditated in it enough that it's beginning to take root)
   B. But what do they get occupied with? (The cares of this life, the deceitfulness of riches, and the lusts of other things)
2. What is not conducive to spirituality? (Busyness)
3. A. If we squeeze just five or ten minutes in, trying to hear the Lord's voice and stay our minds on the things of God, but the rest of the day we are running around at a frantic pace, what will happen? (We aren't going to have the Word of God produce itself in our lives)
   B. Read Psalm 46:10. If Andrew gets really involved, busy, and going at a frantic pace, it takes a period of time for him to sit down and do what? (Slow himself down and get to where he can hear God from his heart)
   C. What limits our perception of the spiritual world? (Busyness with this natural world)
4. Read Mark 6:31. Even though Jesus' goal was to reach people and He desired to touch as many lives as He could, what did He do? (After He and His disciples had been out on this missionary tour, He was telling them to come apart, rest awhile, and go over to this desert place)

5. We need some time where we can separate ourselves from all the busy activities of daily life and just spend time focused on God. Now, we don't necessarily have to have our noses buried in the Bible. To a degree, we will because we can't meditate on scriptures that we don't know. But if we've already been reading the Bible, we might be able to just go sit on the porch for a while and pray about what's been going on during that day. We could meditate on the scriptures He's been giving us and ask Him to show us things.

6. Working our jobs and spending time with our families are good and right in their place, but it's not good if we cram so much into our lives that we have very little or no time left for God and His Word. I wish I could somehow or another make people understand this because Satan is really using this to hinder people's personal growth. He draws them into being so busy that they short-circuit God's provision for them to change. They just get so preoccupied that they don't take the time to be in the Word and in fellowship with Him. This hinders the change God wants to bring to pass. If I can become too preoccupied and busy with ministry—things that are good and that help other people—so that the Word of God is being choked and hindered in my life, what can happen in other people's lives who are occupied with pursuing their careers and running their kids all over town all week long?

7. We may be one of these people who love God, place an importance on His Word, and want to see the fruit, but are so occupied with all kinds of "good" things that the seed of God's Word is being choked out in our lives. If we're not careful, these things will keep us from being productive. They're like weeds sprouting up all around the stalk of corn we planted. The soil (our hearts) only has so much nourishment for the seed (God's Word). Those weeds will suck much of the moisture and nutrients out of the soil, which will keep the seed that we want to grow from really producing and bearing fruit.

8. Many people are cramming so much into their lives, and these things aren't improving the quality of their lives. That lifestyle needs to change. Are you seeing the change in your life that you desire? Are you bearing the fruit that you know God wants you to bear? If not, I challenge you to start spending some quantity time just focused on the things of the Lord. Perhaps you've already been spending time, and the Lord is drawing you deeper. You just need to make a decision that you are going to start taking away all of these things that choke the Word of God in your life.

5. What scriptures can't we meditate on? (The ones that we don't know)
6. A. Working our jobs and spending time with our families are good and right in their place, but it's not good if we what? (If we cram so much into our lives that we have very little or no time left for God and His Word)
   B. Satan draws people into what? (Being so busy that they short-circuit God's provision for them to change)
7. A. What are the "good" things like that we can be so occupied with? (They're like weeds sprouting up all around the stalk of corn we planted)
   B. Our hearts only have so much _____ for God's Word. (Nourishment)
   C. What will the weeds do? (They will suck much of the moisture and nutrients out of the soil, which will keep the seed that we want to grow from really producing and bearing fruit)
8. A. What is not improving the quality of people's lives? (The things they cram into their lives)
   B. What needs to change? (That lifestyle)
   C. What decision do we need to make if we need to spend more quantity time focused on the things of the Lord? (We need to decide that we are going to start taking away all of these things that choke the Word of God in our lives)

CHOKED!
Lesson 16 – DISCIPLESHIP QUESTIONS

1. Read Mark 4:18-19. The cares of this world, the deceitfulness of riches, and the lusts of other things _____ in.

2. What do these things choke?
   A. The Word
   B. The one who didn't pay me what he owed
   C. The cares of this world, the deceitfulness of riches, and the lusts of other things
   D. All of the above
   E. None of the above

3. According to Psalm 46:10, what two things are you to do?

4. **"I will be exalted among the _____, I will be exalted in the earth."**
   A. "Pagan"
   B. "Jew"
   C. "Gentile"
   D. "Heathen"
   E. "Follower"

5. Read Mark 6:31. Why did Jesus tell the disciples to come apart into a deserted place and rest awhile?

Lesson 16
CHOKED! – ANSWER KEY

1. Enter

2. A. The Word

3. Be still and know that the Lord is God

4. D. **"Heathen"**

5. Because there were many people coming and going, and Jesus and the disciples did not even have time to eat

CHOKED!
Lesson 16 – SCRIPTURES

MARK 4:18-19

And these are they which are sown among thorns; such as hear the word, [19] And the cares of this world, and the deceitfulness of riches, and the lusts of other things entering in, choke the word, and it becometh unfruitful.

PSALM 46:10

Be still, and know that I am God: I will be exalted among the heathen, I will be exalted in the earth.

MARK 6:31

And he said unto them, Come ye yourselves apart into a desert place, and rest a while: for there were many coming and going, and they had no leisure so much as to eat.

Less
LESSON 17

In the parable of the sower, there was only one soil that really produced the intended fruit. It's this last type of heart that the Word of God was sown into:

> **And these are they which are sown on good ground; such as hear the word, and receive it, and bring forth fruit, some thirtyfold, some sixty, and some an hundred.**
>
> **Mark 4:20**

We all want to be this last type of ground. We all want to produce an abundant crop of good fruit. However, the best type of ground didn't have more; it had less.

First Place

When the Lord showed this truth to me, I was just starting out in ministry. It impacted me deeply because I was acutely aware that I was just a hick from Texas. My voice is not what you would call a voice for radio and television. God chooses the weak things of this world to confound the wise (1 Cor. 1:26-28). If I were picking people to be on radio and television, I wouldn't have picked me, that's for sure! So, I knew about all my liabilities—my voice, the way I look, that I'm a hick from Texas, and that I don't have the "charisma" that a lot of other people have. Because of this, I honestly doubted that God could use me. But the Lord really encouraged me through this parable.

He showed me that it was the seed—the Word—that produced the fruit. And the ground that produced the best fruit wasn't the ground that had more; it was the ground that had less—less stones, less thorns, and less weeds. The really productive soil didn't have more than everything else; it had less.

This told me that in order to be fruitful, I didn't necessarily need all of these external talents that people normally emphasize; it's really just a matter of the heart. If I would rid myself of the stones, thorns, and weeds, I could bear much fruit. I just needed to eliminate the things that occupy my attention and instead devote myself completely to God. If I put the Word of God first place in my heart, then that Word would produce an abundant harvest in my life.

This really encouraged me. I prayed, "God, if what really makes Your Word become fruitful is being less, then I can certainly be less. I may not be able to be more, but I can definitely be less. I can get rid of these things that hinder me."

You may not feel like you're the sharpest knife in the drawer. You may be acutely aware that you have all kinds of liabilities that other people don't have. Yet you can commit yourself to the Word of God and meditate in it until it takes deep root in your heart. You can refuse to allow anything else to divert your attention or sap the strength from your heart that could be going to the Lord. If you devote yourself completely to His Word, it will make you a success. It will cause fruit to come in whatever area He has called and anointed you to minister.

An Asset

Luke's account says,

> **But that on the good ground are they, which in an honest and good heart, having heard the word, keep it, and bring forth fruit with patience.**
>
> **Luke 8:15**

If you stop to think about it, this whole parable has been about patience. It's about a seed being planted and then reaping a harvest. Anyone who has ever dealt with seeds knows they have to give the seeds time to work. Time is actually an asset. It's a benefit to a farmer. It's not a negative but a positive.

When you put a seed in the ground, you don't know what's happening. But if you'll leave that seed in the ground, keeping it watered and weeded, God has just made it so that over time, it'll germinate and take root. The crop will come up, and the fruit will mature. Time is actually a benefit. Instead of looking at time negatively, you need to see it as a friend.

After speaking along these lines about the growth process and it taking time, I remember one of our Bible college students getting mad, saying, "I don't have ten years to mature. God has told me that I'm supposed to lead a million people to the Lord. Jesus is coming back soon!" So, in spite of all the scriptures that talk about not putting a novice in a position of authority, all the scriptures that speak of growth over time, this guy just determined that he was going to violate all of that and get it done on his own. He actually quit school so he could go ahead and change the world in a short period of time. This was years ago, and it hasn't come to pass yet. He saw time as a negative and had the attitude of "I can't afford to wait!"

Now that I've been in the ministry for over forty years, I look at time as an asset. I've been sowing the Word of God in my life for decades. I've been meditating on these truths for years. I'm still reaping today because of the time I invested in the kingdom of God decades ago.

Reproduction and Multiplication

Once a seed is sown, it'll grow and multiply over time. Consider the dandelion. If you were to sow a dandelion seed in your yard, over time, that dandelion would reproduce itself and completely fill your yard. That's how seeds work. Time is actually a friend to a seed because it allows reproduction and multiplication.

Don't think, *Oh, man, I have to spend time growing, maturing, and letting the Word take root on the inside of me.* View it positively. Every second you spend meditating in the Word of God and planting these seeds into your heart, you're putting in motion a process that cannot be stopped. Seeds are powerful.

It's been over twenty years since Mount St. Helens erupted. Because of the devastation, all the scientists back then were predicting it would take hundreds of years for the area to reforest itself, for the animals to come back, and for the flowers to return. Now they're just shocked that things have regenerated like they have after only a little more than twenty years. It's far beyond everyone's expectations. They didn't understand the power that's in those seeds. There was so much heat and so many mudslides, yet those seeds are doing what God created them to do: They started producing, and by the very next year, there were already signs of regeneration sprouting up here and there.

God has put seeds in His Word. We need to take these seeds, plant them in our hearts, and just leave them there. If we keep the Word of God fresh and alive on the inside of us, it'll continue benefiting us twenty, thirty, fifty years from now, should the Lord tarry.

This is how the kingdom of God works. Once you understand this principle, you can take the Word of God, sow it into your life, and keep it there. Instead of being discouraged that it takes time, you can be encouraged. Once you get this system going and you've invested that time, the Word of God will supernaturally change you. You'll be changed effortlessly by the Word of God. It'll just spring forth and grow up in your life. You'll be transformed.

I live in the mountains of Colorado. There is a 250-foot-vertical rise from the road that runs in front of our house up to our house. Our property is so steep that it's hard to walk on, especially in winter with the snow. Add to that the fact that our altitude is 9,000 feet, and it really taxes your breathing to climb these hills. Therefore, I decided to build a trail with switchbacks across my property so I could walk up and down without losing my breath.

I started building that trail with only hand tools in 1994. Most of my property is decomposed granite, and I averaged only ten feet per hour. My trail is 2.5 miles, round trip. So, it looked like it was going to take me forever to finish that trail. I worked on it till the year 2000 and still maintain it today.

But here's my point in sharing that: Now, every time I go walking on my trail, I am reaping the benefits of that labor I did back in 1994-2000. Yes, it took me six years to build that trail, but I've been using it for nearly two decades now. That wasn't wasted time; I'm reaping benefits from it every day. Likewise, the time you take getting God's Word rooted and grounded in you isn't wasted time; you will reap its rewards for the rest of your life.

Less

LESSON 17 – OUTLINE

I. In the parable of the sower, there was only one soil that really produced the intended fruit:

> **And these are they which are sown on good ground; such as hear the word, and receive it, and bring forth fruit, some thirtyfold, some sixty, and some an hundred.**
>
> **Mark 4:20**

A. The Lord really encouraged me through this parable.

B. He showed me that it was the seed—the Word—that produced the fruit. And the ground that produced the best fruit wasn't the ground that had more; it was the ground that had less—less stones, less thorns, and less weeds.

C. This told me that in order to be fruitful, I didn't necessarily need all of these external talents that people normally emphasize; it's really just a matter of the heart.

D. I prayed, "God, if what really makes Your Word become fruitful is being less, then I can certainly be less. I may not be able to be more, but I can definitely be less. I can get rid of these things that hinder me."

II. You may not feel like you're the sharpest knife in the drawer.

A. You may be acutely aware that you have all kinds of liabilities that other people don't have.

B. Yet you can commit yourself to the Word of God and meditate in it until it takes deep root in your heart.

C. You can refuse to allow anything else to divert your attention or sap the strength from your heart that could be going to the Lord.

D. If you devote yourself completely to His Word, it will make you a success.

E. It will cause fruit to come in whatever area He has called and anointed you to minister.

III. If you stop to think about it, this whole parable has been about patience (Luke 8:15).

A. Anyone who has ever dealt with seeds knows they have to give the seeds time to work.

B. Time is actually an asset.

C. It's a benefit.

D. Instead of looking at time negatively, you need to see it as a friend to a seed because it allows reproduction and multiplication.

IV. Every second you spend meditating in the Word of God and planting these seeds into your heart, you're putting in motion a process that cannot be stopped.

A. Seeds are powerful.

B. If we keep the Word of God fresh and alive on the inside of us, it'll continue benefiting us twenty, thirty, fifty years from now, should the Lord tarry.

C. Once you get this system going and you've invested that time, you'll be changed effortlessly by the Word of God.

D. It'll just spring forth and grow up in your life.

E. You'll be transformed.

F. The time you take getting God's Word rooted and grounded in you isn't wasted time; you will reap its rewards for the rest of your life.

Less

LESSON 17 – TEACHER'S GUIDE

1. In the parable of the sower, there was only one soil that really produced the intended fruit (Mark 4:20). The Lord really encouraged me through this parable. He showed me that it was the seed—the Word—that produced the fruit. And the ground that produced the best fruit wasn't the ground that had more; it was the ground that had less—less stones, less thorns, and less weeds. This told me that in order to be fruitful, I didn't necessarily need all of these external talents that people normally emphasize; it's really just a matter of the heart. I prayed, "God, if what really makes Your Word become fruitful is being less, then I can certainly be less. I may not be able to be more, but I can definitely be less. I can get rid of these things that hinder me."

2. We may not feel like we're the sharpest knives in the drawer. We may be acutely aware that we have all kinds of liabilities that other people don't have. Yet we can commit ourselves to the Word of God and meditate in it until it takes deep root in our hearts. We can refuse to allow anything else to divert our attention or sap the strength from our hearts that could be going to the Lord. If we devote ourselves completely to His Word, it will make us a success. It will cause fruit to come in whatever area He has called and anointed us to minister.

3. If we stop to think about it, this whole parable has been about patience (Luke 8:15). Anyone who has ever dealt with seeds knows they have to give the seeds time to work. Time is actually an asset. It's a benefit. Instead of looking at time negatively, we need to see it as a friend to a seed because it allows reproduction and multiplication.

1. A. Read Mark 4:20. What did the ground have that produced the best fruit? (It had less—less stones, less thorns, and less weeds)
   B. If it's not really about external talents in order to be fruitful, what is it about? (The heart)
2. A. Even if we're acutely aware that we have all kinds of liabilities that other people don't have, what can we do? (We can commit ourselves to the Word of God and meditate in it until it takes deep root in our hearts)
   B. What can we refuse to allow? (Anything else to divert our attention or sap the strength from our hearts that could be going to the Lord)
   C. The Word will cause fruit to come where? (In whatever area He has called and anointed us to minister)
3. A. Read Luke 8:15. What has this whole parable been about? (Patience)
   B. What do we need to see time as? (A friend to a seed)
   C. Why? (Because it allows reproduction and multiplication)

4. Every second we spend meditating in the Word of God and planting these seeds into our hearts, we're putting in motion a process that cannot be stopped. Seeds are powerful. If we keep the Word of God fresh and alive on the inside of us, it'll continue benefiting us twenty, thirty, fifty years from now, should the Lord tarry. Once we get this system going and we've invested that time, we'll be changed effortlessly by the Word of God. It'll just spring forth and grow up in our lives. We'll be transformed. The time we take getting God's Word rooted and grounded in us isn't wasted time; we will reap its rewards for the rest of our lives.

4. A. What happens every second we spend meditating in the Word of God and planting these seeds in our hearts? (We're putting in motion a process that cannot be stopped)
   B. If we keep the Word of God fresh and alive on the inside of us, what will it do? (It'll continue benefiting us twenty, thirty, fifty years from now, should the Lord tarry)
   C. We'll be changed effortlessly once we what? (Get this system going and we've invested that time)
   D. Therefore, the time we take getting God's Word rooted and grounded in us isn't what? (Wasted time)

Less

LESSON 17 – DISCIPLESHIP QUESTIONS

1. According to Mark 4:20, what kind of ground was the Word sown into?
   A. Holy
   B. Peat
   C. Good
   D. All of the above
   E. None of the above

2. Read 1 Corinthians 1:26-28. Are all wise, mighty, or noble not called?

3. **"But God hath chosen the _____ things of the world to confound the wise; and God hath chosen the _____ things of the world to confound the things which are mighty."**
   A. "Foolish," "weak"
   B. "Simple," "peaceful"
   C. "Wise, "strong"
   D. "Noble," "attractive"
   E. "Gifted," "qualified"

4. What has God done with the base, the despised, and the things that are not?

5. Read Luke 8:15. Those with honest and good hearts are those who do what with the Word?

Less
LESSON 17 – ANSWER KEY

1. C. Good

2. No, not many of them are called

3. A. **"Foolish," "weak"**

4. He has chosen them

5. They keep it and bring forth fruit with patience

Less
LESSON 17 – SCRIPTURES

MARK 4:20
And these are they which are sown on good ground; such as hear the word, and receive it, and bring forth fruit, some thirtyfold, some sixty, and some an hundred.

1 CORINTHIANS 1:26-28
For ye see your calling, brethren, how that not many wise men after the flesh, not many mighty, not many noble, are called: [27] **But God hath chosen the foolish things of the world to confound the wise; and God hath chosen the weak things of the world to confound the things which are mighty;** [28] **And base things of the world, and things which are despised, hath God chosen, yea, and things which are not, to bring to nought things that are.**

LUKE 8:15
But that on the good ground are they, which in an honest and good heart, having heard the word, keep it, and bring forth fruit with patience.

The Growth Process
LESSON 18

On the same day that Jesus taught the parable of the sower sowing the seed, He also said,

> **So is the kingdom of God, as if a man should cast seed into the ground; And should sleep, and rise night and day, and the seed should spring and grow up, he knoweth not how. For the earth bringeth forth fruit of herself; first the blade, then the ear, after that the full corn in the ear. But when the fruit is brought forth, immediately he putteth in the sickle, because the harvest is come.**
>
> **Mark 4:26-29**

Although this is a simple passage of Scripture, it's very profound. It's packed with meaning.

First of all, it says that the kingdom of God is as if a man should cast seed into the ground. This is the same principle as the parable of the sower sowing the seed. God's Word is like a seed planted in the ground of our hearts.

Cooperate and Reap

Then verse 27 says,

> **And should sleep, and rise night and day, and the seed should spring and grow up, he knoweth not how.**
>
> **Mark 4:27**

In the same way that we plant a seed in the ground and don't really know what's happening, so it is with the Word. Man, with all his knowledge, has put satellites in orbit, people on the moon, and sent spacecraft to other planets. For all that man has accomplished and all of his cumulative knowledge, he cannot manufacture a seed. Oh, he can make something that looks like a seed, with the same size, color, and chemicals. It could have the same everything, and fool people. But if you take a manmade seed and plant it in the ground, it won't germinate or reproduce itself. Why? There isn't any life in it.

Despite all of our knowledge, we have not been able to figure out why a seed does what it does. It's just because God created it that way. However, even though we don't understand it, that doesn't keep us from taking seeds and planting them in the ground. We've learned a few things about how long it takes for a seed to germinate and produce a harvest. We've learned about what weeds to keep out. We've learned about what kind of temperature and how much water it needs. We've learned enough about a seed to be able to cooperate with it, but we still don't understand it. Yet it works. Every one of us benefits from seeds sown around the world when we eat our bread, fruit, and vegetables. We don't understand it, but we still benefit from it.

This is a tremendous comfort to me. I don't have to understand everything about how the Word works. I don't have to understand why just shutting myself in with the Lord, studying His Word, and listening to Him speak to me does what it does. The fact that I can't totally explain it doesn't keep me from cooperating and reaping the benefits of it.

You don't have to be a rocket scientist or the sharpest person around. You don't have to understand everything to get God's Word working in your life. Just start sowing the Word into your heart. Begin meditating on it day and night. The Word of God will germinate, take root, spring forth, and grow up of itself.

Everything Jesus Provided

God put life in those seeds. Man cannot figure it out, but God spoke life into physical seeds. God has also spoken life into the spiritual seed of His Word.

Proverbs 4:20-22 says,

> **My son, attend to my words; incline thine ear unto my sayings. Let them not depart from thine eyes; keep them in the midst of thine heart. For they are life unto those that find them, and health to all their flesh.**

God's Word contains His life in it. If you would take His words, His sayings, and put them on the inside of you, then God's kind of life would start flowing through you. You would find that healing, prosperity, joy, peace—everything Jesus provided—are contained in His Word.

The Bible isn't like any other book. It's different. It's alive:

> **For the word of God is quick** [alive]**, and powerful, and sharper than any twoedged sword.**
>
> **Hebrews 4:12, brackets mine**

God's Word is alive. It's different than reading any other book—even books about the Bible. The Word of God is different. There's life in it. If you take it, the Word will give you life where there's been death. It gives light where there was darkness. It's that simple.

Patience

In light of this truth, I don't know why people don't spend more time studying the Word of God. I don't know why they spend so much time occupied with all these other things. The only way I can understand it is that they really don't believe it. They really don't believe the power and authority that's in God's Word. If you understand what I'm saying, then you'll realize that the most important thing you could ever do is just to take God's Word and begin planting it in your life.

God has created His Word just like a physical seed. It brings forth fruit of itself. Yet the Word doesn't work until it's sown into your heart, just like a seed doesn't work until it's sown into the ground.

They've found seeds in pyramids that had been lying there for 4,000 years. They were dormant, never sprouting because they weren't in the ground. But once they were planted with the right temperature, nutrients, and water, they started sprouting and producing plants. All of a sudden, the life that was in them came forth. That's a miracle!

God's Word has been recorded for thousands of years. If you would take it and sow it into your heart, it will begin to produce. But the seed has to be in the ground. The Word has to be in your heart for it to begin to release that life. You can't just read it with your eyes and take a little truth into your brain; you have to put it down deep on the inside of you. You must meditate the Word until it literally takes root on the inside of you. That's when it will just start supernaturally producing.

In this parable, Jesus was saying that the kingdom of God is like a man that takes a seed and puts it in the ground. He sleeps and rises night and day, so this implies time is involved. You have to exercise patience.

Act in Faith

If you put a seed in the ground and then go out and dig it up every day to see if anything is happening, you'll kill that seed. That seed has to be left in the ground for a period of time. There has to be faith. Farmers may not use this terminology, but it's true. The person who plants the seed has to believe that the seed is germinating, putting roots down, and producing. You just have to leave that seed there by faith, and over a period of time, it produces.

It's the same with the Word of God. You can't just take a promise, plant it into your heart, and expect to reap a harvest right away. You can't just hear 1 Peter 2:24 for the first time, then confess "By His stripes I am healed. I claim it in the name of Jesus," and if you aren't healed in the next ten minutes, go dig that seed up by saying, "Well, nothing's happening." Then the next day, you go back and do it again. That's not abiding in the Word and letting the Word abide in you (John 15:5).

You must come to a place where the Word is a part of you. It's not something you study for a little bit and then go out and live your whole day contrary to. I'm not against specific devotion and prayer times, but you need to keep focused on the Lord and His Word all day long. It does you no good to spend ten or twenty minutes in "devotion mode," being sweet and kind and listening to God, but once it's over, you go back to being a piranha the rest of the day—as mean, angry, and vicious in your relationships and business dealings as anyone else in the world. You may have planted the Word in your devotion time, but you dug that Word up. It's not working on the inside of you. It's not staying in your heart, and because of that, you aren't going to see it produce. It takes more than that.

You can't just consider God's Word during your devotion time and expect that to all of a sudden change the way you act that day; you have to take the truths about loving people (John 13:34-35), turning the other cheek (Matt. 5:39), and thinking more highly of others than you think of yourself (Phil. 2:3) and leave that seed in your heart over time. Then, whenever somebody rubs you the wrong way, you need to act in faith and let that Word continue to affect you. You must abide in the Word and let the Word abide in you for it to release its power and for it to impact your life.

Yet many people are trying church, trying prayer lines, and trying everything else except taking God's Word and meditating on it. And they wonder why they aren't getting the right results. This is so simple that you have to have somebody help you misunderstand it. You take the Word of God, put it in your heart, leave it there, meditate on it, and it just produces.

Full-Blown Manifestation

Mark 4:28 goes on to say,

> **For the earth bringeth forth fruit of herself; first the blade, then the ear, after that the full corn in the ear.**

It takes time for the Word of God to work, and when it starts working, you don't get the full-blown manifestation at first. There's first the blade, then the ear, and then the full corn in the ear. In other words, there's growth. Just like when you plant a seed in the ground, it doesn't just stay there for a week or a month and then—BOOM—instantly you get a full-grown tree. No, there's a growth period.

First we see a tiny shoot sticking up out of the ground. Then it begins to grow and develop. We recognize that this is the way it works in the physical realm, but many people haven't realized that it's also how it works in the spiritual realm.

People who have spent virtually no time getting established in the Word of God come to me all the time. They hear me talking about how the Word works, how I've seen God set me free, seen people healed and raised from the dead, and seen other great testimonies. They ask, "What scriptures promise that?" I give them a seed and they plant it, but if they don't have the same results by that time the next day, then they say, "I don't believe that works. The Word doesn't work. I did exactly the same thing you did, and it didn't work for me."

You need to recognize that I've been walking with the Lord now for over forty years. It's been over four decades since I had my life-changing encounter with the Lord, received my call to ministry, and things really began to work. I have spent some time meditating and seeking the Lord. But I didn't start off seeing some of the results that I am getting today.

No Shortcuts

Today Andrew Wommack Ministries needs about two million dollars a month just to pay our bills and keep things going. I didn't start at that level. I remember the very first time Jamie and I ever prayed together and agreed for a certain amount of money. We prayed and agreed for $250 a month. Back then, that would pay our rent, all of our utilities, and allow us to give $75 a month. That was our total needs.

When my wife and I moved to Manitou Springs, Colorado, we started this ministry and I began traveling. I remember that Jamie and I agreed for $3,000 a month. That would pay all of my employees, rent, cassette tape bills, and everything else. There was a growth process. Sometimes when I'm talking about the millions of dollars we need to operate today, people think, *I'm going to take those scriptures and try it.* Then if it isn't working for them by this time next week, they say, "That health-and-wealth, name-it-and-claim-it, blab-it-and-grab-it stuff doesn't work." They become critical because they don't understand that there's a growth process. There was a growth process in my life, and there will be a growth process in your life.

You may not like that because you just want to jump ahead. You want to skip all the intermediate steps and go from where you are to full maturity. You can desire that all you want. You can pray and beg God. You can even get a thousand people to agree with you in prayer, but it doesn't matter. You cannot circumvent the process. It's first the blade, then the ear, then the full corn in the ear. That's the way the kingdom of God works. There are no shortcuts.

Personally, I believe that by the degree of seeking you do, God might be able to speed up the process a little bit, but there's still going to be these steps, stages, and growth. You can accelerate it to a degree, but you can't stop this process. You aren't going to go from having never seen the Word of God work in your life to seeing a hundredfold return. There is first the blade, then the ear, and then the full corn in the ear.

I once had a Bible college student who was a lovely man. He had a great heart, and I really liked him. But he had spent most of his life in psychiatric hospitals, and he had a lot of problems. He had no social skills. But I decided to take him on as a project and see him change through God's Word. I shared a lot of things with him. And he really grabbed hold of the teaching on prosperity. He began to dream big.

He came to me one day and gave me his plans for buying and restoring an old, hundred-room, partially burned hotel so we could use it as a dormitory for Charis Bible College students. He had done his homework. He had the cost of buying the building, how much money he would have to borrow, what his payments would be, and how much income he could produce by renting out the rooms. It was well thought out. And he wanted to know what I thought of it.

I told him I was really glad he was beginning to think of being productive and trusting God for bigger things. But I told him this definitely wasn't God's will for him at that time. He was crushed and asked what was wrong with his plan.

This man had lived off government payments his whole life. He was attending Charis Bible College on a government program. He had never worked a job a single day in his life. He had never made a dollar before. And on the basis of this parable, you don't go from a seed to full harvest without any intermediate steps. You can't go from 0 to 100 mph instantly. That's not acceleration. That's a wreck.

So, I complimented him for moving in that direction. But I made it clear that he couldn't believe for millions of dollars until he believed for one dollar. He couldn't manage a large hotel until he managed to get a job and became faithful in a small thing first. He went on to graduate, and the last time I saw him, he had a job and was making it on his own. He's not arrived, but he's left.

You must realize that seed, time, and harvest is a process. It takes time. And time is your friend, not your enemy.

The Growth Process
LESSON 18 – OUTLINE

I. The kingdom of God is as if a man should cast seed into the ground (Mark 4:26-29).

A. This is the same principle as the parable of the sower sowing the seed.

> **And should sleep, and rise night and day, and the seed should spring and grow up, he knoweth not how.**
>
> **Mark 4:27**

B. In the same way that we plant a seed in the ground and don't really know what's happening, so it is with the Word.

C. Despite all of our knowledge, we have not been able to figure out why a seed does what it does.

D. However, that doesn't keep us from taking seeds and planting them in the ground.

E. We've learned enough about a seed to be able to cooperate with it.

F. We benefit from it.

G. This is a tremendous comfort to me.

II. I don't have to understand everything about how the Word works.

A. I don't have to understand why just shutting myself in with the Lord, studying His Word, and listening to Him speak to me does what it does.

B. The fact that I can't totally explain it doesn't keep me from cooperating and reaping the benefits of it.

C. You don't have to understand everything to get God's Word working in your life.

D. Just start sowing it into your heart.

E. Begin meditating on it day and night.

F. The Word of God will germinate, take root, spring forth, and grow up of itself.

III. God's Word contains His life in it.

   A. If you would take His words, His sayings, and put them on the inside of you, then God's kind of life would start flowing through you.

   B. You would find that healing, prosperity, joy, peace—everything Jesus provided—are contained in His Word.

   C. It's different than reading any other book—even books about the Bible.

   D. If you take it, the Word will give you life where there's been death.

   E. It gives light where there was darkness.

   F. It's that simple.

IV. In this parable, Jesus was saying that the kingdom of God is like a man that takes a seed and puts it in the ground.

   A. He sleeps and rises night and day, so this implies time is involved.

   B. You have to exercise patience.

   C. That seed has to be left in the ground for a period of time.

   D. There has to be faith.

   E. The person who plants the seed has to believe that the seed is germinating, putting roots down, and producing.

   F. It's the same with the Word of God.

   G. You can't just take a promise, plant it in your heart, and expect to reap a harvest right away.

   H. That's not abiding in the Word and letting the Word abide in you (John 15:5).

V. You must come to a place where the Word is a part of you.

   A. It does you no good to spend ten or twenty minutes in "devotion mode," being sweet and kind and listening to God, but once it's over, you go back to being a piranha the rest of the day—as mean, angry, and vicious in your relationships and business dealings as anyone else in the world.

B. You may have planted the Word in your devotion time, but you dug that Word up.

C. It's not working on the inside of you.

D. It's not staying in your heart, and because of that, you aren't going to see it produce.

E. You have to take the truths about loving people (John 13:34-35), turning the other cheek (Matt. 5:39), and thinking more highly of others than you think of yourself (Phil. 2:3) and leave that seed in your heart over time.

F. Then, whenever somebody rubs you the wrong way, you need to act in faith and let that Word continue to affect you.

G. You must abide in the Word and let the Word abide in you for it to release its power and for it to impact your life.

VI. People who have spent virtually no time getting established in the Word of God come to me all the time.

A. They hear me talking about how the Word works, how I've seen God set me free, seen people healed and raised from the dead, and seen other great testimonies.

B. They ask, "What scriptures promise that?"

C. I give them a seed and they plant it, but if they don't have the same results by that time the next day, then they say, "I don't believe that works. The Word doesn't work. I did exactly the same thing you did, and it didn't work for me."

D. They become critical because they don't understand that there's a growth process.

E. There was a growth process in my life, and there will be a growth process in your life.

VII. You can get a thousand people to agree with you in prayer, but you cannot circumvent the process.

A. Personally, I believe that by the degree of seeking you do, God might be able to speed up the process a little bit, but there's still going to be these steps, stages, and growth.

B. You aren't going to go from having never seen the Word of God work in your life to seeing a hundredfold return.

C. You can't go from 0 to 100 mph instantly.

D. You must realize that seed, time, and harvest is a process.

The Growth Process
LESSON 18 – TEACHER'S GUIDE

1. The kingdom of God is as if a man should cast seed into the ground (Mark 4:26-29). This is the same principle as the parable of the sower sowing the seed. In the same way that we plant a seed in the ground and don't really know what's happening, so it is with the Word (Mark 4:27). Despite all of our knowledge, we have not been able to figure out why a seed does what it does. However, that doesn't keep us from taking seeds and planting them in the ground. We've learned enough about a seed to be able to cooperate with it. We benefit from it. This is a tremendous comfort to me.

2. I don't have to understand everything about how the Word works. I don't have to understand why just shutting myself in with the Lord, studying His Word, and listening to Him speak to me does what it does. The fact that I can't totally explain it doesn't keep me from cooperating and reaping the benefits of it. We don't have to understand everything to get God's Word working in our lives. We just need to start sowing it into our hearts. And then we need to begin meditating on it day and night. The Word of God will germinate, take root, spring forth, and grow up of itself.

3. God's Word contains His life in it. If we would take His words, His sayings, and put them on the inside of us, then God's kind of life would start flowing through us. We would find that healing, prosperity, joy, peace—everything Jesus provided—are contained in His Word. It's different than reading any other book—even books about the Bible. If we take it, the Word will give us life where there's been death. It gives light where there was darkness. It's that simple.

1. Read Mark 4:27. In the same way that we plant a seed in the ground and don't really know what's happening, so it is with what? (The Word)
2. A. The fact that Andrew can't totally explain why shutting himself in with the Lord, studying His Word, and listening to Him speak to him does what it does, that doesn't keep him from what? (Cooperating and reaping the benefits of it)
   B. If we start sowing God's Word into our hearts and begin meditating on it day and night, it will germinate, take root, spring forth, and grow up _____. (Of itself)
3. A. What are contained in God's Word? (Healing, prosperity, joy, peace—everything Jesus provided)
   B. If we take it, the Word will what? (It will give us life where there's been death)
   C. What else does it give? (Light where there was darkness)

4. In this parable, Jesus was saying that the kingdom of God is like a man that takes a seed and puts it in the ground. He sleeps and rises night and day, so this implies time is involved. We have to exercise patience. That seed has to be left in the ground for a period of time. There has to be faith. The person who plants the seed has to believe that the seed is germinating, putting roots down, and producing. It's the same with the Word of God. We can't just take a promise, plant it in our hearts, and expect to reap a harvest right away. That's not abiding in the Word and letting the Word abide in us (John 15:5).

5. We must come to a place where the Word is a part of us. It does us no good to spend ten or twenty minutes in "devotion mode," being sweet and kind and listening to God, but once it's over, we go back to being a piranha the rest of the day—as mean, angry, and vicious in our relationships and business dealings as anyone else in the world. We may have planted the Word in our devotion times, but we dug that Word up. It's not working on the inside of us. It's not staying in our hearts, and because of that, we aren't going to see it produce. We have to take the truths about loving people (John 13:34-35), turning the other cheek (Matt. 5:39), and thinking more highly of others than we think of ourselves (Phil. 2:3) and leave that seed in our hearts over time. Then, whenever somebody rubs us the wrong way, we need to act in faith and let that Word continue to affect us. We must abide in the Word and let the Word abide in us for it to release its power and for it to impact our lives.

6. People who have spent virtually no time getting established in the Word of God come to me all the time. They hear me talking about how the Word works, how I've seen God set me free, seen people healed and raised from the dead, and seen other great testimonies. They ask, "What scriptures promise that?" I give them a seed and they plant it, but if they don't have the same results by that time the next day, then they say, "I don't believe that works. The Word doesn't work. I did exactly the same thing you did, and it didn't work for me." They become critical because they don't understand that there's a growth process. There was a growth process in my life, and there will be a growth process in your life.

4. A. What does the person who plants the seed have to believe? (That the seed is germinating, putting roots down, and producing)
   B. Is it the same with the Word of God? (Yes)
   C. What can't we expect? (To reap a harvest right away after we take a promise and plant it in our hearts)
5. A. What place must we come to? (Where the Word is a part of us)
   B. Read John 13:34-35, Matthew 5:39, and Philippians 2:3. What do we have to do? (Take the truths about loving people, turning the other cheek, and thinking more highly of others than we think of ourselves and leave that seed in our hearts over time)
   C. Then, whenever somebody rubs us the wrong way, what do we need to do? (Act in faith and let that Word continue to affect us)
   D. We must _____ in the Word and _____ the Word abide in us for it to release its power and for it to impact our lives. (Abide, let)
6. There was growth process in Andrew's life, and there will be a growth process where? (In our lives)

7. We can get a thousand people to agree with us in prayer, but we cannot circumvent the process. Personally, I believe that by the degree of seeking we do, God might be able to speed up the process a little bit, but there's still going to be these steps, stages, and growth. We aren't going to go from having never seen the Word of God work in our lives to seeing a hundredfold return. We can't go from 0 to 100 mph instantly. We must realize that seed, time, and harvest is a process.

7. A. We aren't going to go from having never seen the Word of God work in our lives to what? (Seeing a hundredfold return)
   B. What must we realize about seed, time, and harvest? (It is a process)

The Growth Process
LESSON 18 – DISCIPLESHIP QUESTIONS

1. Read Mark 4:26-29. What doesn't the man know?

2. **"The _____ bringeth forth fruit of herself."**

3. When the fruit comes forth, when does he put in the sickle?
   A. When it's convenient
   B. He doesn't need to because the fruit harvests itself
   C. Immediately
   D. All of the above
   E. None of the above

4. According to Proverbs 4:20-22, are these commands to a stranger?

5. Read Hebrews 4:12. What does the Word of God pierce even to the diving asunder?

6. Read 1 Peter 2:24. If you **"should"** live unto righteousness, who is better for it?
   A. God
   B. Me
   C. My spouse
   D. The pastor
   E. Others

7. According to John 15:5, to bring forth much fruit, Jesus only needs to abide in you?

8. Read John 13:34-35. What is the new commandment?

9. What will all people know by this?

10. Read Matthew 5:39. If someone strikes you on one cheek, what should you do?

11. According to Philippians 2:3, you are to let _____ be done through strife or vainglory (conceit).

12. In lowliness of mind, you are to esteem _____ better than yourself.

The Growth Process
LESSON 18 – ANSWER KEY

1. How the seed springs and grows up
2. **"Earth"**
3. C. Immediately
4. No, to a son (one's child)
5. Soul and spirit, and joints and marrow
6. B. Me
7. No, I need to abide in Him as well
8. That I should love others, as Jesus has loved me
9. That I am Jesus' disciple
10. Turn the other cheek to them as well
11. Nothing
12. Others

The Growth Process
LESSON 18 – SCRIPTURES

MARK 4:26-29
And he said, So is the kingdom of God, as if a man should cast seed into the ground; [27] And should sleep, and rise night and day, and the seed should spring and grow up, he knoweth not how. [28] For the earth bringeth forth fruit of herself; first the blade, then the ear, after that the full corn in the ear. [29] But when the fruit is brought forth, immediately he putteth in the sickle, because the harvest is come.

PROVERBS 4:20-22
My son, attend to my words; incline thine ear unto my sayings. [21] Let them not depart from thine eyes; keep them in the midst of thine heart. [22] For they are life unto those that find them, and health to all their flesh.

HEBREWS 4:12
For the word of God is quick, and powerful, and sharper than any twoedged sword, piercing even to the dividing asunder of soul and spirit, and of the joints and marrow, and is a discerner of the thoughts and intents of the heart.

1 PETER 2:24
Who his own self bare our sins in his own body on the tree, that we, being dead to sins, should live unto righteousness: by whose stripes ye were healed.

JOHN 15:5
I am the vine, ye are the branches: He that abideth in me, and I in him, the same bringeth forth much fruit: for without me ye can do nothing.

JOHN 13:34-35
A new commandment I give unto you, That ye love one another; as I have loved you, that ye also love one another. [35] By this shall all men know that ye are my disciples, if ye have love one to another.

MATTHEW 5:39
But I say unto you, That ye resist not evil: but whosoever shall smite thee on thy right cheek, turn to him the other also.

PHILIPPIANS 2:3
Let nothing be done through strife or vainglory; but in lowliness of mind let each esteem other better than themselves.

Life and Power
LESSON 19

On the same day that Jesus taught these ten parables of the kingdom, including the parable of the sower sowing the seed, which emphasized the significance and power of His Word, the Lord also told His disciples to get in a boat and go over to the other side of the Sea of Galilee:

> **And the same day, when the even was come, he saith unto them, Let us pass over unto the other side. And when they had sent away the multitude, they took him even as he was in the ship. And there were also with him other little ships. And there arose a great storm of wind, and the waves beat into the ship, so that it was now full. And he was in the hinder part of the ship, asleep on a pillow: and they awake him, and say unto him, Master, carest thou not that we perish? And he arose, and rebuked the wind, and said unto the sea, Peace, be still. And the wind ceased, and there was a great calm. And he said unto them, Why are ye so fearful? how is it that ye have no faith? And they feared exceedingly, and said one to another, What manner of man is this, that even the wind and the sea obey him?**
>
> **Mark 4:35-41**

Now remember, Jesus had spent the better part of this same day teaching these disciples that the Word of God is like a seed. You sow this seed into your heart. The seed has the life of God in it, and you don't need to go somewhere else. If you want a tree in your yard, you don't have to go get a tree; just plant a seed, and that seed will turn into a tree. The seed has life in itself.

The Creator Said

So, Jesus had been teaching these truths from a number of different angles. Then, that same day, He said in verse 35, **"Let us pass over unto the other side."** Do you realize what Jesus was doing? He was the Word made flesh who dwelt among us (John 1:14). Jesus was the incarnate Word of God. He had just been talking about the power of the Word. So, what did He do? He gave them a seed. He gave them a word.

Jesus said,

> **Let us pass over unto the other side.**
>
> **Mark 4:35**

Jesus didn't tell the disciples, "Let's get into the boat, go halfway, and then drown. Let's get in there and be overwhelmed by this storm. We're never going to make it to the other side." No, He gave them a word.

This was the Creator of that Sea of Galilee. He's the one who created the heavens, and the earth, and everything in the natural realm that was coming against them. And the Creator said, "Let's get into the boat and go to the other side." He gave the disciples a seed. Jesus gave them a word and then proceeded to the back part of the ship and fell asleep.

While Jesus was asleep, a great wind came up. A great storm arose, and the waves beat into the ship so that it was now full. You have to remember that this wasn't a huge ocean liner, or even a cabin cruiser with berths below deck that were dry and warm. No, this was a little open boat.

As a matter of fact, I've been out on a tour of the Sea of Galilee in what was called the "Jesus Boat." It wasn't the exact vessel that Jesus used, but they said it was a replica of the type of fishing boats they used at that time. We had about thirty or so people on this boat. It was all open. There was nothing below deck. If Jesus was in the back end of this boat asleep on a pillow and the boat was now full of water, then that means He was sloshing around in the water. He was aware of what was going on, but instead of getting up and taking care of the situation, He just stayed sleeping. That's amazing!

Never, Ever Your Problem

Look at how the disciples responded to this:

> **And he was in the hinder part of the ship, asleep on a pillow: and they awake him, and say unto him, Master, carest thou not that we perish?**
>
> **Mark 4:38**

This is so typical—not only of these disciples but also of people today. You come into a problem and the doctor tells you that you're going to die, the banker tells you that you're going to have something repossessed, your spouse tells you they're going to divorce you. Somebody tells you bad news, and all of a sudden the depression starts. These storms come and you say to the Lord, "God, I thought You loved me. Why aren't You doing anything? Don't You care if I perish?" You basically put it all off on God as if it's His fault. God's not the one that sent this storm.

Religion has caused a lot of confusion in this area by teaching that God is "sovereign," meaning that He controls everything. They say that God is the one who caused or allowed your sickness, poverty, divorce, or whatever. That's not true. God didn't cause this storm in Mark 4. The Lord doesn't control everything.

Now, Jesus did have the power and authority to do something about this storm. He exercised that power by rebuking the wind and speaking to the sea, **"Peace, be still."** The Lord has the power, but not every problem that comes into your life is God ordained. He didn't make these problems. So, for you to say "God, why did You let this happen?" is wrong. In the first place, you're imputing iniquity and error unto the Lord, and you need to stop it. God is a good God. He's not the source of your problems. Don't blame God, saying, "How come You haven't healed me? Why did You let this person die?" God is never, ever your problem.

These disciples in the boat started saying, "Lord, wake up! Don't You care that we perish? Get a bucket and bail. Row. Do something to help us! You aren't pulling Your weight. If it wasn't for us, we would have already been sunk. You haven't done anything!" Sounds very similar to what people are saying to the Lord today: "Why haven't You healed me? I've prayed, I've done this, and yet You haven't done Your part. Lord, don't You care about me?" The truth is that Jesus had done His part. He gave the disciples that word. Then it was up to them to take that word and release the life that's in it through believing and speaking it out. But they didn't do that.

Rebuked

It's the same with us today. We are praying and asking God to heal us, saying, "O Lord, what's wrong? Don't You love me? Haven't You heard what the doctors said? Please, please heal me." We're going to the Lord as beggars instead of sons who have already received our inheritance. Instead of claiming what is rightfully ours, we're begging for what He could do but hasn't done. We think it's God's responsibility, it's His turn to fix this problem, when the truth is that God has done His part. He gave us the seeds of His Word, which will grow the solution to our problems. He's given words that have life in them. All we have to do is take that Word, stand on it, and begin to release the life that is in that seed—the Word of God.

These disciples typify where much of the body of Christ is today. They're whining, crying, and saying, "Lord, don't You care about me? Why haven't You done this? Please touch me!" They're begging, pleading, and doubting the goodness of God. These disciples were moaning and groaning, griping and complaining. Look what Jesus did and said when they woke Him. He rebuked the wind, spoke peace to the sea, and then turned to them and asked,

> **Why are ye so fearful? how is it that ye have no faith?**
>
> **Mark 4:40**

Jesus didn't get up and say, "Guys, I'm sorry. I was tired and just trying to catch a few winks. It's My fault. I got you into this. I apologize for not getting up and taking care of it." No, He didn't say that. Jesus didn't placate them. He didn't just sit there and approve of their panic, griping, and complaining. Instead, the Lord asked, "Why are you so fearful? How is it that you have no faith?" He was angry at their carnality and disappointed by their unbelief. By His words, you can see that He didn't approve of their powerlessness.

It would be unjust of Jesus to be critical of these disciples if there was nothing they could have done. If it was just a matter of them waking the Lord up and Him solving the situation, then Jesus should have been apologetic, saying, "Guys, I'm sorry that I wasn't already awake and there for you." But that's not the response He had. Instead, Jesus basically rebuked them, saying, "Why are you operating in fear?"

Someone might say, "Well, most people would say they were about to drown. Why shouldn't they be operating in fear?"

If these disciples would have understood what Jesus had been teaching them all day long, they could have done something about this storm. Jesus had just given them ten parables about the kingdom of God. He had told them that the seed of God's Word contains power and life. When Jesus said "Let's go over to the other side," He gave them a seed. He gave them His Word, a promise. If they would have had any understanding at all, they could have taken that Word and stood on it. They could have taken their authority and commanded the boat to go to the other side. They could have rebuked the wind and commanded the waves to stop. Jesus did not approve of their ineffectiveness. He rebuked them, saying, "Guys, you ought to be doing better than this."

A Sharp, Two-Edged Sword

Brothers and sisters, we ought to be doing better than this! The body of Christ is going to God crying, asking for help, and wondering why He isn't releasing His power. They're saying, "God, what's wrong with You?" So, they organize a hundred thousand people to intercede in order to force God, to twist His arm a little more, and to put additional pressure on Him until they make Him send revival, heal this person, or whatever. That's an offense to the Lord!

Praying "O God, please pour out Your Spirit. O God, have mercy on our country. Please don't judge us!" is an offense against God. The Lord has already poured out His Spirit and had mercy on our country. In fact, God has already had mercy on the entire world because He put that judgment on His Son at the cross. Jesus already paid for it—in full. The only reason we don't have red-hot revival flowing in the land isn't because God hasn't poured out His Spirit; it's because we, as the body of Christ, aren't doing what He told us to do.

We're asking God to do what He told us to do. He told us to go preach the Gospel and teach His Word (Mark 16:15 and Matt. 28:18-20). He told us to go heal the sick. He told us to advance His kingdom upon the earth (Luke 19:13). Jesus gave us these words. The life is in the Word, and the problem is we aren't planting the Word. We don't want to take time to plant the Word into our hearts, keep it in there, and meditate on it so it can take root, mature, and bear fruit. That's work! God isn't asleep; we are. We aren't doing what He told us to do. We're asking Him to do it, but it's not going to work that way.

Do you want to see the power of God? Do you want to see change manifest in your life? This is how you do it. God has spoken His Word. He has released His life and power by His words. Every word that comes from God is a faith-filled word and has the power in it to change everything.

When the Lord comes back at the end times, Revelation 19:15 says a sharp, two-edged sword will come out of His mouth with which He'll strike the nations. I don't believe that's describing a physical sword, but that the sword represents the Word of God.

That Same Word

Hebrews 4:12 says,

> **The word of God is quick, and powerful, and sharper than any twoedged sword.**

God is going to speak words out of His mouth, and those words will have so much life in them. The Word of God will be the greatest display of power in the history of the universe, and He's given it to you. The Lord will destroy His enemies and set everything straight by His Word. You have that same Word right now.

You don't need a tree to just drop out of the sky. What you need to do is take the seed that God has given you, plant it, and give it some time. You can grow any tree that you want. You don't need a miracle to just fall out of the sky. What you need to do is take the Word of God, plant that seed into your heart, and let it grow. Then the supernatural life and miraculous power of God will come right up out of the midst of you!

I believe the seeds of God's Word that I've sown in you through this **Study Guide** will not be choked out but will produce up to a hundredfold. Amen! So be it!

Life and Power
LESSON 19 – OUTLINE

I. On the same day that Jesus taught these ten parables of the kingdom, the Lord also told His disciples to get in a boat and go over to the other side of the Sea of Galilee:

> **And the same day, when the even was come, he saith unto them, Let us pass over unto the other side. And when they had sent away the multitude, they took him even as he was in the ship. And there were also with him other little ships. And there arose a great storm of wind, and the waves beat into the ship, so that it was now full. And he was in the hinder part of the ship, asleep on a pillow: and they awake him, and say unto him, Master, carest thou not that we perish? And he arose, and rebuked the wind, and said unto the sea, Peace, be still. And the wind ceased, and there was a great calm. And he said unto them, Why are ye so fearful? how is it that ye have no faith? And they feared exceedingly, and said one to another, What manner of man is this, that even the wind and the sea obey him?**
>
> **Mark 4:35-41**

A. Jesus said in verse 35, **"Let us pass over unto the other side."**

B. Do you realize what He was doing?

C. He had just been talking about the power of the Word.

D. So, He gave His disciples a seed. He gave them a word.

E. He didn't tell the disciples, "Let's get into the boat, go halfway, and then drown. Let's get in there and be overwhelmed by this storm. We're never going to make it to the other side."

II. God didn't cause this storm in Mark 4.

A. So, for you to say "God, why did You let this happen?" is wrong.

B. In the first place, you're imputing iniquity and error unto the Lord, and you need to stop it.

C. God is a good God.

D. He's not the source of your problems.

III. These disciples in the boat started saying, "Lord, wake up! Don't You care that we perish? Get a bucket and bail. Row. Do something to help us! You aren't pulling Your weight. If it wasn't for us, we would have already been sunk. You haven't done anything!"

A. Sounds very similar to what people are saying to the Lord today: "Why haven't You healed me? I've prayed, I've done this, and yet You haven't done Your part. Lord, don't You care about me?"

B. The truth is that Jesus had done His part.

C. He gave the disciples that word.

D. Then it was up to them to take that word and release the life that's in it through believing and speaking it out.

E. It's the same with us today.

F. God gave us the seeds of His Word, which will grow the solution to our problems.

IV. Jesus didn't get up and say, "Guys, I'm sorry. I was tired and just trying to catch a few winks. It's My fault. I got you into this. I apologize for not getting up and taking care of it."

A. Instead, the Lord asked, "Why are you so fearful? How is it that you have no faith?"

B. He was angry at their carnality and disappointed by their unbelief.

C. It would be unjust of Jesus to be critical of these disciples if there was nothing they could have done.

V. If these disciples would have understood what Jesus had been teaching them all day long, they could have done something about this storm.

A. If they would have had any understanding at all, they could have taken that Word and stood on it.

B. They could have taken their authority and commanded the boat to go to the other side.

C. They could have rebuked the wind and commanded the waves to stop.

D. Jesus rebuked them, saying, "Guys, you ought to be doing better than this."

E. Brothers and sisters, we ought to be doing better than this!

VI. Praying "O God, please pour out Your Spirit. O God, have mercy on our country. Please don't judge us!" is an offense against God.

   A. The Lord has already poured out His Spirit and had mercy on our country.

   B. The only reason we don't have red-hot revival flowing in the land is because we, as the body of Christ, aren't doing what He told us to do.

   C. He told us to go preach the Gospel and teach His Word (Mark 16:15 and Matt. 28:18-20).

   D. He told us to go heal the sick.

   E. He told us to advance His kingdom upon the earth (Luke 19:13).

   F. Jesus gave us these words.

   G. The problem is we don't want to take time to plant the Word into our hearts, keep it in there, and meditate on it so it can take root, mature, and bear fruit.

   H. That's work!

   I. We're asking Him to do it, but it's not going to work that way.

VII. When the Lord comes back at the end times, Revelation 19:15 says a sharp, two-edged sword will come out of His mouth with which He'll strike the nations.

   A. I don't believe that's describing a physical sword, but that the sword represents the Word of God (Heb. 4:12).

   B. The Word of God will be the greatest display of power in the history of the universe, and He's given it to you.

   C. You have that same Word right now.

   D. You don't need a miracle to just fall out of the sky.

   E. What you need to do is take the Word of God, plant that seed into your heart, and let it grow.

   F. Then the supernatural life and miraculous power of God will come right up out of the midst of you!

G. I believe the seeds of God's Word that I've sown in you through this **Study Guide** will not be choked out but will produce up to a hundredfold.

H. Amen! So be it!

Life and Power
LESSON 19 – TEACHER'S GUIDE

1. On the same day that Jesus taught these ten parables of the kingdom, the Lord also told His disciples to get in a boat and go over to the other side of the Sea of Galilee (Mark 4:35-41). Jesus said in verse 35, **"Let us pass over unto the other side."** Do you realize what He was doing? He had just been talking about the power of the Word. So, He gave His disciples a seed. He gave them a word. He didn't tell the disciples, "Let's get into the boat, go halfway, and then drown. Let's get in there and be overwhelmed by this storm. We're never going to make it to the other side."

2. God didn't cause this storm in Mark 4. So, for us to say "God, why did You let this happen?" is wrong. In the first place, we're imputing iniquity and error unto the Lord, and we need to stop it. God is a good God. He's not the source of our problems.

3. These disciples in the boat started saying, "Lord, wake up! Don't You care that we perish? Get a bucket and bail. Row. Do something to help us! You aren't pulling Your weight. If it wasn't for us, we would have already been sunk. You haven't done anything!" Sounds very similar to what people are saying to the Lord today: "Why haven't You healed me? I've prayed, I've done this, and yet You haven't done Your part. Lord, don't You care about me?" The truth is that Jesus had done His part. He gave the disciples that word. Then it was up to them to take that word and release the life that's in it through believing and speaking it out. It's the same with us today. God gave us the seeds of His Word, which will grow the solution to our problems.

4. Jesus didn't get up and say, "Guys, I'm sorry. I was tired and just trying to catch a few winks. It's My fault. I got you into this. I apologize for not getting up and taking care of it." Instead, the Lord asked, "Why are you so fearful? How is it that you have no faith?" He was angry at their carnality and disappointed by their unbelief. It would be unjust of Jesus to be critical of these disciples if there was nothing they could have done.

1. A. Read Mark 4:35-42. When Jesus said in verse 35 **"Let us pass over unto the other side,"** what was He doing? (He was giving His disciples a seed. He was giving them a word)
   B. What didn't He tell the disciples? ("Let's get into the boat, go halfway, and then drown. Let's get in there and be overwhelmed by this storm. We're never going to make it to the other side")
2. A. Did God cause this storm? (No)
   B. What kind of God is God? (A good God)
   C. What isn't He the source of? (Our problems)
3. A. It was up to the disciples to do what? (To take the word Jesus gave them and release the life that's in it through believing and speaking it out)
   B. The seeds of God's Word will _____ the solution to our problems. (Grow)
4. A. Jesus was angry at their _____ and disappointed by their _____. (Carnality, unbelief)
   B. It would have been unjust of Jesus to do what? (To be critical of these disciples if there was nothing they could have done)

5. If these disciples would have understood what Jesus had been teaching them all day long, they could have done something about this storm. If they would have had any understanding at all, they could have taken that Word and stood on it. They could have taken their authority and commanded the boat to go to the other side. They could have rebuked the wind and commanded the waves to stop. Jesus rebuked them, saying, "Guys, you ought to be doing better than this." Brothers and sisters, we ought to be doing better than this!

6. Praying "O God, please pour out Your Spirit. O God, have mercy on our country. Please don't judge us!" is an offense against God. The Lord has already poured out His Spirit and had mercy on our country. The only reason we don't have red-hot revival flowing in the land is because we, as the body of Christ, aren't doing what He told us to do. He told us to go preach the Gospel and teach His Word (Mark 16:15 and Matt. 28:18-20). He told us to go heal the sick. He told us to advance His kingdom upon the earth (Luke 19:13). Jesus gave us these words. The problem is we don't want to take time to plant the Word into our hearts, keep it in there, and meditate on it so it can take root, mature, and bear fruit. That's work! We're asking Him to do it, but it's not going to work that way.

7. When the Lord comes back at the end times, Revelation 19:15 says a sharp, two-edged sword will come out of His mouth with which He'll strike the nations. I don't believe that's describing a physical sword, but that the sword represents the Word of God (Heb. 4:12). The Word of God will be the greatest display of power in the history of the universe, and He's given it to you. You have that same Word right now. You don't need a miracle to just fall out of the sky. What you need to do is take the Word of God, plant that seed into your heart, and let it grow. Then the supernatural life and miraculous power of God will come right up out of the midst of you! I believe the seeds of God's Word that I've sown in you through this **Study Guide** will not be choked out but will produce up to a hundredfold. Amen! So be it!

5. A. The disciples could have done something about the storm if they would have what? (Understood what Jesus had been teaching them all day long)
   B. What could they have done? (They could have taken that Word and stood on it. They could have taken their authority and commanded the boat to go to the other side. They could have rebuked the wind and commanded the waves to stop)
   C. As brothers and sisters, we ought to what? (Be doing better than this)
6. A. Why don't we have red-hot revival flowing in the land? (Because we, as the body of Christ, aren't doing what the Lord told us to do)
   B. Read Mark 16:15, Matthew 28:18-20, and Luke 19:13. What did He tell us to do? (He told us to go preach the Gospel and teach His Word. He told us to go heal the sick. He told us to advance His kingdom upon the earth)
   C. What do we need to take the time to do? (Plant the Word in our hearts, keep it in there, and meditate on it so it can take root, mature, and bear fruit)
7. A. What do we have right now? (The Word of God, which will be the greatest display of power in the history of the universe)
   B. When we take the Word of God, plant that seed into our hearts, and let it grow, what will happen? (The supernatural life and miraculous power of God will come right up out of the midst of us)

Life and Power

LESSON 19 – DISCIPLESHIP QUESTIONS

1. Read Mark 4:35-41. What arose while Jesus and the disciples were crossing the sea?
   A. A great windstorm
   B. A great famine
   C. A great wave
   D. All of the above
   E. None of the above

2. The waves beat into the ship so that the ship was what?

3. What was Jesus sleeping on?
   A. A wooden plank
   B. On the breast of the disciple whom He loved
   C. The fishing net
   D. A full stomach
   E. A pillow

4. What did Jesus rebuke?

5. What did He say to the sea?

6. How much faith did Jesus say the disciples had?

7. When the disciples saw what He did, what were they?

8. According to John 1:14, what did John and others behold?

9. Read Mark 16:15. You are to go into _____ the world and preach the _____ to _____ creature.

10. According to Matthew 28:18-20, all power is _____ to Jesus in heaven and in earth.

11. You are to teach all nations all things whatsoever who has commanded you?

12. Read Luke 19:13. How many pounds did he give each servant?

13. Read Revelation 19:15. Who is this verse talking about?

14. Read Hebrews 4:12. Does the Word of God only discern the thoughts of the heart?

Life and Power
LESSON 19 – ANSWER KEY

1. A. A great windstorm
2. Full of water
3. E. A pillow
4. The wind
5. **"Peace, be still"**
6. None
7. Very afraid
8. Jesus' glory, the glory as of the only begotten of the Father
9. All, Gospel, every
10. Given
11. Jesus
12. One
13. Jesus
14. No, it also discerns the intents

Life and Power
LESSON 19 – SCRIPTURES

MARK 4:35-41
And the same day, when the even was come, he saith unto them, Let us pass over unto the other side. [36] And when they had sent away the multitude, they took him even as he was in the ship. And there were also with him other little ships. [37] And there arose a great storm of wind, and the waves beat into the ship, so that it was now full. [38] And he was in the hinder part of the ship, asleep on a pillow: and they awake him, and say unto him, Master, carest thou not that we perish? [39] And he arose, and rebuked the wind, and said unto the sea, Peace, be still. And the wind ceased, and there was a great calm. [40] And he said unto them, Why are ye so fearful? how is it that ye have no faith? [41] And they feared exceedingly, and said one to another, What manner of man is this, that even the wind and the sea obey him?

JOHN 1:14
And the Word was made flesh, and dwelt among us, (and we beheld his glory, the glory as of the only begotten of the Father,) full of grace and truth.

MARK 16:15
And he said unto them, Go ye into all the world, and preach the gospel to every creature.

MATTHEW 28:18-20
And Jesus came and spake unto them, saying, All power is given unto me in heaven and in earth. [19] Go ye therefore, and teach all nations, baptizing them in the name of the Father, and of the Son, and of the Holy Ghost: [20] Teaching them to observe all things whatsoever I have commanded you: and, lo, I am with you alway, even unto the end of the world. Amen.

LUKE 19:13
And he called his ten servants, and delivered them ten pounds, and said unto them, Occupy till I come.

REVELATION 19:15
And out of his mouth goeth a sharp sword, that with it he should smite the nations: and he shall rule them with a rod of iron: and he treadeth the winepress of the fierceness and wrath of Almighty God.

HEBREWS 4:12

For the word of God is quick, and powerful, and sharper than any twoedged sword, piercing even to the dividing asunder of soul and spirit, and of the joints and marrow, and is a discerner of the thoughts and intents of the heart.

About the Author

For over four decades, Andrew Wommack has traveled America and the world teaching the truth of the Gospel. His profound revelation of the Word of God is taught with clarity and simplicity, emphasizing God's unconditional love and the balance between grace and faith. He reaches millions of people through the daily *Gospel Truth* radio and television programs, broadcast both domestically and internationally. He founded Charis Bible College in 1994 and has since established Charis Bible College extension schools in other major cities of America and around the world. Andrew has produced a library of teaching materials, available in print, audio, and visual formats. And, as it has been from the beginning, his ministry continues to distribute free audio materials to those who cannot afford them.

Receive Jesus as Your Savior

Choosing to receive Jesus Christ as your Lord and Savior is the most important decision you'll ever make!

God's Word promises **"that if thou shalt confess with thy mouth the Lord Jesus, and shalt believe in thine heart that God hath raised him from the dead, thou shalt be saved. For with the heart man believeth unto righteousness; and with the mouth confession is made unto salvation"** (Rom. 10:9-10). **"For whosoever shall call upon the name of the Lord shall be saved" (Rom. 10:13).**

By His grace, God has already done everything to provide salvation. Your part is simply to believe and receive.

Pray out loud, ***"Jesus, I confess that You are my Lord and Savior. I believe in my heart that God raised You from the dead. By faith in Your Word, I receive salvation now. Thank You for saving me!"***

The very moment you commit your life to Jesus Christ, the truth of His Word instantly comes to pass in your spirit. Now that you're born again, there's a brand-new you!

It doesn't really matter whether you felt anything or not when you prayed to receive the Lord. If you believed in your heart that you received, then God's Word promises that you did. **"Therefore I say unto you, What things soever ye desire, when ye pray, believe that ye receive them, and ye shall have them"** (Mark 11:24). God always honors His Word. Believe it!

Please contact me and let me know that you've prayed to receive Jesus as your Savior . I would like to rejoice with you and help you understand more fully what has taken place in your life. *Welcome to your new life!*

Receive the Holy Spirit

As His child, your loving heavenly Father wants to give you the supernatural power you need to live this new life.

"For every one that asketh receiveth; and he that seeketh findeth; and to him that knocketh it shall be opened...how much more shall your heavenly Father give the Holy Spirit to them that ask him?" (Luke 11:10 and 13).

All you have to do is ask, believe, and receive!

Pray, ***"Father, I recognize my need for Your power to live this new life. Please fill me with Your Holy Spirit. By faith, I receive it right now! Thank You for baptizing me! Holy Spirit, You are welcome in my life!"***

Congratulations—now you're filled with God's supernatural power!

Some syllables from a language you don't recognize will rise up from your heart to your mouth (1 Cor. 14:14). As you speak them out loud by faith, you're releasing God's power from within and building yourself up in the spirit (1 Cor. 14:4). You can do this whenever and wherever you like!

It doesn't really matter whether you felt anything or not when you prayed to receive His Spirit. If you believed in your heart that you received, then God's Word promises that you did. **"Therefore I say unto you, What things soever ye desire, when ye pray, believe that ye receive them, and ye shall have them"** (Mark 11:24). God always honors His Word. Believe it!

Please contact me and let me know that you've prayed to be filled with the Holy Spirit. I would like to rejoice with you and help you understand more fully what has taken place in your life. *Welcome to your new life!*